A DICTIONARY OF
CREATIVE ACTIVITIES
FOR SCHOOL USE

By the same author:
Modern Art Education in the Primary School

MAX DIMMACK

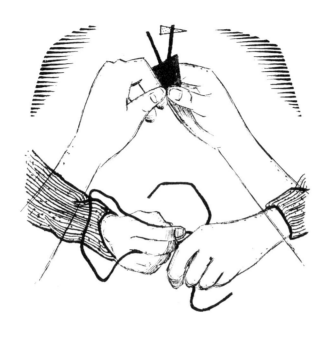

A DICTIONARY OF
CREATIVE ACTIVITIES
FOR SCHOOL USE

MACMILLAN AND CO. LTD.   1966

MACMILLAN & CO. LIMITED
LONDON—BOMBAY—CALCUTTA—MADRAS
MELBOURNE

THE MACMILLAN COMPANY OF CANADA LTD.
TORONTO

ST. MARTIN'S PRESS INC.
NEW YORK

Wholly set up and printed in Australia at The Griffin Press, Marion Road, Netley, S.A.
Registered at the General Post Office, Melbourne, for transmission through the post as a book.

Foreword

It is hoped that this book will meet an expressed need of many teachers. During Education Week displays at Burwood Teachers' College over recent years visitors frequently have commented, "It's all very well to show us examples, but where can we find out how to do these things?" That and similar questions have prompted the writing of this book.

It is designed as a teacher's handbook. The contents, therefore, are arranged in two sections. Section I forms a brief introduction to current concepts and classroom practices, for only by considering and acknowledging modern educational advances can the introduction of the activities listed in Section 2 achieve maximum personal and social benefits. Section I, in effect, forms an educational background to Section 2, which comprises a comprehensive dictionary of creative activities suitable for use in a modern programme of art education growing from, and directly related to, children's needs and interests. It does not profess to contain all the information available on the techniques listed but simply to supply sufficient details to enable the teacher to introduce a desired activity. Activities are listed alphabetically so that teachers can refer to them without having to read the whole book, and a system of cross-reference is included where activities are similar or related. The practice of tabulating the required materials for each activity also is included to help teachers to organize listed supplies or to plan substitutes. The book is closely related to existing classroom conditions, and an indication of the probable age group and suggested number of participants is given with each activity.

While the book is addressed in the main to the primary teacher, for whom the writer maintains a continuing empathy, most of the activities listed can be introduced at any level in the school system. The techniques will remain substantially the same; the end products will differ, of course, to the extent that the children who created them differ. Thus, it is felt that an alphabetical listing of creative activities will prove valuable not only to the secondary school teacher but to all others who are interested in the art education of children, including parents, youth leaders, and the like.

The book as written represents the collective contributions of many people. A great number of teachers and children in Victorian schools have supplied stimulation and ideas, and the writer expresses his warm appreciation of this source of help. Where research findings are used in Section I the authors and their studies are acknowledged. The material in Section 2, however, has been compiled over a decade or more from personal experience and from reference works of all kinds; the assistance and guidance of these authors, many of whose names have not been recorded, is acknowledged with gratitude.

Nearer to home, a number of people also have helped. The writer is deeply indebted to two people in particular for their direct assistance. Mrs. M. Melbourne, of the Craft staff at the Burwood Teachers' College, undertook the onerous task of checking the information accompanying the listed activities; her criticism, suggestions, and the discussions which followed, have added considerably to the comprehensiveness of the book. Mr. Graham Allen, B.Com., B.Ed., Lecturer in Social Studies at Burwood Teachers' College, willingly edited the manuscript, offering valuable advice and insisting on numerous improvements. Two other members of staff at Burwood Teachers' College also assisted. Mr. Arthur Reynolds, A.T.C., T.T.C. (Man.Arts), Head of the Craft Department, gave guidance and information for the section on Weaving, and Mr. W. Barnett, with painstaking care, completed the necessary photography. The indirect contribution of the former Principal of the College, Mr. D. M. Waller, B.A., Dip.Ed., also must be recognized in this book as well as in the writer's earlier work; by his example and his philosophy he generated at the College an educational atmosphere conducive to the writing of books.

The illustrations to the text have been obtained from a number of sources. Miss Marion Scott, of the Junior School at the Scotch College, Melbourne, generously permitted the writer to photograph examples of the work of boys in that school, and her willing co-operation is appreciated. Similarly, Mr. A. L. Bell, formerly a member of staff at the Box Hill South Primary School, kindly made available a collection of the work of his class. Examples have been obtained from other schools also, and these sources are identified where possible. The line illustrations, in the main, have been taken from examples of creative activities made by first year students at the Burwood Teachers' College, to whom the writer expresses his thanks.

Finally, to my wife and children, who surrendered their Christmas vacation so that this book could be written, I express my appreciation of their understanding and forbearance.

MAX DIMMACK.

June, 1961,
Moorabbin.

CONTENTS

Page.

The format, cover design, and line illustrations are the work of the author.

INTRODUCTION

SOME CONSIDERATIONS IN THE TEACHING OF ART TO CHILDREN

Current Concepts and their Bases

Classroom Practices

INTRODUCTION

SOME CONSIDERATIONS IN THE TEACHING OF ART TO CHILDREN

Until comparatively recent times art and craft (or handwork) were taught as separate subjects in the primary school. In most educational centres today, however, this distinction has been recognized as artificial, and eliminated; and art and craft appear as an integrated area of the curriculum designated by the term "art." For the purposes of this book, therefore, the term "art education" should be interpreted broadly to encompass a wide variety of art experiences, both two-dimensional and three-dimensional, and to include those activities variously called "craft" or "handwork activities" when these are truly creative, appropriate to the primary age level, and conform to modern educational principles.

Current Concepts and their Bases

The great changes apparent in the character, scope, and purpose of modern art education in a programme of total child development can be attributed to a number of causes. Gaitskell (1, p. 4) identifies three main influences which have effected the evolution of art education as a contributing area of the primary school curriculum. These are (a) the nature or tradition of art itself; (b) the influence of the philosophy of democracy; and (c) the impact of the discoveries of psychology upon teaching theory and practice. The collective effect of these influences has been to revolutionize art education in a comparatively short time; individually, they constitute the bases of most of the concepts and practices which characterise modern art teaching.

THE TRADITION OF ART ITSELF

A study of the history of art reveals a succession of periods in which current ideas of the nature of art resulted in changes in the modes of expression. It is significant, however, than an ingredient of the great and enduring art of these periods is the *personal* nature of the expression, regardless of differences in place and appearance. The great masterpieces of both past and present impress with the *personalities* of their creators. Dewey (2, pp. 64, 65) asserts that *art is a significant expression giving form and order to a human being's reaction to his environment.* It is precisely this concept that has fundamentally influenced the nature of art education in the primary school. Art as an area of the school programme is now a matter of self-expression; it is the child's personal reaction to significant aspects of his environment expressed either pictorially or in some other visual form.

In addition, it should be remembered that new methods of reproduction, which have introduced the personal forms of expression and the many styles and developments

I

in contemporary art to almost every school and home, have themselves made a transformation of art teaching inevitable.

THE PHILOSOPHY OF DEMOCRACY

In a democratic society the worth of the individual is held sacrosanct. He enjoys the privileges of freedom of thought, of expression, of action; he also enjoys additional freedoms such as freedom from fear, or from interference. These freedoms—and the responsibilities that accompany them—are characteristic of the liberty inherent in democratic living. They are also characteristic of the liberty essential to the child in the classroom if genuine and beneficial self-expression is to occur. Art education cannot operate successfully unless it is presented in an atmosphere of democratic freedom. The child must be self-directing, making his own decisions and expressing his own concepts and experiences by his own means and in terms appropriate to his own age level. He must learn to work independently, and to co-operate. He must learn to share and to exchange. He must learn to respect. He must learn to be tolerant, and to show sympathy when necessary towards others. He must learn how to lead and when to follow. These characteristics of democratic living—and others—are attainable in a modern programme of art experiences to a degree rarely permitted elsewhere in the primary curriculum. Gaitskell (1, p. 20) claims, in fact, " . . . . . that art educators have been among the pioneers in developing a pedagogy which is compatible with democratic practices."

A principal concern of modern art education is to provide opportunities for the development of those social habits, attitudes and values acceptable in a democratic society, at the same time nurturing personal attributes such as initiative, inventiveness, resourcefulness, self-reliance, sense of responsibility, creative thinking, and the capacity to act constructively, which are essential to the maintenance of the democratic way of life. Thus art education, in embracing the philosophy of democracy, contributes in its own right towards the preparation of our school population for adulthood in such a society.

THE IMPACT OF PSYCHOLOGY ON TEACHING THEORY AND PRACTICES

An increasing volume of research in such fields as psychology, education, and medicine, provides a clearer picture of the child as an individual, of his needs, his behaviour, his similarities and his differences, how he learns, and what education should do for him. There appear to have evolved a number of educational concepts or developments based on psychological findings. Certain of these seem to suggest that what education *should* do for the child and what education does for the child are by no means synonymous. This applies equally to art education as to other areas of the primary curriculum. The more important of these concepts which are influencing art education now, or appear likely to do so in the near future, follow.

A. THE LEARNING PROCESS

In its study of what is involved in learning, experimental psychology has made a significant contribution to educational practice. The learning process is currently held to embrace *perception* (perceiving by one or more of the senses), *association* (or thinking), *emotional involvement* (or feeling), and *action* (or acting or doing); learning is defined as the gaining of knowledge or skills or attitudes in a manner which modifies behaviour through experience. Learning, to be fully effective, should incorporate some form of action. Education that is passive or based on submissive step-by-step procedures is held to be incompatible with learning in the fullest sense. "Activity" methods, therefore, characterise modern education. In art education it is essential that the action aspect of learning should be *creative*. Creativeness becomes, in effect, both a concomitant and an outcome of the learning process. It becomes the child's personal and inventive expression and, as such, opposes sterile imitation of another's concepts and work. This concept of learning as a creative process is having a profound effect on the theory of art education. As it becomes more widely adopted and applied in the classroom, its influence on teaching practices is likely to be considerable.

B. CREATIVENESS

Much research is needed before a clear concept of the nature of "creativeness" will emerge. Kilpatrick (3), as early as 1935, asserted that creativeness is characteristic of all learning. Dewey (4, p. 187) supports this view. The recent studies of Guilford (5, p. 80) and Brittain (6, p. 39) suggest that creativeness is a complex whole made up of basic creative abilities common to all fields, but varying from field to field. The creative person, the evidence suggests, is generally more individual in behaviour, more emotional, more self-sufficient, reveals a higher degree of facility, flexibility, and originality, and is more prone to frustration. These studies indicate that those attributes which contribute to general creativeness in the individual are the same attributes revealed in any creative art activity. It can be claimed, therefore, that creative art experiences promote creativeness in general. One of the prime objectives of modern art teaching is to use creative activities to make people more creative regardless of the field in which the creativeness will be applied; hence the importance of creative art education in a democratic community. In art education, art is used simply as a means to this end. It is not an end in itself.

The former concept of creativeness as a special "ability" possessed by a gifted minority is no longer tenable. This is important to current practices in art education. It is accepted now that creativeness in some form or other is possessed by all people and that creative activity is a basic, common need. Any modern system of education is obliged to accommodate this need. Within the scope of current primary education, it is clear that this creative urge in children can best be satisfied through self-expression in a broad programme of art experiences. Classroom procedures which deny or stifle creativeness are contrary to the welfare both of the individual child and of

3

the community. In the freedom and variety of their personal expression, acceptable to and understood by a sympathetic teacher, *all* children become creative.

C. IMITATION

That much current art teaching in primary classrooms makes use of step-by-step procedures, copying of concepts and techniques, and imitative colouring exercises, cannot be disputed. While it is conceded that imitation is an important factor in learning, two recent studies, by Russell and Waugaman (7, p. 16) and by Heilman (8, p. 16), show convincingly the detrimental effect of imitative procedures on children's creative ability. In both studies, at different grade levels, comparative analyses were made of children's drawings before, and after, exposure to copying devices. The drawings made after exposure showed strongly derivative influences and a marked deterioration in the children's creative concepts and in their confidence to express their own ideas. Prolonged interference with the child's ideas and the replacement of his *own* naturally evolved concepts by imposed stereotypes can cause not only mental and emotional disturbances but also can affect seriously his whole subsequent creative output. The problem would be disturbing, educationally, if confined to art education alone. But when it is considered that similar practices are standard procedures in the primary school, both in the infant grades (for example, in reading and number activities) and in higher grades (in most subjects), the dimensions of the problem are multiplied. For the duration of their schooling, day in and day out, children are being conditioned to dependency by an insistence on the use of concepts, forms, techniques and methods *which are not their own*. Clearly this is incompatible with the preceding concept of "creativeness" and with the stated educational objective of producing a self-directing adult for life in a democratic community.

D. PROBLEM-SOLVING EXPERIENCES

Increasing recognition is being accorded the concept that children learn more readily through individual participation and experiment in classroom situations in which they are confronted by a variety of problems which they must solve in order to progress further. Such a principle is basic to progressive teaching in certain subject areas elsewhere in the primary curriculum. It is being adopted increasingly in modern art education where the provision of such "situations" is considered an integral part of classroom method, and the planning of them an essential part of the teacher's role. Problem-solving experiences are devised wherein the child is encouraged to make decisions, to think individually and creatively, and to act independently or, if the experience demands, co-operatively with others in the social unit. Wickiser (9, p. 17) claims, "Problem-solving is an important part of education. The child grows and develops as he becomes able to solve all kinds of problems. Behaviour changes resulting from the solution of meaningful problems indicate that learning has taken place and that desirable attitudes are being established." The problems a child encounters may originate in an experience of materials (for example, discovering a way to achieve structural strength in a three-dimensional construction), from the needs of expression (clarifying, and then representing, personal concepts in a visual statement of an experience), from the employment of group techniques (resolving social frictions that might occur in combining ideas and efforts to produce a communal picture), or even from class routines and habits (overcoming problems that accompany the sharing of limited supplies). The *planned* use of problem-solving experiences not only contributes to the child's immediate growth, but it also anticipates and prepares for his future role as a self-directing adult in a democratic society.

E. SELF-IDENTIFICATION WITH EXPERIENCE

A further principle concerns the self-identification of the child with the experience —experience being interpreted to include both the subject-matter chosen for expression and also the materials and process used to achieve the expression. For self-identification to occur, the experiences employed should be personally familiar and fully comprehensible to the child. "Experiences of the child," writes Jefferson (10, p. 231), "are simply the things that have happened to him, such as the things he has done, seen, read, heard, imagined, felt, or dreamed." Lowenfeld (11, p. 26) claims that the child has to be able to identify himself with his own experience before he can be motivated to produce creatively, and the greater the degree of self-identification on the part of the child with the experience, the richer and more beneficial the creative expression which follows.

The child's identification of himself with the experience is strengthened considerably if his sense of that experience can be enlarged to make it more meaningful. In other words, it becomes more *real*. The child is able to project himself into the activity or situation of the experience, to re-live it, to draw upon his store of passive knowledge, and so to evolve the personal, detailed mental imagery essential to satisfactory creative expression. Lowenfeld (11, p. 5) calls this "extending the child's frame of reference," and proceeds to demonstrate the importance of starting at the child's present level before attempting to stimulate his thinking to the point where new concepts and relationships transform his initial set of concepts of the experience. It is one of the most important tasks of the teacher in art to enlarge the child's sense of his experience by motivating him to heightened individual interest and emotional relationships. Thus, the child who is enabled to re-live the joy and excitement of "The Night Dad Brought Home Our New Car" generally experiences little difficulty in expressing his personal reaction in the subsequent expression.

The significance of this concept of self-identification to the development of the child requires emphasis. It assists the clarification of his conceptual knowledge and developing relationships, challenges his intellectual response, and promotes creative thinking. It is essential if the child's individuality is to be preserved in his work.

5

It is also essential, in a wide view, to the production of a well-adjusted, integrated individual within a social group. Self-identification with the needs, the difficulties, the endeavours, and the hopes of others is fundamental to effective social living in a democratic community.

F. THE PERSONAL FACTOR

Recent research, for example by McVitty (12, p. 82), suggests that the forms of motivation most likely to achieve self-identification are those based on the "personal factor," that is, the co-operative exchange of ideas between pupils and a sympathetic teacher. McVitty expresses the opinion that the "personal factor" of pupil-teacher participation is the basis of a desirable learning situation, and that individual growth is more pronounced where the co-operation of pupil and teacher has been the source for motivation. Mechanical devices, such as a film or a recording, or even dramatization, are still only supplementary to, and can never replace, the personality of the teacher in the educational experience. Lowenfeld (11, p. 3) supports this finding, which questions the value of a number of motivational devices currently employed, and also the suitability of many of the topics or experiences selected for children's creative expression.

G. INDIVIDUAL DIFFERENCES

While the principle of individual differences has been accepted theoretically, a broad application of it to classroom practice has yet to be achieved. It is possibly one of the most important contributions of psychology to modern teaching. It has been clearly established that individual differences, developing from heredity, environment, and experiences, influence and determine both the child's behaviour and his performance. The present primary curriculum offers little opportunity for the encouragement and cultivation of these differences. However, a broad and varied programme of creative activities, as an area of the curriculum, permits the exercise of individual variation. The encouragement of the child's individuality of performance and the preservation of the uniqueness of his expression are of vital importance to the development of a complete and balanced personality. If the child is to grow as an individual, he must be free to express himself as an individual. Modern art teaching cultivates individual differences and, through communal experiences and group activities, assists the child's assimilation into his social unit where the existence and exercise of these differences enables him to become a useful and productive member.

H. TOTAL GROWTH

It is now accepted that a child grows in many ways. Growth has many facets. One of these, intellectual growth, has been emphasised to such a degree that other important aspects of growth virtually have been neglected until recently. To preserve a balanced growth, education must consider the *total* growth process in all its aspects, and provide accordingly. de Francesco (13, p. 147) comments, "Experiences of various types, materials of many sorts, learnings gained in many ways, participation in group enterprises, and other educational means need to be utilised to make more effective the teacher-learning situation. All these efforts are employed in order to develop, through appeal to diverse personal interests and capacities, a resourceful, self-reliant individual." Numerous educational authorities acknowledge the value of creative art experiences to the growing child. Lowenfeld (11, pp. 48-59) lists seven areas of growth claimed to be discernible in children's art, all seven of which are important in an art education aimed at educating the whole child. His list reads—1) intellectual growth, 2) emotional growth, 3) social growth, 4) perceptual growth, 5) physical growth, 6) aesthetic growth, and 7) creative growth. The teacher who can detect evidence of growth in any of these areas after an analysis of a child's work is in the position of having a clearer understanding of that child as an individual. He is then able to use the understanding gained in better teaching of the child. But while a picture of the total growth of the child can be obtained by studying in isolation the several components of growth as they are revealed in his expressions, Lowenfeld stresses the importance of relating these phases in classroom practice so that growth is regarded as an entity. Classroom methods should be designed to stimulate growth in all phases rather than growth in certain areas. Lowenfeld's view of the contribution that enlightened art education can make towards the total growth of the child is shared by Gaitskell (14, p. 3) who writes, "Art supplies a unique, efficient and indispensable method of learning. Through art activities a young child may exercise his senses, his emotions, his intellect, and his perceptive powers to great advantage."

When the concept of total growth becomes widely accepted in the primary school, it seems certain that art education will be called upon to make a significant contribution towards the balanced development of the individual child.

I. NATURAL STANDARDS

The modern approach to art education incorporates a healthy appreciation of the nature of children's art and a more accurate recognition of the child's capacity and performance at his own level of ability. "Traditional" art teaching, in introducing adult concepts and skills, and even adult experiences, presents standards of comprehension and performance beyond the capacity of the children. As a result, much of this art teaching fails as education. Modern art teaching takes materials and activities that are normal and natural to growing children, adapts them for use in the classroom, and directs them towards worthwhile individual or social objectives. Areas of activity, information, and skills are presented in a manner at once interesting and attractive to the child, related to both his range of experience and to his level of comprehension. The creative work which follows is personal and natural. The standards of achievement involved are *natural* standards; the individual child's expression is appreciated on its merits. There is no place for external or artificial criteria. Since the child's art merely serves him as a means of expression, and since in creative expression both the various stages of development and the personal form of the expression may differ widely, it is considered normal that a child's work may differ greatly from that of other children. Thus there can be no fixed or standard performance; each child establishes his *own* standard. He is expected simply to give of his best in a natural performance. This acceptance of the child's natural performance as an aid to his development is an educational advance not yet apparent in all subjects. It represents a change in concept that holds wide implications for teaching generally.

J. A REVALUATION

Because modern art education takes into account the latest knowledge of children and the meeting of their needs, modern concepts in teaching practice, the existing school system, and the requirements of a rapidly changing democratic society, it is achieving surprising educational results in the classroom. The transformation that has occurred, and its value to education in general, are described by Clegg (15, p. 23) in the following words: "These new processes which evoke from the child rather than impose upon it, which throw a child upon his own resources rather than require from him a response dictated by the teacher, which convert teaching into a process of stimulation and guidance rather than instruction, are, I think, likely to have a profound effect on the teaching of the future, and to secure a higher standard particularly from the average and less able child, than we would have dreamed possible a few years ago."

A revaluation is taking place of the role and value of creative art experiences in a programme of general education. Art is being regarded increasingly as an essential component in a balanced education and less as a cultural "frill" to the educational fabric. Some writers, in fact, regard it as a core subject. A scholar of the eminence of Herbert Read (16), for instance, advocates that the whole of the educational process should be based on what he calls "creativeness," and he recognises that in a broad programme of creative art experiences lies the best means of developing this quality.

Classroom Practices

That the nature of art education has been fundamentally transformed is clear. It follows then that classroom practices inevitably must be modified and adapted to the changed circumstances so that art education is permitted to make its maximum contribution to the task of educating the growing child. It is proposed now to examine some of these changes in so far as they concern the teacher and the educational process.

A. THE LEARNING SITUATION

It is clear that the formal, teacher-dominated lesson in which the whole class engages in a single activity without regard to individual differences or varying needs and performances is now obsolete. The malpractices that accompany it are incompatible with important principles of modern teaching. The former "teaching" situation has been superseded by a "learning" situation. The art lesson now becomes a creative venture in which the child actively and individually participates, encountering problems and difficult situations, examining them, discovering feasible solutions, and applying them logically in materials of his own selection. Wickiser (9, p. 208) believes, "It is up to the teacher, then, to establish productive learning situations, to 'set the stage' for creativity, by creating a visually interesting situation, exciting in feeling, an art activity that challenges the imagination of the child, so it can be accomplished within his span of interest and attention, and yet reaches out a little beyond his abilities to keep him interested in trying to improve."

B. THE FUNCTION OF THE TEACHER

The replacement of the teacher-dominated lesson by the child-centred approach, however, does not mean that the teacher is absolved from teaching. The teacher's contribution to the learning process is more subtle, unobtrusive, and flexible. It becomes more a process of stimulating than teaching. The teacher finds himself devoting much of his time to stimulating the child's interest in what is to be the subject of his work. He seeks to give him as wide and as deep an experience of that particular subject as is possible, in order that creative expression may emerge from an abundance of enthusiasm and interest. The emphasis is very much on making the child want to learn.

The function of the teacher becomes that of a guide rather than that of an instructor. He is compelled to adopt an attitude sympathetic to the needs of the individual child. As Clegg (15, p. 22) puts it, "In short, the teacher has perforce to know why he is teaching what he is teaching in the way that he is teaching it and what he expects his teaching to do for each of his children." This necessarily eliminates the aimless and thoughtless teaching that frequently characterises traditional art education, where the teacher in many cases simply teaches what he was taught at school in the way that he was taught it.

C. METHODS OF TEACHING

Methods of teaching in art form an educational field almost wholly untouched by research. There is no single method. But art educators generally agree that sound art teaching is evocative—it evokes the maximum creative response from the individual child. Jefferson (10, ch. 1) identifies six methods currently employed in art teaching, some of which possess values that contribute to child growth, while others do not. *Creative expression* is a method of teaching which gives the child the opportunity to choose his own ideas or subject-matter, the freedom to express it in his own way and the right to organise it in his own way. *Assigned topics* describes the method where the teacher or the children decide upon a topic that all in the group will use but which permits them freedom of both expression and organisation. *Directed methods* are those in which a prescribed course is set by the teacher and controlled in a step-by-step procedure, the whole class working in the same way, at the same time, at the same speed, to produce identical end-products. *Copying* as a method occurs when a child is required to duplicate a picture or form as accurately as he can, and the method is used individually or on a class basis. *Patterns* refers to a method in which prepared patterns or shapes are given to children to reproduce, often in step-by-step procedures, and uses devices such as tracing, templates, and cut-outs. *Prepared outlines* in colouring books or on prepared sheets are supplied to the children who are required simply to colour or paint within the prescribed limitations.

Two of these methods, *creative expression* and *assigned topics*, because they give to each child opportunities for personal, creative expression, are liberal, modern methods of art teaching. The other four, educationally unsound and undesirable, are to be discouraged.

On the matter of method, Lowenfeld (11, p. 3) observes, "It is quite impossible to say that any one approach .... is good for all. At one time it may be better to have the children divided in groups working on group projects, at another simultaneously with different materials in one classroom, or individually on the same motivation. This all depends on individual needs ..... The teaching situation as well as the need of the children should always be the decisive factor in choosing the method of approach, for it is the effect the creative process has on the child and not the final product which is of decisive significance."

The approach that is most suited to present concepts should be informal, flexible, and capable of individual application. After considering the personality, the needs, the problems of the individual child, and the materials to be used, the teacher adapts his teaching accordingly, thinking in terms of the growing child rather than of the end-product of the activity. Experience suggests that if teachers adopt such an approach, the end-products, in fact, become better; they show not only increased spontaneity, variety, and individuality of performance, but also a noticeable improvement in quality.

D. CHANGED PROCEDURES

The new approach to art education is characterised by innovations and new procedures. The use of the *diversified programme*, in which a number of activities is carried on in the same room and at the same time, has as its aim the most economic use of the time available so that the greatest possible contribution to individual development can be made. It enables a considerably increased number of activities to be introduced in the art programme for the year, for, instead of the entire class engaging in a single experience, groups of children participate in a number of separate activities or variations of an activity. A *developmental treatment of units of study*, involving series of graded experiences, enables the study to be more intensely pursued. Thus, four successive and related pattern-making experiences, because of their greater impact upon the child, prove more effective educationally than four isolated experiences. Continuity of experience, of thought, of activity, assists learning, strengthens performance, and conserves teaching effort. The setting up and equipping of a part of the classroom or school building as a *work centre* for a particular activity, with storage for the essential materials located nearby, reduces the number of problems accompanying preparation, organisation, distribution and collection of materials, and class management in general. Such work centres are more or less permanently prepared for their respective activities. To permit satisfactory use of the various materials, a simple system of *decentralised storage* should be devised, using clearly labelled cartons, boxes or shelving, readily accessible to the children. *Different sized activity groups* are used frequently in this new approach. The size of the groups participating in the planned experiences depends, in the main, on the nature of the experience and the needs of the children. Times will occur when provision must be made for participation on an individual, small group, or class basis. Group or *communal experiences* develop those socially desirable attributes indicated on p. 2. Art education of the type advocated here also makes far greater use of *planned displays* and *illustrative material* to achieve a visual presentation. The simple actions of looking, seeing, observing, and comparing are considered fundamental to successful art education.

E. MOTIVATION

Reference already has been made to motivation, and the term as used here denotes those means or devices employed by the teacher to evoke interest and an enthusiasm to participate in the activities planned, and also to secure a co-operative class response conducive to creative expression. McVitty's study shows the importance of the teacher in motivation. Motivations which use active participation and a good relationship between teacher and pupils help the children individually to become closely identified with the experience, and result in more meaningful expression. But it has been shown that the same motivation may have different effects under different conditions and treatment. Thus, on occasions, teachers may have to motivate children on an individual basis; at other times, it might prove advantageous to motivate a group or the whole class simultaneously by a single experience. Whatever form the motivation takes, the important consideration is that the child retains the freedom to use his *own* form of expression. His creativeness thus remains free.

F. HELP AND INTERFERENCE

There is a school of thought which claims that the child needs no help; he simply is given the materials and opportunities to use them. Such a claim runs contrary to

11

the spirit of true education. If art education is to make a genuine contribution to child growth, then the child can and should be helped. There is in current teaching, however, an urgent need to distinguish between help and interference.

Help, in art education, means meeting individual needs of expression as they arise. Children may require help in a number of directions and a teacher should be able to recognise these and to offer guidance accordingly. Thus, motivation, in enabling a child to re-live an experience so that it becomes meaningful for him, becomes a form of help. Individual children will need help with the organisation of their work; in picture-making, for example, few children are satisfied with a random distribution of forms over the paper, and guidance from the teacher may assist them to achieve a satisfactory pictorial expression. Primary children need guidance in the use, care and maintenance of the various materials introduced. They will need individual assistance in mastering the many processes and activities. They will need help in developing desirable working habits and attitudes that make for agreeable working conditions within their social group and within the classroom at large. They will need encouragement, sympathy, and understanding. They will need recognition of their work so that they enjoy status among their class mates. These forms of help are essential to the development of confidence and a sense of achievement that lead to improved individual performance. But any help in the matter of *expression* becomes a hindrance.

Help degenerates into interference when it adversely influences or hinders the child's natural mode of reasoning and expression, or when it prevents him from fully participating in an activity or situation, or when it deprives him of the educational experience of individually discovering a feasible solution to an art problem by imposing a solution prematurely. The motives underlying such interference are generally well-meant, but the fact remains that it causes unintentional and insidious damage to the child's natural, individual expression, to his creative ability in general, and ultimately to his normal development.

For a detailed account of the adverse effects on child development of the various forms of interference currently practised, the reader is referred to Lowenfeld's "Your Child and His Art," (1954), pages 10-23.

G. REVISION AND REMEDIAL TEACHING

A conspicuous defect in much current art teaching is the neglect of teachers to revise known activities, to introduce useful variations of familiar techniques, or to consolidate previous teaching. A similar neglect in other subjects would incur strong condemnation. This should apply equally to art education. Probably as a result of inadequate background knowledge and misapplication, art in the classroom at times degenerates into mere entertainment without educational purpose or benefit—as if the function of the subject is to entertain the children with "something new" each lesson. The revision of known knowledge and processes, so that they can be related to new material, is characteristic of sound teaching, regardless of subject. In introducing new areas of information or activity in the art programme sufficient time and the necessary number of experiences should be provided to permit adequate comprehension and satisfactory individual performance. The planning of areas of study or units of work, involving short graded series of related experiences, makes this possible. With children of primary age, it is futile to introduce new activities until children have developed reasonable facility in the activities already introduced, or to introduce more than one *new* activity or material at a time.

In cases of partial comprehension, or inadequate mastery of a necessary skill, or misuse of a technique, remedial teaching may be needed. This may be done on an individual basis as the need arises during the activity, or it can be accomplished to a group or class during the exhibition period which normally terminates the lesson.

H. ASSESSMENT AND EVALUATION

The problem of marking or grading in art causes concern to many teachers. The common practice of awarding a mark (numeral or letter) cannot be justified. Research to date has produced no accurate or acceptable method of measuring children's art work. Numerous approaches have been tried, and rejected. Some have been shown to be harmful, emotionally and in other ways, to children. Olson (17, p. 312), in fact, claims, "The marking system may be emphasised to the extent that it constitutes a major frustration in the lives of many children." The emphasis in modern art education is on personal and social growth. There is no way yet of assessing the development of qualities such as imagination, inventiveness, initiative, or adaptability. It is accepted that a creative art programme contributes to the development of these qualities, and others, but the value of that contribution cannot be measured.

Evaluation is a different matter. It refers to the process of determining both the quality and the amount of growth that has occurred in each pupil as a result of his participation in the various activities. As such it concerns both pupils and teacher. Children quite naturally are interested in their own performances and progress, and in the expressions of others. When they view their work they examine, compare, and react towards it according to their individual capacities and experiences. This self-examination leads to self-criticism, possibly to re-direction of effort, to greater confidence, and to further growth. Evaluation becomes part of the process of learning and growing. It is the teacher's responsibility to involve the pupil actively in this process.

For the teacher, evaluation involves his own personal estimate of the success or otherwise of his teaching efforts in guiding and assisting pupil growth. Reference has been made to the concept of total growth, in which growth is seen as a simultaneous process involving a number of facets. In evaluating his teaching, the teacher should keep all the facets in mind so that the greatest contribution to the welfare of the pupil is made. Those aspects of growth seemingly neglected or under-developed can be strengthened through special guidance, remedial teaching, or further

13

participation. In this sense evaluation for the teacher assumes a *diagnostic* function in that it is aimed at an improvement in teaching and a strengthening of child growth.

I. DISCIPLINE

A disservice has been done to the cause of art education through a misunderstanding of the term "freedom of expression." The abuse of this concept in classroom practice at times has produced conditions bordering on chaos. Learning cannot occur in chaos. On this point Holmes and Collinson (18, p. 8) comment, "Nor must it be thought that children should be allowed to do just what they please in the interest of freedom and imagination, with no guidance and discipline." Lowenfeld (11, p. 83) prefers what he calls "self-discipline," a discipline which grows from an understanding of the situation and a desire on the part of the child to relate himself to it. The new approach to art education makes this "self-discipline" possible. The fascination the activities hold for children, their enjoyment of the work, the informality that pervades the classroom, the absence of teacher domination, all combine to induce a different form of discipline and a happier classroom climate. Imposed discipline is replaced by a discipline of work and interest. There results an improved teacher-class relationship and a re-assessment by the children of their attitude towards their teacher. They respond more readily, co-operate enthusiastically, and work harder. They not only work harder, but they perform at a higher level. Because of the change in approach, art education now is getting more in terms of response and performance from all children. The so-called lower ability groups are being brought into active production —and the educational significance of this needs no emphasis. Because natural standards are accepted all children derive pleasure and satisfaction from their participation. The individual child becomes conscious of a sense of achievement and avoids the sense of constant failure. As a result, those behaviour and disciplinary problems that accompany perpetual failure, prolonged frustration, unacceptable performance, or inability to participate, are eliminated.

.   .   .   .

The foregoing indicates the educational background which must determine and influence the use in the classroom of the creative activities which follow. For unless such educational advances are reflected in the introduction of these activities they surely must fail to achieve their maximum contribution to the total growth of the child.

Bibliography

1. Gaitskell, C. D. "Children and Their Art." N.Y., Harcourt, Brace and Co., 1958.
2. Dewey, J. "Art as Experience." N.Y., Minton Balch and Co., 1934.
3. Kilpatrick, W. H. "A Reconstructed Theory of the Educative Process." N.Y., Teachers' College, 1935.
4. Dewey, J. "Experience and Education." N.Y., Macmillan, 1938.
5. Guilford, J. P. series of articles. Psychological Laboratory. University of Southern California, 1951-1957. In Encyclopedia of Educational Research, N.Y., Macmillan, 1960.
6. Brittain, W. L. "An Experiment Toward Measuring Creativity." in Research in Art Education. 7th Year Book. National Art Education Association, Kutztown, Pennsylvania, 1956.
7. Russell, I. and Waugaman, B. "A Study of the Effect of Workbook Copy Experiences on the Creative Concepts of Children." Research Bulletin, The Eastern Arts Association, Vol. 3, No. 1. In Lowenfeld V. "Creative and Mental Growth."
8. Heilman, H. "The Effect of Workbook Stereotypes on the Creativeness of Children." Doctoral Thesis. Pennsylvania State University, 1954. In Lowenfeld, V. "Creative and Mental Growth" and Enc. of Educational Research, 1960.
9. Wickiser, R. L. "An Introduction to Art Education." N.Y., World Book Co., 1957.
10. Jefferson, B. "Teaching Art to Children." Boston, Allyn and Bacon, 1959.
11. Lowenfeld, V. "Creative and Mental Growth." N.Y., Macmillan, 1957.
12. McVitty, L. F. "An Experimental Study on Various Methods in Art Motivations at the Fifth Grade Level." In Research in Art Education. 7th Year Book. National Art Education Association. Kutztown, Pennsylvania, 1956.
13. de Francesco, I. L. "Art Education: Its Means and Ends." N.Y., Harper and Bros., 1958.
14. Ontario Department of Education. "Art Education in the Kindergarten." Toronto, The Ryerson Press, 1952.
15. Clegg, A. B. "Filling Pots and Lighting Fires." In New Horizons, No. 18., Sydney, New Education Fellowship, 1958.
16. Read, H. "Education Through Art." London, Faber and Faber, 1943.
17. Olson, W. C. "Child Development." Boston, Heath and Co., 1949.
18. Holmes, K. and Collinson, H. "Child Art Grows up." London, Studio Publications, 1952.

A DICTIONARY OF
CREATIVE ACTIVITIES
FOR SCHOOL USE

CREATIVE ACTIVITY

21

.   .   .   .

ABSTRACT PATTERNS (see Figs. 1 and 2)

As the name implies, these patterns are not based on recognisable forms or subject-matter. Instead, they make use of shapes, colours, lines, and directions. When introduced with an understanding of their nature and educational objectives, they require a considerable intellectual response from the child who must exercise imagination, reasoning, and judgment, to produce a satisfactory result. For this reason they are more appropriate as an activity for older children, and any number of children can participate if suitable materials are available.

MATERIALS

A number of materials can be used, all common and familiar to the child. They include powder, poster, or tempera paints, used with a variety of brushes ranging from large bristle brushes on large sheets of paper to sable-type brushes on smaller sheets; pastels; oil pastels; crayons or coloured pencils; on cartridge paper, cover paper, ticket paper, and similar papers of an appropriate size (both the nature of the medium and the time allotment can influence the size of the paper). Probably the medium with the greatest benefit for the child—and which certainly produces the most spectacular results—is coloured paper (cover paper, flint paper, foil paper, poster paper, coloured surface squares, collected wrappings of all kinds and magazine pieces) cut, arranged, and pasted on either cartridge paper or black cover paper. Coloured backing sheets can be used, but black or white impart a dramatic finish to the completed arrangement because of the contrast they afford. Office or school paste should be available, and each child should have a pasting brush. Newspapers should be used to cover desk-tops; this practice restricts the amount of mess made, and simplifies the cleaning-up process.

TECHNIQUE

The precise technique, of course, will depend on the materials being used but as these usually are familiar to the child, difficulties in their handling are few. If the technique involves pasting, the distribution of the various parts and their satisfactory arrangement should be evolved before pasting commences; premature pasting prevents alterations and adjustments being made as the child analyses relationships and makes decisions. To enable pasted arrangements to dry flat, they can be arranged in a pile, each pattern separated by a sheet of waxed paper obtained from a cereal packet, under a piece of strawboard on which a suitable weight has been placed. When dry, the waxed sheets are removed and stored for future use, as they can be used many times for the same purpose.

23

The problem of the abstract pattern is to place *agreeably* within a given shape such as a square, rectangle, or circle, a pleasing and coherent arrangement of shapes and colours. The arrangement need *not* fill or occupy the whole area, and thus it forms a self-contained unit in contrast to all-over patterns (see p. 24) and border patterns (see p. 34) with their regular and continuous repetition. The general effect should be one of harmony of shapes and colours, and a dominant centre of interest or focal point should be established. A series of problems will arise. The child will need to consider the kinds and sizes of shapes, the range of colours and their balanced distribution, ways and means of relating the component parts, the type of detail needed to give interest, how much to include and what to reject, the amount of background area to be utilised, and so on. The child will encounter difficulties which he should overcome as far as possible unaided. The teacher should be on hand, nevertheless, to help by suggestion or comment when the child is unable to proceed, or requests guidance. It is important that help should be offered in such a way that the child is not deprived of a problem-solving experience; decisions made should be those of the child.

ALL-OVER PATTERNS (see Fig. 3)

An all-over pattern should give the impression of being a small portion of a much larger area in which the pattern has been applied "all over" the surface. As such it is designed to repeat regularly in several directions, horizontally, vertically, or diagonally, in contrast to the border pattern (see p. 34) which repeats in a single direction.

MATERIALS

All-over patterns can be created in a wide range of materials. The following are common in primary classrooms—coloured papers of all kinds, cut, torn, arranged, and pasted; powder, poster, or tempera paints, using both bristle and sable-type brushes; felt-tipped pens; finger paint; pastel and oil pastel; crayons; coloured pencils; on cartridge paper, litho paper, cover paper, ticket paper, bulky newsprint, or similar papers, of a size appropriate to the materials and the nature of the pattern. At times certain waste materials (such as pieces of fabric, rick-rack, wool, string, or newspaper shapes, coloured wrappings and confectionery papers) can be introduced to give interest and variety to the patterns made; in this case a range of common adhesives (paste, mucilage, tube glue, etc.) should be available in the classroom.

In addition, all-over patterns can be produced by simple printing techniques, such as Block Printing (see p. 30), Cork Printing (see p. 58), Linoleum Printing (see p. 92), Peg Printing (see p. 131), Potato Printing (see p. 141), Stick Printing (see p. 175), String Printing (see p. 180), or combinations of these, or by stencilling (see p. 174).

TECHNIQUE

Wherever possible, pattern-making activities should involve the planning or designing of patterns for specific purposes or situations. Thus, an all-over pattern in poster paints could be designed for a bright wrapping paper, or oil pastels could be used to create a bold and colourful arrangement of lines and areas suitable for a patterned fabric. Actual examples, which are readily available, should be shown so that children understand clearly the nature of the pattern they are required to make.

With some types of pattern, and with older children, patterns can be evolved on cheap newsprint or scrap paper first. This practice offers a freedom and a security that encourages children to work individually, to clarify ideas and to make changes, and to establish satisfactory relationships between the parts of the pattern. It is at this stage that the teacher can offer individual guidance through questioning or by suggestion. Principles of design such as repetition, alternation, dominance, or balance, and terms such as major motif, minor motif, can be introduced simply in language appropriate to the age group. It is important that both the motifs and the intervening background shapes be carefully considered; there appears a tendency on the part of many children to leave too much background so that the pattern seems sparse and uninteresting. The actual form of the motifs similarly should be considered, for their shape will depend on the nature and purpose of the pattern. Generally, accurate reproductions of natural forms such as flowers and leaves lead to unimaginative and non-creative pattern making. Therefore, children should be encouraged to depart from natural appearances, to alter and to distort, in the interests of the pattern. In other words, they should *design* the motif.

When the pattern worked out on scrap paper is considered satisfactory by the child, it can be transferred to better quality paper such as cartridge paper to form an all-over pattern in whatever medium is most appropriate. This stage should be completed *without tracing* or mechanical assistance, each motif being repeated by hand as a creative act. It is important that the child should feel free from any pressure from the teacher to reproduce each motif exactly, the slight irregularities that occur in drawing and in the repetition of the motifs adding a unique charm and interest to the work.

There will be many occasions, however, when the initial planning on scrap paper is not necessary, or even possible, and children can create the required pattern in a suitable medium directly on the paper.

Colour is an important ingredient of pattern-making. Children should be encouraged to consider the suitability of the colours they employ, and guidance by the teacher can draw attention to the requirements of a particular pattern. Children should feel free to experiment with colour, and to depart from standard colours available in the classroom by mixing additional colours. In this way their knowledge and appreciation of colour is extended and they develop individuality in its use. This growth must take place naturally, without adult imposition or coercion.

25

For a fuller treatment of types of all-over patterns and techniques, the reader is directed to "Graphic Design," by M. Baranski (Davis Publications Inc., 1960).

APPLIQUE PICTURES

The applique technique involves the application or affixing of an arrangement of materials to the surface of another material which serves as a backing. There are several kinds of applique work, and two, cloth applique and paper applique, are particularly suited to the primary school. For details of these techniques see Cloth Applique (p. 50) and Paper Applique (p. 120).

AREA-FILLING EXERCISES (see Fig. 4)

These are similar in many respects to the making of abstract patterns (see p. 23), for they are essentially abstract in nature and the same materials can be used. They are suitable for almost any grade level of the primary school, and, depending on the materials being used, any number of children can participate, working in their desks.

MATERIALS

Any common and easily manipulated fluid or graphic media which permit the free colouring of areas can be used—powder, poster, and tempera paints, with sable-type brushes; coloured papers, cut, arranged and pasted; pastels; oil pastels; and crayons. Coloured pencils tend to be laborious and slow, causing the activity to become tedious for the child; they also make even application of colour difficult. White cartridge paper, approximately 10 inches by $7\frac{1}{2}$ inches, is the most suitable paper for the materials normally used, although coloured papers can achieve striking effects when used on black cover paper. Working areas should be protected by the use of newspapers.

TECHNIQUE

The area-filling exercise presents a problem different from that of the abstract pattern in that the *whole* area is used; hence, the name, *area-filling*. In a rectangle or square, intersecting vertical and horizontal lines provide a basis for an arrangement of small rectangles of varying areas and proportions, and these are then coloured to establish a centre of interest and to achieve chromatic balance. In a later exercise, oblique and curved lines can be introduced and used in conjunction with horizontal and vertical lines. When the area to be filled is circular, an arrangement of predominantly curved lines seems more appropriate.

26

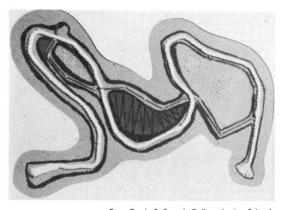

Boy, Grade 5, Scotch College Junior School.

FIG. I. Abstract Arrangement, using rope, cotton and paint.

Student, Burwood Teachers' College.

FIG. 2. Abstract Arrangement, using coloured papers.

Boy, Grade 7, Scotch College Junior School.

FIG. 3.
All-over Pattern
using stencilling
technique.

Student, Burwood Teachers' College.

FIG. 4. Area-Filling Exercise, using coloured paper.

Boy, Form I, Hampton High School.

FIG. 5. Batik Picture, using floatation
method.

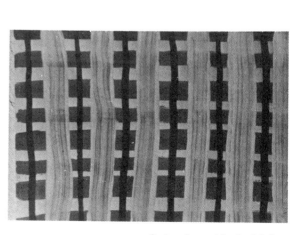

Student, Burwood Teachers' College.

FIG. 6. Broad Brush Pattern.

So that the full educational value of the exercise is realised children should be encouraged to work in a restricted range of from four to five colours, such as the three primary colours plus black and white; or black, blue, grey, and white; or in autumn colours of brown, tan, yellow/green, and cream. Narrow strips (approximately 1/16 inch wide) of background left between colour areas adds an animation and a sparkle to the completed exercise, and prevents areas of colour merging when paint is being used. Thus the colouring of areas can proceed without delay.

Area-filling exercises are experiences in design and pattern-making, and readily relate to the use of colour in modern architecture, to contemporary mosaic wall and floor treatments, to modern publicity such as pamphlets and book-jackets, to floor rugs, and to other aspects of the child's environment. Such illustrations, apart from making visual the nature of the activity, serve to emphasise that area-filling exercises are essentially experiences in pattern; the child should be conscious of the fact that he is creating an abstract pattern as he engages in the experience of dividing and colouring the given area.

ARRANGING DISPLAYS OF SCHOOL WORK

As a result of discussion and examination of specific classroom situations, children can be led to devise pleasing arrangements of teaching material, and certain items of equipment in the room, to produce an attractive environment conducive to creative activities. One of the beneficial results of such responsibility is that children show a personal interest in the appearance of their classroom, and what goes on in it. A valuable part of such activity is the training in decision-making which it affords. To arrange, for example, a display of paintings or social studies material, the children (or preferably, a group of children) must consider the mass of material available; they must examine it, consider quality, size, and quantity, exercise judgments, make selections and rejections. In doing this they develop standards and a sense of values. At first children's efforts will seem crude and unsatisfactory by *adult* criteria, but where the teacher shows patience and understanding, and gives the necessary guidance and encouragement, rapid progress results. For a fuller discussion of the displaying of pictures, the reader should refer to Displays of Pictures (p. 64).

Discussions on specific problems, such as the most attractive and efficient way to arrange the contents of cupboards or where to mass floral decorations for the best effect, should be conducted on a class basis as a rule, but the implementation of the agreed solution is best conducted as a group experience.

BATIK PICTURES (bar-teek) (see Fig. 5)

Batik pictures use simplified adaptations of the traditional Indonesian method of printing coloured designs on fabrics by waxing the parts not to be dyed. The resistance principle is basic to the method; the materials used, being incompatible, resist each other. There are a number of adaptations available for school use, and two, the floatation method and the crayon-resist method, are suitable for primary school children.

Crayon-resist Method (for all grade levels)

MATERIALS

Wax crayons; transparent water paints and sable-type brushes; cartridge paper of medium size, approximately 10 inches by $7\frac{1}{2}$ inches; water in jars; newspapers to cover desks.

TECHNIQUE

The crayon-resist method is particularly suitable for young children, or for larger groups. On the white cartridge paper a design or drawing is made in full colour using good quality wax crayons or marking crayons, firmly applied. Both light and dark colours can be used, but parts of the paper should be left white. Over this crayon drawing a wash of dark transparent water colour (purple, blue, black, etc.) is gently applied using sable-type brushes, to cover the whole sheet. The water colour, repelled by the wax crayon, colours only those parts of the paper left white. Striking colour contrasts can result, and the colours used in the original design or drawing are enhanced by the superimposition of the dark wash.

Floatation Method (for older children) (see Fig. 5)

MATERIALS

Poster paints and sable-type brushes; Indian ink; cartridge paper, 10 inches by $7\frac{1}{2}$ inches, or smaller; tap and running water; newspapers.

TECHNIQUE

A picture or design is painted in poster paint on cartridge paper, leaving areas or parts of the paper unpainted, and allowed to dry. (A portable electric heater is extremely useful at this stage to hasten the drying process). When dry, the painting is covered completely with indian ink which is also allowed to dry, after which it is gently washed under a tap. As no bonding occurs between the ink and the underlying poster paint, the ink floats off to expose the original paint areas, but remains

29

on the unpainted areas of the paper. The batik picture obtained thus shows a combination of painted areas and inked areas, and the effect is not only unusual but cannot be duplicated by any other media or process. The amount of paint exposed can be controlled by the amount of washing done; thus there is great scope for individual experiment and personal expression.

Because of the nature of the materials used and the process, the floatation method can cause problems when large numbers of children are involved. It is advisable, therefore, to limit the number of children using the method at any one time to between six and ten, working in a group.

BLOCK PRINTING

Block printing, in the sense used here, can be considered an adaptation of the familiar Linoleum Block Printing method (see p. 92). The technique is similar, but the nature of the block differs for linoleum is not used. Block printing, for which the blocks can be made easily by primary school children, is used in making all-over patterns on a large scale, either on paper or on cheap fabrics, such as cotton.

MATERIALS

Printer's inks in tubes, or student quality oil paints; rubber lino rollers; piece of $\frac{1}{4}$-inch plate glass, size approximately 12 inches by 10 inches, or smooth masonite, or linoleum; palette knife, or similar knife with pliant blade; materials and glue to make printing blocks (see under Technique); white or light coloured paper, such as litho paper, in large sheets, the size depending on the purpose; rags for cleaning purposes; mineral turpentine or kerosene; newspapers to cover working area.

TECHNIQUE

The first task is to construct the block. A piece of flat board, plywood, masonite, or heavy strawboard, is cut to a convenient shape and size, normally a rectangle, approximately 4 inches by 3 inches. This forms the backing to the block. On this is glued a considered arrangement of materials of different shapes and surface textures, such as several pieces of strawboard cut in abstract shapes, one or two pieces of coarse sandpaper, and a length of string. If a quick-drying adhesive is used, the block can be prepared in a few moments.

Next, printer's ink or oil paint is squeezed onto the plate glass or masonite and rolled across the surface to ensure even inking of the roller. The inked roller is then rolled several times in all directions over the surface of the prepared block, so that the glued materials are thoroughly inked. The inked block is taken and firmly pressed, inked side down, on the paper, using an even pressure, and repeated regularly to form the pattern. To ensure clear printing, the block should be re-inked each time it is used. Sharper registration can be obtained sometimes if several layers of newspaper are placed under the paper, and the printing, of course, should be done on a flat-topped table or bench. Variations in pattern can be achieved by reversing or inverting the block, or two blocks can be used alternately with changes of colour, or superimposed. Children should be encouraged to explore fully the possibilities of the method, and to experiment.

The teacher should prepare the table and working area with newspaper and arrange the materials so that the printing can be undertaken conveniently. The activity is best conducted with six or eight children operating as a group.

The working area should be kept tidy, and soiled paper and trial prints should be disposed of as work proceeds. The inked glass and roller can be cleaned after printing with newspaper in the first instance, and afterwards wiped clean with cloths moistened in mineral turpentine or kerosene. The inked block can be cleaned similarly by wiping.

To facilitate drying of large, printed patterns a drying line of string or wire can be erected, perhaps at the back or side of the classroom. The patterns can be pegged with small plastic pegs or paper fasteners to this line, like washing, or simply draped across and allowed to hang.

BLOTTER LITHOGRAPHY PICTURES

This activity, a little more complicated than the customary art activity found in the primary school, introduces variety and offers a challenge to those children who are eager to participate in new activities which test their developing abilities and energies. Older primary school children using this technique can obtain interesting results.

MATERIALS

Powder paints and sable-type brushes; wax crayons or marking crayons; sheets of blotting paper of medium size (approximately 8 inches by 5 inches); water in a dish, or a tap; a clean sponge is useful, but not essential; newspapers.

TECHNIQUE

On one of the pieces of blotting paper an outline drawing is made in wax crayons firmly applied so that bold lines result; these lines later will be used to separate areas of paint. The blotting paper is then liberally wet and placed on several sheets of wet newspaper so that it does not dry out. Powder paints, or other paints which contain a low gum content, are used to paint in the areas between the crayon lines.

31

A second sheet of blotting paper, also wet, is then placed on the wet painting, and, by rubbing evenly with the hand, a print is produced. If the paints used contain a high gum content it will be found that the two wet sheets of blotting paper frequently will stick, thus destroying the print. The technique can yield interesting results, but it is essential that the working surfaces are continually wet, and that strong colours are used. As a degree of dilution inevitably occurs during the taking of the print, pale colours (or thinned colours) do not print as satisfactorily as strong colours.

Because technical difficulties may occur, so that children will need individual guidance and frequent supervision, the activity is more suitable for small numbers at a work centre.

BLOWING PICTURES

This is a technique which is simple and fascinating for children. Introduced occasionally, and with purpose, it can be creative in nature and individual in result. It can be done by older children sitting in their desks, and by the whole class if the materials are available. Used excessively and without purpose, however, the technique is merely entertaining and the benefits slight.

MATERIALS

Drinking straws; thinned poster colours, water colours, or coloured drawing inks; sable-type brushes; cartridge paper, or other suitable white or light coloured paper, size 10 inches by $7\frac{1}{2}$ inches; newspapers.

TECHNIQUE

Blowing pictures can be made directly on the white surface of the paper; or, if a coloured ground is desired, the paper can be coloured with a transparent water-colour wash, the colour of the wash depending on the kind of picture the child proposes to make and the effect he wants. This wash is allowed to dry before proceeding. On the dry paper a blot of paint or coloured ink is dropped, and the child blows at it through the drinking straw, forcing it to spread across the surface of the paper. If straws are not available, the mouth can be used, but the use of the straw permits greater control of the paint movement and increases the picture-making possibilities.

Weird landscapes and underwater scenes, trees and orchards, flowers, blossoms, strange animal and plant forms, desert landscapes, and colourful flower gardens, are some of the topics possible by the blowing technique. Flowers are made by dipping the straw into the selected colour, shaking it so that only a little paint remains inside the straw, and then blowing directly down over the place where the flower is required.

Large or small flowers can be made according to the strength of the blow through the straw.

Having achieved as much as possible by blowing, children should be allowed to use a brush for a final touching-up, to add accents or detail, to define forms or objects, thus clarifying the pictorial statement.

BOOK DECORATION

There are many types of bookcraft, but most of them are too exacting for primary school children and provide little scope for creative activity and individual expression. Older children at the primary level can make simple booklets, but more opportunities for creative expression are provided by book covering and decoration, using the products of pattern-making activities in a meaningful experience.

MATERIALS

Book cloth, or large sheets of paper such as cartridge paper, litho paper, or similar paper; scissors; rulers and pencils; paste, mucilage, or milliner's solution; large pasting brushes; rubber rollers; clean rags; art materials appropriate to the techniques listed below; newspapers.

TECHNIQUE

Coverings can be made from book cloth or suitable paper sheets which can be decorated by any of the following processes, or combinations of them: Block Printing (p. 30), Colour Mingling on Wet Paper (p. 58), Finger Painting (p. 79), Marbling (p. 96), Paste Graining (p. 128), Potato Printing (p .141), Spatterwork (p. 169), Stippling (p. 58), or Tin Can Printing (p. 185). In any of the normal lessons using these techniques the child might decorate a large sheet of paper (or cloth) for the specific purpose of covering a book, folio, album, or similar article; he is thus engaging in a creative activity that is meaningful, with a clear goal to be attained. When the covering sheet is dry, the book to be covered should be laid, with covers opened out, on the sheet. The sheet is then cut, leaving a margin on all four sides. Two wedged-shaped pieces, at their minimum width as wide as the spine of the book, are cut out of the covering sheet above and below the spine. The edges of the covering paper are now folded over the front and back covers of the book and pasted, and, if the child is able to do so, the corners can be mitred to give a neater appearance.

By substituting two separate pieces of strawboard for the covers of the book and leaving a gap between them to accommodate a spine, the child can make a booklet cover in the same way. To reduce damage by wear, the spine can be re-inforced with cellulose tape, or a strip of linen or cotton fabric can be glued in position to the prepared covering sheet. The pages of the booklet, cut slightly smaller than the strawboard pieces, are lightly stitched with a needle and thread, and inserted between the covers by pasting and pressing the first and last pages to the insides of the covers. A neat label or title can be prepared as a lettering exercise (see p. 89) to complete the booklet.

Individual children might like to create folding or zig-zag booklets by joining sheets of appropriate size along their alternate vertical edges, using strips of book cloth and paste, or cellulose tape or gummed paper, so that the pages can fold flat or expand as a series of connected sheets. Back and front covers can be decorated by any of the processes indicated above. The making and use of zig-zag booklets correlates readily with such subject areas as health, social studies, or even literature.

BORDER PATTERNS

The border pattern, as the name suggests, has its motifs repeating regularly in a *single* direction, usually horizontal, and in this respect it differs from the all-over pattern (see p. 24).

MATERIALS

As with many pattern-making activities, the materials commonly used are familiar to the child—newspapers and coloured papers of all kinds, cut or torn, arranged, and pasted; powder, poster, or tempera paints, with brushes appropriate to the technique and size of paper, and ranging from bristle brushes, round and flat, to smaller sable-type brushes; pastels; oil pastels; crayons; soft coloured pencils; felt-tipped pens; on cartridge paper, cover paper, ticket paper, bulky newsprint, or similar papers. For a 30 to 45 minute lesson to older children, a piece of paper 10 inches by $7\frac{1}{2}$ inches, folded longitudinally, provides a suitable area in which to establish clearly the form and repeat of the pattern and, at the same time, provides a protective flap to fold over the completed work.

TECHNIQUE

Young children can be introduced to the making of border patterns by creating simple rhythmic arrangements using paints and bristle brushes on large sheets of classified advertisements from daily papers. Turned sideways, the columns provide guide lines which assist the child to place his pattern, and the type itself forms an interesting background surface. Newspapers are readily available, cheap, and reduce the amount of preparation. The teaching emphasis at this stage should be on the rhythmic manipulation of the materials to produce a variety of strokes, and the activity for the small child essentially is muscular.

With older children, the border pattern should be seen as an edge defining an area or shape (as around a handkerchief, a silk scarf, or a floor covering) or as a decorative band on an object (as encircling a plate or around a vase). As the nature of the pattern and the forms employed should be appropriate to its purpose, children should create border patterns always for specific applications, and actual examples, which are readily obtainable, should be shown to make visual the nature of the activity and its problems, and to add realism to the experience. Children should not be asked to create types of patterns which cannot be illustrated by familiar and recognisable applications in everyday things.

It is important that a single direction (generally horizontal) be established. The use, therefore, of bands of colour along the top and bottom edges of the area define the direction in which the pattern will repeat, limit the area, and add a finish. These defining bands need not necessarily be simple or in one colour; at the same time they should not become so elaborate that they compete with the pattern itself. Between these bands the motifs comprising the pattern will be arranged. The arrangement may be static in that the major and minor motifs, while conforming to an underlying rhythm or "flow," are not actually in contact; or the motifs may overlap and flow one into another in a continuous and lively rhythm along the border. Both the forms of the pattern and the intervening background shapes require consideration. Both should reflect planning and design. The created pattern should occupy more of the area than the background, and children as a rule are inclined to leave too much background space. Large background areas of irregular shape can not only dominate the pattern—they can destroy it because of the discord and distraction they introduce. Concepts such as major and minor motifs, dominance, alternation, balance, rhythm, appropriateness, and the like, can be explained in simple terms and illustrated by reference to common applications, as in modern wrapping papers, packaging, and fabrics.

Repetition of motifs should be done by hand. Tracing, templates, and similar devices which are educationally harmful, should be avoided. To trace around a kangaroo form a number of times does not produce an original, creative pattern; it simply degrades the activity into a meaningless and mechanical routine and deprives the child of the deep satisfaction that accompanies personal creation. Arrangements produced by these means are invariably unimaginative, lifeless, and impersonal. Satisfactory patterns are produced as a result of the exercise of imagination, thoughtful planning, use of suitable materials, and the personal solution of the problems encountered.

BOTTLE SCULPTURE (see Fig. 7)

In this activity, a form of three-dimensional expression, small bottles are used as supports around which forms are created.

MATERIALS

Small bottles such as those in which medicines, flavourings, essences, cosmetics, lotions, and similar preparations are marketed; papier mache (see p. 125) or clay or other modelling media; modelling aids such as nails, matches, icecream sticks; appropriate waste materials to provide significant detail; newspapers to cover working area and furniture; at a later stage, powder or poster paints and brushes to paint the papier mache or clay when dry.

TECHNIQUE

The selected form in characteristic dress or pose is built up around the small bottle. The use of the bottle reduces the amount of modelling material required, supplies strength and durability to the form, and lessens the risk of breakage when the sculptures are moved about. Often the shape of the bottle can influence the form of the sculpture. Human beings, real or imaginary, are most appropriate; the creation of characters from stories and literature or from social studies topics gives purpose and realism to the activity. Significant detail to assist characterisation can be worked in clay or plasticine with the simple aids or tools indicated, although clay may crack as shrinkage occurs during the drying process. Papier mache and clay can be painted in poster paints when dry. Bottle sculptures in papier mache, as well as taking paint, have an added advantage in that pieces of coloured paper or other appropriate waste materials can be affixed by pinning or pasting to add interest and to enrich the characterisation. They can be used for decorations (for example,

Little Bo-Peep in clay.

Cosmetics bottle around which clay form is modelled.

FIG. 7. BOTTLE SCULPTURE

Christmas figures or party decorations), in dioramas (see p. 63), and in social studies topics to show, for instance, peoples of other lands and the clothes they wear, or to show different occupations, such as butcher, policeman, fireman, and tram conductor.

Older children, desiring greater accuracy and more skilful representation, can use soft wire to construct a skeletal arrangement (or armature) around the bottle to show limbs in characteristic pose or action. The use of the wire increases the possibilities of the technique. Plaster of Paris or patching plaster, mixed to a thick cream in small quantities as needed, is applied by hand to both the wire and the bottle to build up the form, using a modified modelling technique. The plaster sets quickly, so that simple processes like carving, scraping, and rasping, can be used to

36

define the form, to express detail, and generally to finish the bottle sculpture ready for painting, when completely dry.

BOX SCULPTURE (see Fig. 8)

Almost all parents and teachers are aware of the need of growing children to build, to assemble, construct, and dismantle. A whole range of toys is produced to satisfy this need; toys of this nature make a positive contribution to the physical development of the child by exercising motor co-ordination and finer muscle movement. At the same time they develop initiative, resourcefulness, and the ability to think. Box Sculpture, therefore, is a legitimate classroom activity because it enables children to construct shapes and build forms using expendable and readily obtained materials in problem-solving situations. For details of a related activity see Cardboard Sculpture (p. 41).

MATERIALS

Small containers of all kinds—cigarette and sweets packets, tooth-paste boxes, aspirin boxes, match boxes, and the like; liquid glue; colourless cement, or similar household adhesive in tube form; milliner's solution (if available); cellulose tape; gummed paper; scissors; several trimming knives and sharp pocket knives; side-cutting pliers; steel pins and lills; paper fasteners; waste materials such as pipe cleaners, drinking straws, pieces of dowelling, icy-pole sticks, soft wire, etc; newspapers to cover desks and in which to dispose of rubbish; poster or powder paints and brushes to apply finishing touches.

TECHNIQUE

Selected small boxes of varying shapes and sizes, whole or cut, are assembled to represent recognisable forms and objects such as buildings, vehicles, animals, and people. Pieces of wire, pipe cleaners, wooden skewers, drinking straws, and similar materials can be used as connections between the component parts. However, children should be encouraged to discover ways of joining parts without external aids, and there will be times when inserting, folding, or using slots and flaps, will prove satisfactory methods of joining. In addition, unions between parts can be effected by using pins, paper fasteners, or tube adhesive. Children generally display great ingenuity, imagination and resourcefulness in their sculptures. In exploring ways and means of achieving their intentions they learn by experience some of the properties and limitations of the materials they are using, and certain laws governing their use.

In the final stages, expressive detail can be added to the sculptures by painting or using oil pastel, or by affixing coloured paper and suitable waste materials. Frequently

37

details on the boxes, such as trade-marks, labels, or illustrations, can add interest to the final effect. A wide variety of suitable boxes can be obtained by continuous class collection; stored in a large carton, clearly labelled, an ample supply of boxes thus is always available.

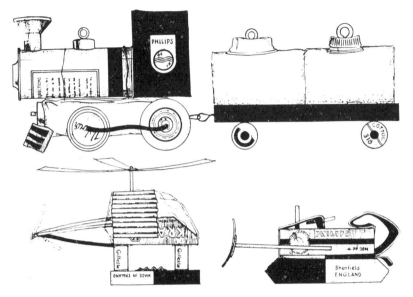

FIG. 8. BOX SCULPTURE TRANSPORT

BROAD BRUSH PATTERNS (see Fig. 6)

The nature of this type of pattern can be explained to children by reference to tartans, checks, or similar patterns produced by bands or stripes of colour in varying widths. Frequently pieces of fabric or the clothing of children can be used as teaching material. Once children understand the nature of the pattern and the broad brush technique, colourful patterns ranging from simple bands in one direction to complex intersecting arrangements can be created.

MATERIALS

Poster, powder, or tempera paints, or drawing inks; a range of brushes of different sizes, from broad flat bristle brushes to smaller sable-type brushes; cartridge paper, cover paper, ticket paper, bulky newsprint, or similar paper, 15 inches by 10 inches, or larger; palettes or suitable surfaces on which to mix colours; water in suitable containers; newspapers on desks or tables to permit free working.

Drawing inks, which are transparent, are best used on white paper, but opaque media such as poster or powder paints can be used on either white or coloured paper provided the colours selected relate agreeably to the background colour. The patterns are created by devising arrangements of bands (or brush strokes) of colour, at first in a single direction, usually vertical. Differences in width add interest, but these variations in width should repeat regularly according to a definite plan. All dimensions of the brush should be employed; with a flat bristle brush strokes of different widths can be made with the full width and also with the edge of the brush. Further variety in widths can be achieved with additional brushes. At this stage, the arrangement of multi-coloured, vertical bands or stripes should present a pattern appropriate for a printed fabric, or even for familiar objects such as canvas awnings and beach umbrellas.

When the first arrangement is dry (and if the child desires), a second arrangement of strokes or bands can be superimposed in a transverse direction, adding to the complexity of the pattern and producing a tartan-like effect. As earlier, these strokes should repeat to a regular plan or the pattern is destroyed.

Broad brush patterns can be created on an individual basis, or as co-operative exercises on large sheets of cheap paper such as litho paper or newsprint and used for decorating puppet theatres, for paper costumes (see p. 59), and for paper curtains, table-cloths, etc., where these are required in classroom dramatisations.

BRUSH AND INK PICTURES

The use of brush and Indian ink is a technique well-known to the adult artist who frequently uses it for quick impressions and preliminary studies. The main virtues of the technique are its speed and its directness. A simplified version is appropriate for older children at the primary school level.

MATERIALS

Indian ink, or ordinary school ink if Indian ink is not available (a combination of both can yield interesting results); sable-type brushes; cartridge paper, bulky news-print, or similar white paper of medium size, approximately 10 inches by $7\frac{1}{2}$ inches; water in suitable jars; newspaper to cover furniture.

TECHNIQUE

The technique is simple and direct; the picture is painted on the paper using Indian ink or writing ink instead of the customary paints. Gradations of tone can be introduced, if desired, by using clean water to dilute the ink, and a monochromatic range from dense black to soft grey is possible.

Brush and ink pictures can serve as a change of activity, and possess the advantage of simple materials which can be used by the whole class if necessary. The simplicity of the technique considerably reduces supervision and the problems of preparation and class management, giving the teacher increased opportunity for individual stimulation and guidance.

CANDLE AND PAINT PICTURES (see Fig. 9)

Interesting pictorial effects can be obtained by this technique which uses mixed media, by nature repellent, so that a resistance occurs. The result shows a combination of both materials. The technique and the materials present little difficulty to older children of primary school age, and permit ready expression of individual concepts and experiences. For related techniques see Batik Pictures (p. 28) and Waxed Paper Pictures (p. 190).

MATERIALS

Household wax candles or white crayon; transparent water paints or thinned poster colours; sable-type brushes; white or light coloured paper of medium size (10 inches by $7\frac{1}{2}$ inches); water in suitable containers; newspapers.

TECHNIQUE

Using the candle as a drawing material, either sharpened or on edge, a line drawing is made on the white paper. Firm pressure is necessary to ensure a bold wax imprint, and the drawing can contain as much detail as the child desires. Over this candle drawing, washes or areas of transparent colour are applied, at random, or as a painted picture. Sable-type brushes should be used for this stage as the stiffer bristle brushes have a tendency to scrub away the wax impression. Since water will not adhere to wax, the invisible wax lines repel the watercolour and the drawing shows through, to afford a strong white contrast. The completed picture, combining characteristics of the water colour painting and the white-lined drawing, reveals a freshness and a luminosity that are not only attractive and interesting but also unique to this technique.

CARBON PAPER DRAWINGS

In many primary grades materials for drawing are limited in range, comprising usually pencils, conventional pastels or the more recent oil pastels. The following simple technique introduces a change of medium and produces drawings which are not only different but which offer increased opportunity for experiment and individual expression.

MATERIALS

Carbon paper (pencil carbon, which is blue, black typewriter carbons, or coloured carbons for spirit duplicators); white cartridge paper of medium size, 10 inches by $7\frac{1}{2}$ inches; a collection of implements to make marks and lines, for example, a hard pencil, nail file, pointed eraser, sharpened stick, top of ball-point pen, etc.; newspapers.

TECHNIQUE

Carbon paper drawings are best done on a hard smooth surface, such as a laminex or polished table-top, or on the smooth side of pieces of masonite. Blue pencil carbon paper and spirit duplicator carbons, which are softer, permit a greater range of lines and effects and, therefore, obtain better results than typing carbons. Carbons preferably should be new, but satisfactory results can be obtained from ones lightly or partially used.

The carbon paper is inserted, inked side down, between two sheets of white cartridge paper pinned together with slide fasteners, or in one sheet folded. On the top sheet, using a firm pressure, a drawing is made using a variety of means to make the lines or marks. If the softer varieties of carbon paper are used almost any pressure applied to the top sheet, or any mark made, should register on the sheet under the carbon, giving scope for endless variety in line treatment or experiment in special effects. Thick lines, thin lines, dots, dashes, squiggles, hatching, and other details made on the top sheet register a corresponding effect on the second sheet. A pencil eraser or finger, for example, rubbed across the top sheet produces a soft scumbled area in contrast to the hard line made by the pressure of a sharpened stick or a finger nail.

The technique, simple and effective, uses few materials and is introduced without difficulty into the classroom, where any number of children working in desks or at tables can participate at the one time. It permits wide variation in individual expression, and obtains results that can be interesting pictorially, both in treatment and in detail.

CARDBOARD SCULPTURE

This activity is related to Box Sculpture (see p. 37), the same techniques and tools being employed. Only the form of the basic material is different, cardboard in sheet form being used instead of small boxes and containers, but the educational benefits advanced for Box Sculpture apply with equal validity.

MATERIALS

Strawboard of medium weight (16 ounces to 20 ounces) in sheets or pieces, and similar boards in varying thicknesses and colours; liquid glue; milliner's solution (if available); mucilage; fast-drying cement or household adhesive in tube form; cellulose tape; gummed paper; scissors; trimming knives, sharp pocket knives, or safe razor blades; cutting boards; side-cutting pliers; small tack hammer; steel pins and lills; paper fasteners; newspaper.

TECHNIQUE

As in box sculpture, the child creates a three-dimensional form to express his personal concept of the selected object or topic. During the early part of the activity the child should be motivated to form an individual visualisation of the form and nature of the object to be created; a clear mental image greatly assists the selection of appropriate materials, in determining shapes and sizes of pieces, and in other details of construction.

Pieces are cut using trimming knives, pocket knives, or similar tools. All cutting should be done on cutting boards of plywood, masonite, or even heavyweight strawboard, to prevent damage to school furniture. Joins are effected by pinning, using lills as miniature nails, or by adhesives of the range indicated. External junctions between pieces or areas can be finished neatly and strengthened by the use of gummed paper strips. When all adhesives used are dry the cardboard sculptures can be completed by the addition of coloured papers, or by painting, to add significant detail and to increase individual variation.

Difficulties encountered by the children during construction should be overcome, as far as possible, without direct assistance from the teacher. The teacher may offer guidance when requested, but the educational benefits of the experience are reduced considerably if the teacher solves the problems for the children or anticipates their difficulties. The children, having been told the nature of the activity and what is expected of them, are required to identify the problems involved and to determine their own working methods and techniques. In effect, they learn through direct participation and experience. It is for this reason that no detailed methods of construction can be supplied.

CARVING

There are a number of carving activities that fall within the performance range of children of primary school age. These range from the relatively simple soap carving to the more difficult and challenging techniques involved in wood or stone carving. Several are particularly suitable for boys in the 10 years to 12 years age group. In

42

general, carving activities, because of the nature of the materials and the equipment used and because of problems involved in preparation and class management, are conducted better with small numbers of children. In fact, an activity such as driftwood carving or soft stone carving might be attempted in the classroom by one child.

For details of the different types of carving considered appropriate for primary children see Clay Carving (p. 46), Driftwood Sculpture (p. 68), Plaster Carving (p. 134), Soap Sculpture (p. 165), Stone Sculpture (p. 176), and Wood Sculpture (p. 197).

CHALK PICTURES

Coloured chalks form a very suitable drawing medium, either on an individual basis or for collective pictures, and there are a number of ways in which they can be used. In infant grades especially, chalk possibly is better for small children to use than pastels; it is easier to hold and more responsive to their needs of expression.

MATERIALS

White chalk; coloured chalk in a strong colour range; almost any sort of paper except glossy paper, of an appropriate size, up to 18 inches by 12 inches; newspapers to cover furniture and to minimise mess; old shirts, smocks, or aprons to protect clothing; large sheets approximately 44 inches by 30 inches of wrapping paper or litho paper (rough side) if collective pictures are being made.

TECHNIQUE

There are several ways in which chalk can be used, the most common being in dry form on white or coloured paper of a suitable size and texture, or, in some infant grades, on small individual chalkboards. When a group of children are using chalk, the individual colours can be put out in small boxes, pie tins, saucers, or small paper plates, to provide ready access for the participants. The chalk should be applied boldly and directly to the surface, and older children can blend areas by rubbing. Bright colour effects should be encouraged. The chalk can be used in various ways to gain different results; for example, sharp narrow strokes can be made with the end of the stick, while broad sweeping areas are possible when the chalk is used on its side. Children should be guided to explore the full possibilities of the medium, particularly in ways of suggesting detail and other surface enrichment.

In addition to the dry technique, chalks can be used on wet paper, or dipped in water as they are used and applied to dry paper such as cartridge paper or coloured cover paper. The paper can be wet by dipping in a bucket of water, or by the use of a wet sponge, wettex, or large paint brush, size 2 inch or 3 inch. A number of advantages result from wetting the paper. The use of water transforms the chalk into a

43

semi-fluid medium, making it more responsive to children's needs, binding the chalk particles to the surface of the paper (thus reducing smudging and mess), and generally intensifying the colours used. For group pictures and murals, the areas to be chalked can be wet as they are required by using a piece of sponge or a large paint brush.

A further variation is to dip the chalks as they are used into a powdered milk preparation mixed to a thin, creamy consistency. This serves to permanently fix the chalk to the paper, and eliminates smudging when the picture dries. For large areas the paper can be painted with a thin powdered milk preparation, and the chalks used directly on the wet paper. The same technique is particularly successful with pastels.

Chalk is also a useful medium for "blocking in" murals or other large pictures which are to be completed in another medium, or combination of media, and for quick sketching.

CHARCOAL DRAWINGS

Charcoal is an excellent medium for quick sketching, indoors or outside, and for exercise in rapid working methods. It also has value in supplying variety to the range of drawing materials offered. Charcoal sticks can be made with little difficulty by older children. Dry willow sticks, stripped of bark and of even length, are packed in a tin such as a baking powder tin, curry powder tin, or mustard tin, the ends of which have been perforated. The tin containing the sticks is then placed in a fire or oven, where it remains until the sticks are partly burnt, the black residue being charcoal.

MATERIALS

Charcoal sticks, purchased or made; cartridge paper or light coloured paper, in size up to 15 inches by 10 inches; fixative (white shellac dissolved in methylated spirits and sprayed through a fly spray); newspapers.

TECHNIQUE

Charcoal is used directly on the paper, in a manner similar to chalk and pastels. Variations in pressure produce corresponding variations in line and tone, ranging from soft grey to black in a variety of widths. Masses of charcoal can be blended and edges softened by rubbing with a finger. Children should discover the possibilities and the limitations of the medium through individual experiment.

Charcoal is a very soft medium prone to smudging, and completed drawings, to be kept in good condition, require immediate fixing.

CHARCOAL AND PEN PICTURES

This technique, by combining two media, extends the possibilities of charcoal. Because the simple materials are easily provided, the making of pictures in charcoal and pen becomes an ideal drawing activity for children in the upper grades of the primary school.

MATERIALS

Charcoal; cartridge paper, or similar light coloured paper, size approximately 10 inches by $7\frac{1}{2}$ inches; Indian ink, or ordinary school ink; mapping pens, or ordinary school pens, including fountain pens and ball-point pens; fixative; newspapers.

TECHNIQUE

A charcoal drawing is made in the manner previously indicated. Increased definition of detail, dramatic or meaningful accents, and surface enrichment, are achieved by the addition of pen strokes of varying quality and thickness. On completion, the drawing is sprayed with fixative to prevent smudging of the charcoal areas.

CHARCOAL AND WASH PICTURES

Charcoal and wash is a two-stage process like charcoal and pen, and forms an additional variation of the charcoal drawing technique.

MATERIALS

Charcoal; cartridge paper, or similar light coloured paper, size 10 inches by $7\frac{1}{2}$ inches; transparent watercolours; sable-type brushes; water in suitable containers; newspapers.

TECHNIQUE

On a prepared charcoal drawing, areas and accents of transparent colour are applied gently with soft brushes to introduce colour, to distinguish component areas, and to add interest. Exposed areas of charcoal are liable to smudge, and a light spraying with fixative may be necessary.

CHARCOAL AND SHARPENED ERASER PICTURES (see Fig. 11)

More difficulty is experienced in achieving a satisfactory personal expression in this technique using charcoal, but it is well within the performance range of older children at the primary level, and can produce monochromatic pictures of unusual appearance and interest.

MATERIALS

Charcoal; cartridge paper, size 10 inches by $7\frac{1}{2}$ inches, or smaller; sharpened erasers or typewriter rubbers; small pieces of sandpaper; fixative; newspapers to cover furniture.

TECHNIQUE

A small or medium sized piece of cartridge paper is covered entirely with a layer of charcoal, rubbed with the fingers to produce an even dark-grey surface, and to remove excess charcoal. On this prepared surface, a design or picture is created by removing the charcoal with a pencil eraser sharpened to a chisel-end, or with a typewriter rubber, to expose the white paper and to produce striking contrasts of dark areas and light accents and details. The amount of white paper exposed depends on the nature of the drawing and the topic, but the amount of erasing can be controlled by the young artist so that there exists great scope for varied personal performance and expression.

Care must be exercised in handling the blackened sheet to prevent smudging, and tidy working habits should be encouraged. The erasers quickly become soiled by the charcoal, and to keep them sharp and clean they should be rubbed frequently on fine sandpaper, a small piece of which should be kept nearby.

When the erasing stage is completed and immediately the child expresses satisfaction with his picture, it should be sprayed with fixative.

CLAY CARVING

Clay in lump form is a responsive carving medium requiring simple tools to achieve satisfactory results. It forms a useful activity for children, especially boys, in the upper primary grades where it is best introduced to small groups. Lump clay generally can be obtained from clay quarries, brick kilns or potteries, frequently from local excavations and site works, and in creek banks and cuttings in country districts.

MATERIALS

Lump clay; simple carving implements such as pocket knives or boot knives; several rasps of different sizes; old files and chisels; large nails and similar tools

Boy, Grade 3, Scotch College Junior School.

FIG. 9.
Candle and Paint
Picture.

Student, Burwood Teachers' College.

FIG. 10. Coloured Cellulose Tape Picture.

FIG. 11.
Charcoal and Eraser
Picture.

Boy, Grade 6, Scotch College Junior School.

Girl, Grade 6, Box Hill South Primary School.

FIG. 12. Cloth Applique Picture.

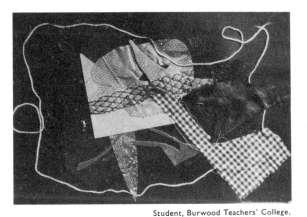

Student, Burwood Teachers' College.

FIG. 13. Collage Exercise.

Girl, Grade 6, Box Hill South Primary School.

FIG. 14. Coloured Paper Picture.

for incising detail; cutting boards of plywood or heavy strawboard; newspapers to contain mess.

TECHNIQUE

There is no prescribed technique or method. Children evolve their own techniques to meet their own needs and they solve their problems as they encounter them. The teacher should be on hand to offer advice and suggestions when guidance is requested, or when a child is obviously in difficulties and unable to proceed.

Children should approach the activity imaginatively and creatively. They should be urged to look for forms suggested in the lump itself. One piece of clay, for example, might suggest a crouching rabbit while another might contain the form of a lumbering elephant. Carving is then directed towards establishing clearly the form sensed, and to achieving appropriate surface treatment and detail. Children need not always carve recognisable objects or forms; they might prefer at times to carve purely abstract forms relying for their effect on related shapes, contours, and textures.

As lump clay is liable to fracture, unwanted portions should be carved away in small pieces. To attempt to remove large pieces is to risk damage. Children should develop all sides of the lump as they work, from the initial "blocking in" of the form to its final detailed definition and finish. The tendency shown by some children to concentrate on, and to overwork, one aspect of the form is not good three-dimensional carving and can prove detrimental to a unified and consistent expression. Shapes can be defined and surfaces finished by using rasps, files, old chisels, nails, improvised scrapers, and the like. Surface detail can be incised by cutting with a pocket knife, or scratching with a nail or nail file.

Because of the nature of the material, forms carved should be simple and blocky, with their greatest dimensions and weight near the base. The full size of the lump should be utilised to minimise the amount of carving and to achieve solidity and strength. Extended projections, excessive undercutting, and thin unions should be avoided. Realism and natural proportions should be disregarded, and distortions and simplifications incorporated in the interests of structural strength and sound technique.

Completed carvings can be left in the natural state or they can be painted with poster or similar paints, which dry matt, or with household enamelised paints, which give a gloss finish. If soundly-conceived simple forms are carved they will last indefinitely on condition they are not subjected to harsh treatment, or dampness.

CLAY MODELLING

Clay Carving (p. 46) is a subtractive process in that the form is produced by cutting away the mass; clay modelling is an additive technique in that the form is built up from the mass of pliable clay. It is the ideal modelling medium for the primary school.

Prepared clay generally can be purchased cheaply from potteries, brick kilns, and art supply stores. Clay in powder form is obtainable from mineral earth millers, and is prepared by mixing the powder with water. The powder is placed in a bucket or dish and water is added. Sufficient time should be allowed for the powder to absorb the maximum quantity of water. The excess water is then drained or siphoned off, and by evaporation the mixture is brought to a firm consistency. The firm clay can be removed from the bucket, formed in to small cylinders or spheres, and stored. A simpler method is to spread the powder on a board, add water, and mix like dough until the right consistency is attained. Satisfactory clay supplies can also be prepared from local deposits. Local clay should be crushed by pounding, and then emptied on to a flat container such as an old sand-tray so that stones, roots and other foreign matter can be removed. The crushed clay is reduced to a powder by rolling (an old wooden rolling pin can be used), and then prepared as indicated. An alternative method of preparing local clay is to soak it in water until it reduces to a soft mud, which can be strained through fly-wire netting to remove foreign matter and stones, and then dried out to a firm modelling consistency.

A plastic or a galvanised garbage can makes an excellent clay storage bin provided the clay is covered continually with a damp cloth or piece of hessian. Small quantities can be stored in plastic bags or other small plastic containers kept air-tight by rubber bands.

MATERIALS

Clay in plastic form; modelling boards of plywood, masonite, pieces of plastic, or linoleum; water, either in a bucket or from a tap; improvised modelling tools such as plastic or wooden ice-cream sticks, split wooden pegs, large nails, or pieces of comb, are useful but not essential; newspapers to contain mess and to protect furniture.

TECHNIQUE

When clay is being used in the classroom under normal conditions, tops of desks or tables should always be covered with newspapers. Any mess which might result is then simply wrapped in the newspaper and removed. Children should provide themselves with modelling boards of the kind indicated above, and a bucket of water will be required to permit occasional moistening of the clay and also for washing. If reasonable precautions are observed and a routine established for the distribution and collection of materials clay modelling makes less mess than does the use of pastels.

Modelling tools are not necessary in the primary school. Uninhibited and imaginative young children can achieve completely adequate three-dimensional expression using only hands and fingers. Should older children require tools for special surface effects and textures, however, ice-cream sticks, large nails, pieces of comb and similar aids can be used. Splendid modelling tools can be made from old pine rulers and other pieces of soft timber provided these are waxed to make them impervious.

49

The teaching emphasis should be on the modelling by the children of free-standing three-dimensional expressions individually conceived. Forms evolved should be structurally strong and capable of being viewed from all sides; as in clay carving, the greatest dimensions and weight should be near the base. Relief modelling or modelling that is relatively flat and level should be discouraged because of its two-dimensional conception.

By nature clay is a heavy, plastic material, and this imposes certain limitations on its use. Realism and natural proportions are not only unattainable by young children, but also undesirable. Children should be encouraged to model their forms accordingly. Human and animal forms must be conventionalised and distorted to achieve structural strength; legs must be made solid and thick to support the weight of the body above, and undercutting must be kept to a minimum to prevent the collapse of the mass above. Surface details can be incorporated by adding pieces of clay, or incised in the existing mass by using nails, sticks, or other simple tools. A considerable degree of individual freedom should be allowed in the interpretation of the topic, and there is a place for free, exploratory experiences for which no topic is assigned.

When completed clay models have dried out to become hard, they can be finished in the ways indicated for clay carvings (see p. 48); otherwise the clay can be reduced to a simple spherical or cylindrical shape, and, after water has been added to a thumb impression in the top, neatly stacked in the storage container and covered with a damp cloth.

CLOTH APPLIQUE PICTURES (see Fig. 12)

The use of sewing skills on collected pieces of fabrics to make applique pictures is an activity similar in some respects to the making of Coloured Paper Pictures (p. 55) and Paper Applique Pictures (p. 120). It is equally suitable for girls and boys once a certain natural though not serious resistance by boys is overcome—and can be introduced almost with any number of children, working in their desks or at tables.

MATERIALS

Fabrics and cloths of all kinds, white and coloured, plain and patterned, from nylon to felt; coloured wools, silks, and cottons; sewing needles; scissors; backing sheets (pieces of felt, flannel, old blanket, hessian, sugar bag, or cartridge paper, cover paper, Kraft paper, size 15 inches by 10 inches, depending on time allotment); pinking shears, if available; newspapers to contain mess.

TECHNIQUE

Pieces of cloth or materials are selected on the basis of suitability of colour, texture and pattern to interpret the topic or subject-matter. Thus a piece of coarse material, grey in colour, might be selected to represent a grey winter sky; a colourful flower garden, on the other hand, might be shown by an area of brightly coloured printed fabric. These pieces are then cut, arranged on the backing sheet to form the picture, and stitched in position, using as appropriate all kinds of wools, silks, and cotton threads. Much interest is imparted by the use of free creative stitching which, in addition to fixing the pieces, can supply significant details such as stars in a dark sky area, or leaf forms in a mass of foliage. As well as fabrics and felt, materials such as ribbons, rick-rack braiding, even small artificial flowers, can be used for varied effects.

Different sized sewing needles should be available to permit use of both coarse wools and fine cottons, each child requiring a large and a small needle, as well as a pair of scissors. The supply of fabric scraps can be accomplished by class collection which maintains a permanent source, or children can bring from home individual collections of suitable materials as required; the latter practice has certain advantages in regard to the preparation and distribution of materials and class management, and enables any number of children to participate, working in their desks.

The technique allows both individual and collective work, and interpretations of familiar nursery rhymes and well-loved stories form splendid topics. More than one period is needed, normally, to complete a picture in cloth applique. Frequently children, having commenced such a picture in class, in their enthusiasm complete the activity at home. As a group experience five or six children can plan and stitch a large applique picture to serve as a decorative wall-hanging. With a wide range of colourful materials from which to choose and with an imaginative approach to the task, these wall-hangings can take on some of the surface richness and fascination of modern tapestries.

COLLAGES (see Fig. 13)

Collages are arrangements of different materials of various textures and colours pasted on backing sheets, the emphasis being on the properties of the materials and their agreeable combination. The word "collage" is derived from the French word "coller" which means to paste or stick. In the restricted sense used here, collages are not concerned with the making of pictures; they are essentially exercises to direct attention to the different qualities, textures, and varieties of surfaces found in everyday materials, and they correlate easily with the planned use of texture in furniture design, interior decoration, architecture, clothing, and similar fields. The same pasting technique, of course, can be used to produce pictures, and is basic to the making of Coloured Paper Pictures (p. 55), Magazine Montage Pictures (p. 95), Mosaic Pictures (p. 110), Paper Applique Pictures (p. 120), Waste Materials Pictures (p. 188), and similar activities.

51

Parents and teachers know that children enjoy collecting and playing with assorted materials—such an activity is an accepted part of childhood. The making of collages in the classroom is a legitimate educational extension of this activity. Small children form many of their impressions as a result of their sense of touch; it can be claimed that the purposeful making of collages helps them develop this sense as they examine and manipulate materials. Experience with materials of different textures, colours, and qualities may help them to become more sensitive to materials in their environment and not only to see beauty in common things but also to appreciate the possibilities of common things as materials for creative expression. A child, arranging assorted materials to make a collage, can learn to organise his visual and tactile responses, creating new forms and combinations as he manipulates the materials. He is given experience in making independent decisions as he selects materials and controls their disposition. He is helped to think creatively and constructively and he exercises imagination and initiative as he solves the problems presented by the activity. He derives satisfaction and enjoyment from participating, as observation of any group of children at work will show.

As an art experience in the primary school, the making of collages can increase in complexity and scope to promote deeper learning as the child passes through the various grade levels. Normally the collages of older children are more carefully related and arranged than those of younger children, and reveal a development in design sense.

MATERIALS

Textured, coloured materials in a wide variety, papers, cardboards, fabrics, ribbons, strings and threads, buttons, matches, and the like, natural and manufactured; backing sheets of cartridge paper, cover paper, pasteboard, etc., size 15 inches by 10 inches, or smaller; liquid glue; milliner's solution (if available); mucilage; colourless cement in tubes; office paste; brushes for pasting; scissors; long armed staplers are useful but not essential; steel pins; newspapers to minimise mess.

TECHNIQUE

The technique is essentially one of selecting, cutting, arranging, and pasting, and offers little technical difficulty. Scissors should be sharp so that all kinds of fabrics and papers can be cut; for this reason kindergarten type scissors generally prove unsatisfactory. Children should be trained to refrain from pasting too soon. Much of the benefit derives from the critical thinking given to the juxtaposition of materials and to the combination of textures, and children need time to select, to experiment, to consider, to reject, to change and to re-form in order to evolve a pleasing arrangement. When they express satisfaction with their individual arrangements, pasting can commence. Where overlapping of materials occurs, the under piece should be pasted first. Office-type pastes stick most varieties of paper, but mucilage is needed for cardboards, fabrics, and heavier materials. Liquid glue and colourless cement will be required for hard materials such as beads, buttons, shells, sticks, etc. Materials such as wool, pieces of string, and ribbon, can be stapled, but stapling should be kept to a minimum. Parts of the collage frequently can be tacked in position, prior to pasting, with pins; this step is recommended when collages cannot be completed in the one lesson.

A wide range of suitable materials should be available in the classroom and the collection of these should be regarded as an integral part of the activity; it is an aspect that awakens the teacher and the children to textures and patterns around them, and extends a classroom experience into everyday life. The collection should be placed on an organised basis and adequate storage provided. Materials can be stored in various categories, such as smooth, rough, hard, soft, fabrics, strings and threads, and so on, in labelled shoe boxes and grocery cartons, on shelves or on the floor. In large classes where storage is limited, certain materials can be kept in large, labelled shopping bags hung on cup hooks. Sheets of patterned wrapping papers, textured wallpapers, and similar papers, can be stored flat in an art folio.

For the actual lesson, storage cartons and boxes can be placed in convenient positions adjacent to the working area so that children can make their selections individually. Smaller materials like beads, buttons, seeds, matches, or small shells, can be placed in heaps on lids of boxes or on small paper plates. In addition, children can be required to bring, for a specific lesson, individual collections of selected materials in paper bags; these can supplement the permanent class collection and provide for personal variation in the collages made.

The materials, having been collected and suitably stored, become available not only for the making of collages but also for other picture making activities which use collected materials.

COLLAGE PRINTS

Collage prints, taken from completed collages which have served their purpose, involve a simple operation which produces fascinating surface effects and patterns according to the nature of the materials employed in the collages.

MATERIALS

Completed collages; printer's inks in tubes or student quality oil paints; rubber lino rollers or brayers; piece of $\frac{1}{4}$ inch plate glass, size approximately 12 inches by 10 inches, or smooth masonite or linoleum; one or two palette knives, or similar knives; white or light coloured paper, such as thin cartridge paper, ticket paper, litho paper, bulky newsprint, of a size sufficient to cover the collage; rags for cleaning purposes; mineral turpentine or kerosene; newspapers to protect working area.

TECHNIQUE

Printer's ink or oil paint is squeezed onto the plate glass or masonite and rolled across the surface to ensure even inking of the roller. Then the inked roller is rolled several times in all directions over the surface of the collage so that the raised portions and textures are inked. A piece of paper is placed on this inked surface, gently pressed with the fingers, and pressure applied by hand or by using a clean roller. The print is lifted gently and then peeled off. On occasions, more than one print can be taken from the single inked collage, and by experimenting with various types and thicknesses of paper a variety of print effects can be obtained.

Added interest can be introduced by using more than one colour. If a child desires two colours, for instance, these can be squeezed onto the glass, blended with the roller, applied to the surface of the collage, and the print taken as indicated.

Printing can prove messy, and simple precautions should be taken. The working area should be protected by a liberal use of newspapers. Inked equipment such as rollers, or glass, can be partially cleaned on newspaper, and finally wiped clean with rags moistened in kerosene or turpentine. Soiled papers and trial prints should be disposed of quickly, as they are produced; this maintains the working table in an uncluttered, tidy condition. Because of the nature of the materials and process, the activity is best taken with small numbers of children, say, six or eight operating as a group at a work centre.

COLOURED CELLULOSE TAPE PICTURES (see Fig.10)

The making of pictures using coloured cellulose tape is essentially an activity for a small group of older children, say, six or eight in number. It is not suggested that schools purchase cellulose tape in the quantities necessary for large scale participation, but it is within the means of a school to provide a roll of each of the available colours to permit participation on a group basis, as suggested. The technique can be quick, depending on the nature of the cutting of the tape and on the complexity of the subject matter, and the results often are spectacular in their bold colour effects. The activity has value as a change of medium, and for the expression of personal concepts by direct and simple means.

MATERIALS

Coloured cellulose tape, in rolls, $\frac{1}{2}$ inch width, all available colours including white and black; scissors; pinking shears, if available; backing sheets such as cartridge paper or cover paper (particularly black), size 10 inches by $7\frac{1}{2}$ inches; newspapers to cover furniture.

TECHNIQUE

The technique is simple and permits rapid working methods. No preliminary drawing is necessary. Children should be encouraged to visualise the forms and appearance of their pictures, and to work creatively. The full width of the tape is used or it is cut in any way desired, and stuck directly onto the paper to build up areas of colour and to define forms. The possibilities of surface treatments and textures are increased by crumpling, wrinkling, or folding the tape. Pinking shears can be used to provide evenly serrated edges which add interest and variety, and contrast with the straight cuts of ordinary scissors. Scissors should be wiped after use with a cloth moistened in cleaning fluid to remove the adhesive residue.

Some thought should be given to the background colour on which the tape is stuck. Neutral colours like grey and fawn are less effective than black and white, which seem to enhance and intensify the colour combination because of the contrasts they afford. Black especially can provide a striking background to the glossy coloured tape.

Nursery rhyme topics, such as Humpty Dumpty, are particularly adaptable to the cellulose tape technique. As a rule topics chosen should be simple, comprising one or two figures or objects in an appropriate setting. Buildings, vehicles, and similar large forms that occur in topics can be massed in quickly using the full width of the tape. Details and finer accents are added by cutting the tape and superimposing the pieces.

A disadvantage of the technique is that it does not allow corrections. Once the tape is stuck down it cannot be removed without damaging the backing sheet. Children should be made aware of this so that they work with care.

COLOURED PAPER PICTURES (see Fig. 14)

The tearing, cutting and pasting of coloured papers to make pictures is one of the most popular art activities with children of primary school age. It can be introduced at any grade level, and with any number of children, providing the preparation and organisation of materials is such that children have individual supplies so that they can work in their desks and movement about the room virtually is eliminated. The activity is eminently suitable for older children whose work displays skill in arrangement and interpretation of subject matter, and a marked development in sense of design. The widest range of coloured papers of all kinds should be provided for the greater the range of paper the greater the pictorial possibilities of the technique and the opportunities for creative personal expression.

55

MATERIALS

Coloured papers of all types, textures, and colours—purchased (such as cover paper, ticket paper, surface squares, flint paper, foil paper, poster paper, and cellophane) and collected (such as sweets wrappings, commercial wrappings, wall papers, etc.); backing sheets of cartridge paper or coloured cover paper, size 15 inches by 10 inches, or smaller, according to time available; office-type paste; mucilage; pasting brushes; scissors; newspapers to contain waste and to restrict mess.

TECHNIQUE

The technique is simple. The subject matter or topic is interpreted in areas and pieces of coloured paper which are cut or torn, as desired, arranged on a backing sheet, and pasted in position. The activity should be creative, and children should experiment with surfaces, colours and shapes of paper as they make their arrangements. No pasting should be attempted until this experimental, manipulative stage is completed. The disadvantages of pasting too soon should be emphasised, and children should be satisfied with their distribution and arrangement of pieces before they commence pasting them down. Pieces at the back (or objects such as hills, buildings or trees, which are distant in space) should be pasted first so that nearer pieces can overlap to show the desired spatial relationships. The value of overlapping to minimise cutting should be demonstrated. Children should be encouraged to explore fully the possibilities of suggesting detail by various cutting techniques, by tearing, and by superimposing pieces to achieve contrasts in colour and texture. The nature of the edge employed should relate to the nature of the object being represented, so that an irregular torn edge is more appropriate to define a mass of foliage while the precision of a cut edge can more convincingly outline the shape of a building.

There are two methods of pasting that can be adopted. Working on a portion of the picture at a time, paste or mucilage is applied to the backing sheet, and the pieces of coloured paper gently pressed into position on the pasted surface; or each piece of paper is pasted separately and then placed in position. The latter method seems more common, although the former is possibly a faster technique. Care should be taken to avoid excess quantities of paste which cause waste and disfigure the work. When excess paste is used, it should be wiped away immediately with a clean cloth or handkerchief, and the child shown a clean pasting technique. Paste or mucilage can be distributed in jars, saucers, or small lids, and brushes (either paint brushes such as round bristle brushes, size 5, or improvised brushes of rolled paper) are the most useful tools for pasting.

Successful performance by the child is assisted by a choice of topics appropriate to the cutting and pasting technique which, at the primary level, precludes complex shapes and intricate outlines but which permits simple shapes in a variety of surfaces and colours. The technique is suitable for individual creative expression, and also for collective work on large murals, friezes, and for co-operative pictures. For details of making coloured paper murals, see Mural Pictures (p. 113).

COLOUR EXPERIENCES

The need of normal children to use bright, strong colour is well known to manufacturers but perhaps not so well known to some teachers and parents. Normal children should use colour fearlessly, creatively, individually, and with pleasure—using colour should be a happy experience for them. Such an approach is developed by encouraging children to experiment with colour in a variety of simple situations so that they themselves discover some of the characteristics and possibilities of its use. As a result of their direct experience they learn to use colour creatively and they discover simple techniques and colour facts that become meaningful to them.

MATERIALS

Cartridge paper, cover paper, ticket paper, bulky newsprint, 15 inches by 10 inches, or smaller according to the nature of the colour experience; paints, coloured inks, wax crayons; bristle brushes and sable-type brushes; synthetic sponges; water in suitable containers; newspapers to protect working areas.

TECHNIQUE

The techniques used are all simple and vary according to the nature of each activity, a list of which follows to indicate the kind of experience which the teacher can devise:

1. *colour observations* whenever the opportunities occur—in the classroom and out-of-doors, particularly in association with seasonal changes; unusual or pleasing colour harmonies, variations and subtleties can be noted and discussed, and related to practical use of colour in art activities in the classroom;

2. *individual, group or class collections* to show variations of a single colour; thus variations of the colour, red, in all kinds of papers and materials can be collected and pasted down to form an interesting arrangement, each variation being checked before inclusion so that duplication is avoided; such an activity demonstrates clearly to children the great range of variations that comprise a single colour "family," and their infinite subtlety;

3. *colour matching* using materials and coloured scraps stored in "colour boxes"; from a colour box containing, say, red scraps only, a child selects a sample of red in an endeavour to match the red of a classmate's cardigan, or the cover of a book, or the like, the activity again increasing and developing the child's appreciation of the subtleties of colour;

57

4. *colour mingling by pressure*, in which the child applies two or three selected colours to paper and, after either folding the paper or placing a second sheet over the colours, exerts pressure so that the colours intermingle to produce new colours and unusual effects;

5. *colour mingling by blowing*, in which the child places drops of selected water paints or drawing inks on paper; by holding the paper flat and blowing across its surface the colours are blown together so that they intermingle to again produce new colours and pleasing combinations; the child should be able to identify both the new colours and the colours which mixed to form them;

6. *colour mingling on wet paper*, preferably white cartridge paper; sable-type brushes are used to drop transparent watercolours or drawing inks on the wet paper which, when tilted, causes the colours to flow together so that they mix, forming additional colours and interesting harmonies;

7. *colour mingling by superimposition*, using transparent watercolours or drawing inks over wax crayons, the combination of the two media leading to richly varied colour effects, especially when white paper is used;

8. *stippling with a sponge* on white and coloured paper, using a limited colour range to produce a colour harmony; thus a child stippling with red and yellow discovers as a result of the experience that these colours produce orange, and the colour fact becomes of significance to him;

9. *stippling with crumpled paper*, which forms a variation of the previous technique, gives a somewhat different effect;

10. *colour matching using paints*; children attempt to match a given colour by mixing paints (or pastels) and afterwards discuss the various colours used in the mixing and the results they produced.

Activities like those above can be completed in a short working time. Thus they lend themselves to the beneficial use of spare time that sometimes occurs for a number of reasons towards the end of other art lessons, while the materials are distributed and the room arranged, or a number of them might be related to comprise a short lesson of, say, 20 or 30 minutes duration. The various materials required for the activities selected can be arranged in work centres around the room, and the children move in an orderly manner from one to another, completing as many as they are able of the experiences provided.

CORK PRINTING

The use of household corks and bottle stoppers to print patterns is a simple technique, presenting no technical difficulties and using materials readily provided. As the technique produces only abstract patterns or arrangements and is not suited to picture making, no problems of subject-matter arise. If the materials can be provided in sufficient quantity, it can be taken as an individual exercise with any number of children, although large numbers create problems of adequate supervision and guidance.

MATERIALS

Household corks and bottle stoppers, all sizes and varieties; cartridge paper or other light coloured paper, size 10 inches by $7\frac{1}{2}$ inches or smaller; poster paints or powder paints; improvised printing pads, which may range from blanket or cotton wool in a saucer, to small pieces of carpet, to felt discs cut to fit lids of jars nailed to a piece of board; cutting tools such as sharp pocket knives and small files; newspapers to cover generously the working area; some paint brushes, spoons, and rags for cleaning, are desirable.

TECHNIQUE

It is important that the cork or bottle stopper has a *flat* end; uneven or damaged corks should be rejected. Corks may be used uncut, or a simple design consisting of one or two cuts across the end of the cork can be made with the pocket knife or small file, the larger the cork the easier the cutting and the greater the design possibilities. The cork can be inked in two main ways. One way is to paint the end with fairly thick poster paint each time it is used, and the process, while quick initially, is inclined to become tedious. A second method is to provide improvised printing pads which are moistened (but not flooded) with poster paint; the cork is pressed onto the paint-moistened material (blanket, flannel, cotton wool, felt, etc.) which comprises the pad, inked, and applied to the paper. Children generally find this technique interesting, and they should be encouraged to explore the numerous possibilities of its use. Two or more corks, large and small, for instance, can be used alternately with changes of colour, or in other ways, and the possibilities of different types and colours of papers should be examined. At times, fluted edges of plastic stoppers and metal bottle tops can be inked and used to impart interest and variety to the printed pattern.

The technique is essentially an exercise in pattern and the imprints on the paper should conform to a rhythmic order. No ruled framework is necessary. The top edge of the paper can serve as a guide when placing the first row of repeats, and other rows follow, repeating regularly to form the pattern. A tendency to leave large background areas should be discouraged. At times, backgrounds can be painted and the cork prints superimposed to impart interest and variety to the technique.

COSTUME MAKING

Costume making, using papers of various sorts supplemented by items of clothing and accessories brought by the children from their homes, is an art activity that enables individual children to realise their personal impressions of characters and

59

familiar figures in their songs, literature, and nursery rhymes. All children enjoy "dressing up," so the activity becomes a useful educational extension of a play activity. In conjunction with Mask Making (p. 98) the making of simple but colourful costumes gives new interest and educational meaning to classroom dramatisations, and correlates readily with other subjects in the curriculum. The activity is more suited to children in the upper grades, and the various costumes and accessories can be made by groups of 3 or 4 children.

MATERIALS

Paper in large sheets or rolls, such as shelf paper, crepe paper, and poster paper, white or coloured; scissors; mucilage or paste; cellulose tape; needles and thread; painting materials to add decorations and other detail; scrap paper; items of clothing and accessories collected by the children; newspapers from which to cut patterns.

TECHNIQUE

As with other forms of three-dimensional expression, a preliminary visualisation by the children of the character is an important prerequisite to successful costume making. Children should form individual "mental pictures" of the character as a personality, with dress, detail, accessories, etc. The next stage is to make quick sketches on scrap paper, trying out ideas, clarifying them, always seeking to crystallise the mental image. From these sketches a child, or children, can select one which offers possibilities, and this is further developed and defined to express the spirit of the character as imagined by the children. All items and details of the complete costume should relate towards this end.

To prevent mistakes and to avoid later waste of effort and materials, patterns should be prepared and cut out in cheap paper such as large newspaper sheets or brown wrapping paper, using the prepared sketches as guides. When the patterns are corrected, methods of joining and fitting considered, difficulties anticipated, and materials selected, the final stage in the making of the costume is reached. Only when these preliminary steps have been completed satisfactorily should the making of the actual costume be commenced.

An unwanted item brought by one of the children, such as an old dinner jacket or a large ribboned hat, might serve as a starting point, supplemented by other articles, so that the children have only to make the missing items to complete the characterisation according to their preparatory sketches. There are many materials the children can use which are relatively inexpensive, such as shelf paper and crepe paper, in large sheets. The required items of costume are cut out using the prepared patterns, stitched, pasted or taped together, and fitted. Details and decoration can be added by painting, using poster or powder paints and large bristle brushes.

60

Accessories such as pirate swords or gypsy ear-rings can be made in appropriate materials and painted. Old clothes brought by the children, such as an old suit or dress, similarly can have colourful decorations added by painting.

To complete the costume—and the characterisation—a suitable mask should be made, perhaps by one of the children in the group while the others are completing final details of the costume. For further information on the making of masks, see Mask Making (p. 98).

CRAYON PICTURES (see Fig. 24)

Crayons are a useful and popular medium with children and possess a special value for the small children in infant grades, where they permit and encourage the manipulative movements which assist the development of the small child's muscular co-ordination. The child is able to follow his motions because the crayon stroke gives a clear, firm impression on the paper. The medium has value not only for young children, however, for crayons can be a responsive and satisfying material for older children in the primary school.

MATERIALS

Crayons, in large *soft* sticks, such as marking crayons; white or light coloured paper, such as cartridge paper, litho paper, or cover paper, size 10 inches by $7\frac{1}{2}$ inches, and of sufficient texture to take the crayon; newspapers.

TECHNIQUE

Crayon drawing is a simple, direct technique offering little difficulty, like drawing in chalk, charcoal or pastels. The crayons used by children should be of a size that permits easy handling, and soft to use; they should leave a liberal and vivid deposit of pigment at each stroke. Crayons that are excessively waxy should be avoided. Both the end and the side of the crayon can be used, and children should press firmly to obtain rich colour effects. Line and mass treatments are possible, but small children experience some difficulty in achieving large colour areas; their colour application is uneven and the effort is often accompanied by muscular fatigue and tediousness. This can be overcome by guiding children to draw their pictures in a way that avoids large areas; skies can be divided by cloud forms or tree branches and foreground areas by rock forms, plants, fence posts, and so on. Working in small areas and applying the crayons firmly, children can produce brightly coloured, richly varied expressions.

61

The texture of the paper can range from smooth to medium. Rough textures should be avoided, for the child is unable to obtain the colour areas he desires and frustration results; even the most persistent child can be defeated by materials that deny his urge for spontaneous expression. Paper that is too thin also proves unsatisfactory.

Crayons can be used in activities other than drawing, and for details of other uses the reader should refer to Fabric Printing (p. 75) and Melted Crayon Activities (p. 102).

CUTTINGS BOOKS

Cuttings books, or scrap books as they are sometimes called, can be compiled by older children to serve growing personal interests in various aspects of art. They possibly achieve best results when introduced on a voluntary basis as an extra-curricular activity. When five or six children enthusiastically commence cuttings books, displaying a lively interest in their contents and using them, perhaps, for brief class talks, other children are inspired to do likewise. In this way interests in art can be generated that extend beyond the processes and experiences of the classroom.

MATERIALS

A suitable book (such as an exercise book containing ruled and plain pages, or an art student's sketch book); scissors; paste; cuttings (see below); writing materials.

TECHNIQUE

The cuttings book becomes a collection of items about art and artists, with illustrations and reproductions, cut from daily papers, magazines and periodicals, and pasted in the book to present a neat, ordered appearance. Simply to paste the cuttings in a book, however, is not sufficient. All items should be labelled and the child should be encouraged to express his own ideas and opinions, in his own terms and at his own level. Educationally, this expression of ideas and shaping of opinions is the most important aspect of the activity, for it leads to the formation of critical judgments and the ability to appraise, to analyse, and to evaluate. Guidance from the teacher will be necessary, and spectacular results should not be expected immediately; children need time for their interests to grow and their opinions to emerge.

There is some risk of vandalism accompanying the making of cuttings books. Children should be trained not to cut or to mutilate valuable books, and magazines and periodicals should not be cut until they are finished with. Old Christmas cards bearing reproductions of paintings, on the other hand, form a useful source of illustrations, while post cards and small reproductions in a wide range are available from gift shops and art galleries in most large cities.

DECORATIVE STITCHING

The terms Decorative Stitching and Embroidery Pictures refer to the same activity. For details of Decorative Stitching, therefore, the reader is directed to Embroidery Pictures (p. 71).

DIORAMAS

The diorama is a three-dimensional interpretation of a topic contained within a setting made from a box or grocery carton. The topic may represent such things as a circus scene, portion of a story or a nursery rhyme, an item from the social studies course, or even such titles as "The Witches' Picnic" or "The Sunken Galleon." The making of a diorama is an excellent co-operative exercise for a group of three or four children at any grade level, so long as the teacher is prepared to accept the children's own level of performance and does not expect adult standards in concept and execution.

MATERIALS

Shoe boxes, cartons of small to medium size, and similar boxes; a wide range of papers, white and coloured; paints; brushes, for painting and for pasting; crayons, coloured pencils, and other common art media; waste materials of all kinds; paste, mucilage, glue; cellulose tape; gummed paper; scissors, trimming knives, sharp pocket knives; pins, lills, paper fasteners; newspapers in generous supply.

TECHNIQUE

The box or carton is prepared as a miniature stage by cutting away one side and the top, and painting the interior in a manner appropriate to the topic; it is important that this painting of the background setting is done before the foreground objects are arranged in position. All kinds of materials can be used to create the objects, figures, and other details placed in this setting, the uses to which materials can be put being unlimited. Many art media, and techniques of drawing, painting, constructing and modelling, are employed. No method of working can be prescribed; the children evolve ways and means of attaining their defined objectives as they proceed and overcome technical difficulties as they encounter them. The teacher's main task is that of stimulation and encouragement, and of giving guidance and advice on request.

The making of dioramas exercise creative thinking and requires an imaginative approach to the work. They can involve much planning and effort. Very rarely can they be finished in one lesson. Normally several lessons are required, and the storage of the unfinished dioramas during this working period presents a real problem in a crowded classroom.

A variation of the diorama technique is the peep show which generally is constructed in a shoe box. In one end of the box a circular opening approximately 1 inch in diameter is cut. Inside and towards the other end a three-dimensional interpretation of a topic is created, in a manner similar to the diorama. The top is then covered with coloured cellophane, tissue paper, or plastic, to produce unusual and interesting lighting effects inside the box. For example, an arrangement of blackened cardboard tree trunks placed against a background of devastation and lit from above through red cellophane, gives a striking and dramatic bush fire effect when viewed through the peep hole. Children can experiment with the use of two or more sheets of coloured cellophane, superimposed in whole or in part, to produce special lighting effects.

The making of dioramas and peep shows as a classroom activity relates to the designing of sets for the legitimate theatre, shop window displays, trade exhibits, and much modern publicity; these applications at the adult level frequently can be used to demonstrate the nature of the activity to children.

DISPLAYS OF PICTURES (see Figs. 15 to 22)

Collecting and making displays of pictures, as a classroom experience, is aimed at developing within the individual child the ability to appraise, to criticise, and to make sound judgments, as well as to assist his enjoyment and understanding of art in some of its many and varied forms.

MATERIALS

Collected pictures, reproductions, or photographs, centred on a common theme, and ranging from examples of children's paintings or reproductions of adult art to newspaper illustrations of furniture, or motor vehicles, or household appliances; display board; white and coloured paper, such as cartridge paper, cover paper or ticket paper, suitable for mounting; steel lills; a wall stapler or long armed stapler, if available; felt-tipped pens, marking crayons, soft black pencils, for labelling purposes.

TECHNIQUE

Arranging displays of pictures is an activity that can at times be left to children working in a group, or to a group working under the supervision of the teacher. But there will be times when, to realise the full educational benefits of the display, the selection and arrangement should be undertaken by the teacher. Perhaps the greatest problem surrounds the selection of material, whether it be children's work or other pictures, and the teacher alone possesses the maturity, experience, and background to decide the worth of individual items. While children may arrange, for example, a display of their own paintings, the teacher should be responsible

FIG. 15. Stapled to Backing
Sheet.

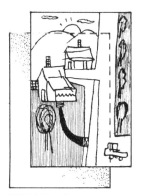

FIG. 16. Overlapping Sheets.

FIG. 17. Window Aperture
cut in Mount Sheet.

FIG. 18. Separate Windows
cut in Mount for Picture
and Title.

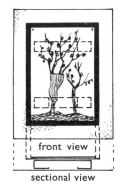

front view

sectional view

FIG. 19. Projecting Forward
from Mount.

FIG. 20. Corrugated Card-
board, Plain or Painted.

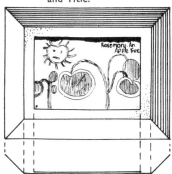

FIG. 21. Bevelled Box Mount.

strawboard
mount

mount cut
and folded
back

mounted
picture

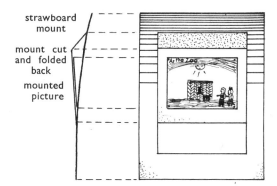

FIG. 22. More Elaborate Mount for Special
Purpose, e.g., "Picture for the Week."

SOME METHODS OF DISPLAYING TWO-DIMENSIONAL WORK

for the selection, or at least assist, so that all children have equal opportunity and the benefits of reward and incentive are available to all. Frequently the teacher can make the selection in consultation with the children, to whom the reasons for the selection should be explained. When children as a group, or an individual child has made a collection of pictures to illustrate a topic of interest, such as design in motor cars, the selection and arrangement can be left to the group or the individual, with the teacher being available for guidance if required.

The pictures for display will show to better advantage and make a greater impact on the viewer if they are mounted on cheap, appropriately coloured background sheets such as ticket paper or cover paper. For standard uniform mounting white cartridge paper is possibly the most useful material. If care is taken so that backing sheets are not subjected to unnecessary damage or mutilation, they can be returned after the display to the stock of art paper. The proportions between the picture and the mount require consideration. The picture should be located on the mount in such a way that the areas of mount showing above and to each side of the picture are equal in width while the area below should be slightly larger, so that the picture lies well up on the mount, and also to accommodate any labelling or captions necessary. An easy method of mounting, though not necessarily the neatest, is simply to place the backing sheet behind the picture and to fix both sheets to the display board (see Fig. 15). A neater method is to cut a "window" or aperture (see Fig. 17), in size slightly smaller than the picture, in the mount; the picture is attached to the back of the mount with tape, thus obscuring torn or rough edges. Sometimes mounts of the same size as the picture can be used, with the picture placed on the mount so that only two edges of the backing show (see Fig. 16). Other methods of mounting are shown in the accompanying drawings.

When arranging pictures the aim should be to produce a display that is attractive and educational, and marked by a neat ordered appearance. Clarity of presentation should be a primary consideration; each picture should be displayed in some measure of isolation so that it makes its impact without distraction, and free use should be made of background spaces. The temptation to show too many pictures should be avoided. Pictures should not overlap or project beyond the limits of the board. The available display space should be pleasantly occupied by a balanced distribution of large and small, or coloured and black-and-white, pictures; the main unit should be placed first and the other pictures arranged around it to produce an effect of order and unity. Meaningful grouping of pictures is important; at times displayed material can be more effective when it is based on (1) a *supplementary* arrangement in which all pictures illustrate a single topic, for example, paintings of summer, (2) a *complementary* arrangement, where the main units show paintings of summer emphasised by contrasting pictures of cold winter, storms and snow, and (3) an *enumerative* arrangement in which the displayed pictures illustrate unrelated objects, all of which are relevant, however, to the central theme. With most arrangements a central theme of some kind is necessary to give the display purpose and unity.

66

Displays generally should be based on a system of vertical and horizontal lines as these harmonise with the main architectural lines of the room, and of the display board itself. Pictures on angles or placed in diagonal arrangements can appear distracting and untidy. Each display should be accompanied by a large clear title telling what the display is about, and it is advisable at times to label individual pictures. The displayed material should not only be in a prominent position but all children should have easy access to it; otherwise the display defeats its primary purpose. Displays should be changed regularly so that the display board remains always an interesting and inviting area of the room, making a positive contribution to the educational process.

If a wall-stapler is not available, an ordinary stapling machine sometimes can be pressed into service to fix pictures to fibre boards such as caneite. Otherwise pictures should be affixed with steel lills, driven in on the angle; these cause less damage to the mount sheets and are less conspicuous than shoe tacks or the customary drawing pins.

DISPLAYS OF THREE-DIMENSIONAL WORK

While the display of pictures presents some problems and difficulties it is generally easier to accomplish in a normal classroom than the display of children's three-dimensional work. Most classrooms are not equipped with glass-fronted display cases or even adequate open shelving, and it becomes necessary to improvise in order to mount a display. The children can be consulted and their suggestions considered; this enables them to take an active interest in the display. A group of children might be given the responsibility of arranging the exhibits, subject to the teacher's supervision and approval.

MATERIALS

Three-dimensional products of art activities, ranging from single clay figures, or carvings, to dioramas or space designs; items of furniture such as a table or open shelving; coloured paper such as cover paper or surface squares to use as display mats; materials for labelling.

TECHNIQUE

As stated, few classrooms possess suitable display cases in which three-dimensional work can be exhibited. Nevertheless, by improvising, much can be done to present such work under favourable circumstances.

In classrooms where space permits, a narrow table or bench, or even a disused desk covered with plywood or masonite, can be placed in front of an existing display board to serve as a surface on which a display of three-dimensional articles can be

67

arranged. In some of the recent prefabricated classrooms the flat window ledges can provide limited space on which selected clay models, simple carvings, space designs and the like can be exhibited for short periods. A group of small shelves of different lengths and intervals between can be attached to an existing display board on right-angle metal brackets; such a device provides some opportunity for the showing of three-dimensional work. Similar sets of shelving can be used against walls, like shadow boxes.

Just as the display of pictures requires care and consideration, so also should a display of three-dimensional work be based on applied principles of design and good layout. The arrangement should be a balanced one. It should have interest and a dominant focal point. Coloured paper can be used to provide an appropriate background, in either a uniform colour or as a varied pattern behind the objects. The objects themselves should be arranged according to their size and height. Tall objects should be placed to the rear so that smaller ones in front show to advantage. All objects, large or small, appear better standing on coloured display mats of simple shape, such as rectangles or circles. If the display fitting permits, objects should not be placed in straight rows which become monotonous; better effects can be obtained by placing articles on different heights, as in open shelving, and even at different distances, as on a table or bench.

Thought should be given to means of introducing unity to the exhibit; the production of a unified appearance should be a governing principle. This can be done by displaying the same kind of objects, such as soap carvings, or by using display mats of the same colour, or by employing a standard background colour, or even by uniform labelling. A sense of ownership and status, as well as the pleasure of reward, is developed in the child if a small card, made by the young artist himself and giving name and title (if any), is placed near each exhibit. When three-dimensional work is displayed against or below an existing display board, and the two displays are related in some ways, the relationship can be emphasised by the use of white strings, coloured wools, paper arrows, and similar devices.

As with the display of pictures the teacher should accept the final responsibility for the arrangement and appearance of the display. This should not be left entirely to immature and inexperienced children. As children gain in experience and judgment, the teacher's role can become less obtrusive. Nevertheless, if the display is to achieve its full impact, only the teacher can provide the mature consideration needed to overcome the problems associated with the display of three-dimensional work.

DRIFTWOOD SCULPTURE (see Fig. 23)

The carving of driftwood and other pieces of wood obtained locally directs the child's attention to the possibilities for creative expression of common materials in his environment. It is a useful activity for older children in seaside and country

68

areas who have had previous carving experience and are familiar with the use of cutting tools. Numbers participating should be small, between one and six children. Driftwood sculpture is a relatively difficult activity presenting a challenge to the creative abilities and imaginative powers of children In upper grades, especially boys for whom carving, whittling and the handling of materials, are strong attractions.

MATERIALS

Driftwood pieces, in the form of weather-beaten or water-worn butts, roots, or broken branches; simple carving implements, such as sharp pocket knives; one or two chisels and a mallet; several rasps of different sizes; sand paper or emery paper; cutting boards, if a craft bench or old table is not available; finishing agent, such as solid wax, or clear varnish and suitable brush; newspapers.

TECHNIQUE

As with Clay Carving (p. 46) children should work creatively, looking for forms in the pieces of driftwood they collect. Driftwood frequently suggests an interesting shape or object, and little carving is needed to work up the form inherent in the piece.

Piece of stick from which sculpture below was made.

Reptile Form, after carving, sand-papering and painting.

FIG. 23. DRIFTWOOD SCULPTURE

Carving tools are available, such as V-cutters, gouges, and chisels, but their purchase by schools is hardly warranted in view of the limited numbers who will participate in driftwood carving. A considerable amount of carving can be done with a sharp pocket knife, and the child can gain much satisfaction from using this simple and familiar tool. If the carving is being done at a desk, a cutting board of plywood should be used. The pocket knife or chisels are used to remove excess and unwanted wood until the form is blocked out; the form is then refined by the use of rasps. All sides of the sculpture should be developed simultaneously. Parts of the surface can be left in the natural driftwood state, but where smooth areas are required these can be obtained by the use of sand paper or emery cloth. The value of tool marks in imparting a certain quality to the surface in contrast to the natural texture of the driftwood should not be overlooked.

The final treatment of the sculpture requires care so that the inherent beauty of the driftwood is preserved. Several coats of solid wax (in the form of furniture polish or floor polish) can be applied and polished vigorously by using a cloth, or the sculpture can be painted with clear varnish or colourless shellac. The completed driftwood sculptures can be displayed effectively on small stands or bases, such as small wooden boxes, painted black or white.

The possibilities of driftwood sculpture are increased if other materials are incorporated to give more freedom of expression. Coloured buttons can serve as eyes on animal forms, for instance, or pieces of teased rope used for tails. However, it is important that this use of additional materials is not overdone, otherwise the essential character of the driftwood sculpture is lost.

DUOPRINTS (see Fig. 25)

The making of duoprints is a fascinating process for children of primary school age, and the activity can be introduced at any grade level from about grade 2 upwards. Providing adequate supplies of marking crayons are available, the making of duoprints is possible with any number of children, working in desks or at tables. As it is not possible to anticipate the exact appearance of the two prints produced, the process often yields results that are accidental and charming. The technique permits performances that can range from simple line treatments to highly complex, detailed pictures. The making of duoprints therefore caters for every level of ability, and all children can participate and achieve success at their own levels.

MATERIALS

Wax crayons, such as marking crayons, with extra quantities of black; cartridge paper, size 10 inches by $7\frac{1}{2}$ inches; hard pointed pencils or ball-point pens; newspapers on desk to provide smooth working surface.

TECHNIQUE

The technique employs two sheets of paper, or a single sheet, size 10 inches by $7\frac{1}{2}$ inches folded to a size 5 inches by $7\frac{1}{2}$ inches. The folded sheet seems easier for small children to handle as the top sheet cannot slide or move. On the under sheet marking crayons are applied with pressure in a random distribution of colours to achieve strong colour areas, and covering the entire sheet; the stronger the colours at this stage the more striking will be the finished duoprint. This random colour application is then covered completely with black crayon, so that there exist two layers of wax crayon, one coloured, one black. A top sheet is either placed or folded over this, and a drawing made with a pointed implement, such as a hard pencil or a ball-point pen. The pressure of the pencil on the top sheet lifts the black crayon so

70

that it adheres to the underside of the sheet, exposing the coloured crayon surface on the first sheet. Thus two prints quite different in appearance are produced, one in colour and one in black and white; hence the name, "duoprint."

The technique is flexible and responsive to children's desires, and they should experiment to discover the various possibilities of working in line and mass. Any kind of mark made on the top sheet should register correspondingly on the sheet below as well as on the underside of the top sheet, and a wide variety of detail is possible. Few difficulties are encountered, but disappointing results follow a weak application of crayons in both the colour stage and the later application of black. The making of duoprints is an ideal activity for short lessons as the complete process can be accomplished comfortably in a 30 minute period.

EMBROIDERY PICTURES (see Fig. 26)

Embroidery pictures differ from Cloth Applique Pictures (p. 50) in that they are linear in treatment, while the latter rely on masses or areas of colour. The same sewing skills, however, are used. The making of embroidery pictures has been revived in recent years as a *creative* activity suitable for older children at the primary level, and any number of children can participate as the materials are simple and readily provided; children can bring almost all that is needed from their homes. The results can be striking and colourful, and often make excellent wall decorations. The activity lends itself to individual as well as to group use.

MATERIALS

Embroidery silks, cottons, wools, in various thicknesses and colours; sewing needles in a range of sizes; scissors; backing materials, such as felt, fine hessian, burlap, and similar coarse fabrics, or sheets of cartridge paper or coloured cover paper, size 15 inches by 10 inches or smaller; newspapers.

TECHNIQUE

The technique is essentially one of sewing, using a variety of threads and stitches in an activity that is creative and which permits wide individual variation. The picture or design can be planned first on scrap paper as a linear arrangement to serve as a guide for the later stitching, or the sewing can be done directly on the backing material. Few children of primary school age, however, possess the design sense to evolve a well balanced and unified arrangement without some initial planning. A favourite drawing or painting might serve as subject matter, or the child might interpret an assigned topic such as a nursery rhyme, or an incident or situation from a well-known story. Embroidery pictures can be made interesting and colourful, and a wealth of detail included, by varying the types of stitches and threads used. Stitches such as

71

chain stitch, blanket stitch, cross stitch, running stitch, outline stitch, stem stitch, buttonhole stitch, feather stitch, long and short stitch, chains and loops, and knots, can all be used, and children should experiment with known stitching techniques in order to evolve additional ways of using thread to meet their needs of expression.

Various coarse fabrics such as those indicated make durable and appropriate backing sheets, but if such fabrics are not available, embroidery pictures can be sewn quite satisfactorily on cover paper, thin card, or even cartridge paper. Edges are protected and a finish added by blanket stitching around the edge of the picture, or by binding the edge with tape, ribbon, or felt.

Groups of 3 or 4 children can combine to work on large stitched pictures. The activity should be conceived as a true group experience in which the children all contribute and share the responsibility. The picture is planned as a collective effort, transferred to hessian, cheap canvas or other coarse fabric, and stitched, each child accepting responsibility for an allotted portion or feature. When completed these large embroidery pictures, like Cloth Applique murals (see p. 51), make colourful and lively wall hangings.

ETCHING (see Fig. 27)

The process of etching as an adult art activity is well-known for it has a long history dating back to the 16th century. The adult technique, of course, is too technical and laborious for school use, but a simplified version of dry-point etching puts the making of simple etchings within the performance range of the older boy or girl in the primary school. The technique, known as celluloid etching, uses printing inks and involves several stages, and is suitable therefore as an activity for small numbers of children who will require continual supervision and guidance at the various stages.

MATERIALS

Pieces of thick celluloid, perspex, or similar clear plastic, size approximately 6 inches by 4 inches, or smaller, to serve as etching "plates"; black printer's ink or student quality oil paint; piece of $\frac{1}{4}$ inch plate glass, tin, or smooth masonite, size 12 inches by 10 inches; pliable knife; ink dabber (see below); improvised etching tools (see below); piece of soft felt for wiping plate; thin absorbent paper, such as blotting paper, cut to a size larger than the "plate"; cellulose tape; scissors; water; press or spoons, for printing; cleaning materials such as mineral turpentine, kerosene, and rags; newspapers to protect clothing and furniture.

TECHNIQUE

The four stages in the simplified etching technique are (1) the preparation of a suitable drawing and its transfer to the plate, (2) the preparation of the paper for

72

Girl, Grade 6, Box Hill South Primary School.

FIG. 24. Crayon Picture.

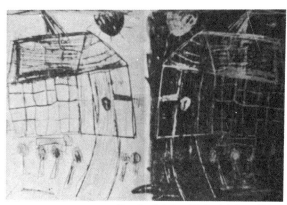

Boy, Grade 1, Box Hill South Primary School.

FIG. 25. Duoprint, showing the linear and mass prints which result.

Boy, Grade 5, Scotch College Junior School.

FIG. 26. Embroidery Picture.

Student, Burwood Teachers' College.

FIG. 27. Simple Etching.

Student, Burwood Teachers' College.

FIG. 28. Felt Applique Picture.

Boy, Grade 3, Scotch College Junior School.

FIG. 29. Finger Paint Picture, cloth fish superimposed.

printing, (3) the inking of the plate, and (4) the printing from the plate. The mounting of the prints could constitute a fifth stage.

An outline drawing in pencil or pen and ink is made on white paper such as cartridge paper or bulky newsprint; this drawing should be slightly smaller in size than the plate of celluloid. The celluloid is placed over this drawing, and the drawing fixed to the underside of the plate with cellulose tape. As the celluloid is transparent, the prepared drawing can be seen clearly. The drawing is then reproduced on the celluloid by incising the lines with improvised etching tools which can be made from discarded dental probes, or by fitting gramophone needles or large sewing needles into wooden handles. Large nails sharpened to a fine point also can be used. Differences in line are achieved by varying the pressure on the tool, and lines ranging from thin to heavy and bold are possible. When the drawing on the plate has been etched satisfactorily, the paper is removed from the back of the plate, and retained for reference.

Now the printing paper can be prepared. Absorbent paper should be cut an inch or so larger than the plate, and dampened thoroughly on both sides by dipping in water or by sponging. A number of sheets should be dampened, piled together wet on wet, and placed between wet newspaper or wet blotting paper so that they remain wet while the plate is being inked. The number of sheets prepared in this way will depend on the number of children participating in the activity, but each celluloid plate is capable of producing 10 to 12 prints; so by multiplying by the number of children engaged an estimate can be made.

When the paper has been prepared, the plate is ready for inking. A small quantity of printer's ink or oil paint (thinned, if necessary, with turpentine) is squeezed onto the plate glass or masonite, and dabbed with an improvised dabber, which can be made by tying several layers of a finely woven material such as cotton around a large cork bottle stopper, or by inserting a wad of cotton-wool inside a piece of old kid glove which is tied at the top. The inked dabber is then used to distribute a layer of ink evenly over the entire surface of the plate and in the incised lines, using partial rotations of the dabber to force the ink into the finer lines. Next, the ink is wiped off, gently using a piece of thin felt, folded; but care is needed so that the ink is not removed from the incised lines. Whether the background areas are completely wiped free of ink depends on the nature of the topic; sometimes a definite mood or atmosphere is created by leaving the plate partially inked. At this stage, the inked drawing becomes clearly visible in the transparent plate, and can be compared with the original drawing for accuracy.

The plate is now ready for printing, either by spoon or by press. Spoon printing is the easier method for young children. The dampened, absorbent paper is placed over the inked plate, and both plate and paper inserted between thin packing sheets. Firm pressure is exerted by pressing on the bowl of a dessert spoon or a wooden mixing spoon so that the dampened paper is forced into the incised lines where it takes up the ink. The spoon should be used in circular or backwards-and-forwards motions so that pressure is applied to the whole surface of the paper, which should be held with the free hand to prevent accidental movement. By gently lifting the paper occasionally the quality of the printing can be checked. Apart from its simplicity, the advantage of spoon printing is that the pressure can be varied as desired, producing gradations of tone and enabling the young artist to experiment with special and unusual effects.

The traditional means of printing, of course, is by a special etching press. Presses suitable for use by older children are available at reasonable prices, but are rarely found in primary schools. Experience suggests that the best results in terms of end-products are obtained on an etching press, but where these are not available alternative means of printing must be explored. An effective substitute press can be made by converting a handle-operated clothes wringer which can be bolted to a table or bench, or even a book press can be pressed into service to obtain reasonably successful results. If a book press is being used the dampened paper and inked plate are placed between pieces of blanket or thick felt, and into the press. By winding the movable jaw down, pressure is exerted on the plate so that the dampened paper is inked. On releasing the pressure, the print is taken from the press. The operation is repeated for each print required.

When a purchased etching press is not available, the teacher and the children are presented with an opportunity to show much initiative and resourcefulness in devising substitute means of printing, and the making of celluloid etchings can still proceed as a worthwhile activity.

Prints are displayed to the best effect when they are mounted in off-white or light coloured mounts. In size, the top and sides of the mount should be between 2 and 3 inches larger than the print, and the bottom larger again. A window or aperture slightly smaller than the print is then cut in the mount, and the print fixed in position at the back by cellulose tape. If a piece of mount paper twice as wide as necessary is used, it can be folded like a book cover to protect the print more adequately. One or two neat pencil lines bordering the aperture add a finished appearance to the mount.

FABRIC PRINTING

The colouring of fabrics dates from ancient times, and for centuries man has attached great importance to the decoration of the numerous fabrics from which his clothing and other cloth goods are manufactured. Today, patterns on fabrics are an accepted and indispensable part of our lives, and fabric printing is a highly organised division of the textile industry. Numerous methods have been evolved to print or otherwise to apply patterns or designs to fabrics, and these range from simple processes to complex technical procedures. Most are too technical for use in schools. Three simplified methods, however, have been developed for school use so that fabric printing can become a creative experience for children of primary school age. These methods are the Crayon and Iron Technique, Fabric Painting, and Screen Printing, and all three are best introduced with small numbers of children. Details of the first two methods follow; for information on Screen Printing, the reader should refer to p. 161.

Crayon and Iron Method

MATERIALS

Soft wax crayons such as marking crayons; electric iron; suitable cloth such as a cotton, calico, or cheap linen; scrap paper and drawing materials, if desired; newspapers.

TECHNIQUE

A design or pattern can be worked out first on scrap paper, or the crayons can be applied directly to the cloth as a creative exercise. The crayon strokes should follow the fibres of the cloth, and bold colour effects and striking contrasts of light and dark areas mean a more spectacular result. If all-over patterns are being applied, the crayons can be used with stencils designed and made by the children.

When the application of the crayons to the fabric is considered satisfactory, the fabric is covered with a damp cloth and lightly ironed backwards and forwards with a warm iron to set the colour. If the fabric coloured in this way is subsequently washed only in warm soapy water the colours should not fade or run. Further interest can be given to the pattern produced by this method if the design is outlined in brightly coloured threads in a variety of stitches. The technique can be used to decorate dinner mats, table centres, and similar cloth articles.

Fabric Painting

MATERIALS

Fabric paints, purchased or made; round bristle brushes in a range of sizes; suitable cloths (as above); electric iron; newspapers to cover furniture and to protect clothing.

TECHNIQUE

Designs or patterns can be painted on fabrics by hand, using free brush work. Several brands of fabric painting colours are on the market. The easiest for primary school children to control appear to be oil-based paints which can be thinned with turpentine if they prove too stiff to use with ease. They are flexible, fadeless, and washable in the normal way for the particular kind of fabric. They can be used with

76

brushes or with stencils, or if the drying rate is suitably retarded by mixing with common paraffin instead of turpentine, they are suitable for Screen Printing (see p. 161).

A fast fabric paint that can be made with little difficulty consists of one part of powdered albumen, or egg white, added to three parts of fluid tempera paint. To this add a few drops of vinegar. The colours can be applied freely to the fabric using a stiff bristle brush. When dry, the painted fabric is placed face down between two sheets of paper and steamed with a hot iron to set the colours.

The decoration and colouring of fabrics by either of the above methods should be regarded essentially as a creative activity. All designs or patterns used should be originated by the children themselves, and repeats effected by hand except when a stencil technique is being used. Ready-made packaged patterns which lead to imitative, impersonal practices should be avoided.

Because considerable supervision is needed and the fact that both processes require the use of a hot iron, they are not recommended for use with large numbers of children. But with small groups of children at the upper grade level, both methods can produce satisfying and individual results.

FELT APPLIQUE PICTURES (see Fig. 28)

As an activity, the making of felt applique pictures is almost identical with the technique used to make cloth applique pictures. In the latter all kinds of cloths and fabrics are legitimate materials, but in the felt applique technique the picture should be composed predominantly of pieces of felt stitched onto a backing material using a variety of stitches and threads. Because few schools can provide large quantities of felt in a wide range of colours, the making of felt applique pictures is best taken with reduced numbers, say, 10 to 15 children. To enable both forms of applique work to be introduced, thus broadening the range of activities offered, it might be possible to have one-third of the class making felt applique pictures while the remainder use the cloth applique technique.

As the technique differs only in the respect indicated above, the reader is referred to the details of procedure given under Cloth Applique Pictures (p. 50).

FELT-TIPPED PEN PICTURES

The felt-tipped pen, consisting of a plastic barrel containing a volatile coloured spirit as the colouring matter which reaches the paper through a felt wick, is a recent addition to the range of art materials available for school use. These pens come in a range of colours, are relatively inexpensive, and enable coloured drawings to be done rapidly and directly. Provided the children have access to sufficient pens, they can be introduced as a class activity as few other materials are needed.

MATERIALS

Felt-tipped pens, in assorted colours; cartridge paper or light coloured paper, size 10 inches by $7\frac{1}{2}$ inches, or larger; newspapers to prevent marking of the furniture.

TECHNIQUE

Like the other forms of drawing listed, the technique is simple, direct, and permits considerable personal variation. No problems in the use of the pens should arise. Children should be encouraged to experiment to discover ways of producing varied line effects and to suggest detail. Differences in pressure effect the type of line, and thick strokes or narrow strokes are possible using either the full width of the tip or the edge.

While the possibilities of these pens for extensive picture-making activities appear limited, they have value in an art programme for quick sketching treatments, for outdoor sketching, for making preliminary studies, or simply in introducing a variation in the existing range of drawing techniques.

FELT TOY MAKING

The making of stuffed felt animals, birds, and dolls is a common activity that can be creative but frequently is not. Where the child impersonally follows patterns issued to him, so that he makes a toy designed by some other person, the activity becomes imitative and the products stereotyped and dull. Children should be encouraged to design their own patterns for a toy of their own selection and to make the toy according to these patterns. In this way the activity becomes creative, the child has a personal interest in the task, his response is heightened, and the products show a rich individual variation.

Although filling and sewing materials can be obtained with little difficulty, the provision of felt in an adequate colour range can be so expensive as to be prohibitive for many schools. In this case, old clean blanket or rug can be used as a substitute. The activity is best introduced with older children, both boys and girls, and the numbers participating will depend on the availability of materials.

MATERIALS

Suitable felt in a wide colour range (or substitute material); scissors; large-eyed sewing needles and threads; filling such as cotton waste; steel pins; common art materials and scrap paper to prepare patterns; selected waste materials to express significant detail or make costumes.

TECHNIQUE

The child should be encouraged to disregard stereotyped patterns and to prepare his own as a preliminary exercise on scrap paper. Having decided on an animal or a character, say, from a nursery rhyme, the child can make small sketches on paper to clarify his concepts and to provide a starting point. One of the sketches, probably, will suggest possibilities, and this is developed further until an indication of the proposed toy takes shape. At this stage, natural proportions and appearances are ignored and a ruthless simplification introduced. Simple outline shapes to full toy size can now be drawn from the developed sketch, giving, say, a side view of an animal toy or a front view of a human characterisation. From these outline shapes the patterns are made in the largest possible pieces to minimise sewing, increasing the size slightly to allow for filling and sewing. To achieve a satisfactory three-dimensional form gusset pieces should be planned where necessary to provide width in, say, an animal form such as an elephant.

When all pieces of the pattern are satisfactory, they are arranged closely on the selected felt to permit economic cutting, pinned in position, and cut out. If the two sides of an animal form are identical, the cutting can be done in felt folded to produce the two shapes from the single cut. Small pieces of felt remaining should be retained for possible use as attached details. The sewing of the felt pieces is then commenced and continued until a portion of the toy is sewn. The sewn portion should then be stuffed tightly with a material such as cotton waste to fill out the form. This process of stitching and filling is followed until all parts of the toy are filled. It should now stand erect.

Expressive detail can be added by decorative stitching (see p.71) and by sewing on additional pieces of felt and other fabrics; selected waste materials also can be sewn or glued in position to assist the characterisation, but some restraint should be exercised in their use. If the toy represents a human character, or a character from nursery rhyme or story, it can be dressed in suitable costume which also can be made by the child.

While felt is the traditional material used (hence, the name), other fabrics can be used equally successfully, including cotton checks, gingham and similar materials, or even velvet and woollen cloths. If cotton waste is not available for filling, old stockings prove satisfactory. Washable toys can be made from cotton, rayon, and nylon fabrics filled with foam rubber. Children need not be restricted exclusively to felt; apart from economic considerations, the use of additional materials increases textural interest and adds variety to the completed toys.

FINGER PAINT ACTIVITIES (see Figs. 29 and 31)

The finger painting technique was invented in 1932 by the famous kindergarten teacher, Ruth Faison Shaw. It is now widely used in kindergartens and primary schools.

It is a valuable medium for small children in infant grades for it can assist muscular development and co-ordination. It allows considerable bodily movement as the child feels the paint and manipulates it with fingers, knuckles, elbows, and arms; finger painting is a rhythmic exercise and the child's whole body is involved. With certain types of children, such as inhibited children or those with poor motor development, finger painting can assist in overcoming their inhibitions, fears, poor co-ordination, and other handicaps. With young children the activity has considerable value from the point of view of individual development, but its artistic value seems limited.

Several finger paint preparations can be purchased, or satisfactory substitutes prepared with little difficulty. The activity by nature is messy, and its use in the classroom basically is an extension of the child's natural impulse to play with mud, water or dirt; therefore a work centre should be prepared and adequate precautions taken to minimise mess. Finger painting in primary classrooms should be regarded essentially as an activity involving small numbers of children at a time.

MATERIALS

Finger paint, purchased or made; a smooth, white non-absorbent paper such as cartridge paper, shelf paper, or litho paper (smooth side), size 15 inches by 10 inches, but preferably much larger if circumstances permit; dishes of water, to wet hands, paper, and to moisten paint; rags for cleaning; protective clothing such as smocks or aprons; newspapers to cover tables and working area.

TECHNIQUE

To gain the full physical benefits of the activity, the child should stand to permit free bodily movement, at a smooth-topped table about hip-high. A plastic-topped table which can be wet is excellent. The top of the table should be wet and a large, smooth sheet of white paper placed on it and flattened out. A sponge can be used to wet the paper; finger painting should always be done on wet paper so that the paint remains fluid and responsive.

A blob of finger paint (about the size of a walnut) is dropped in the middle of the wet paper. This is smoothed over the surface using both hands, and finger painting can commence. Using rhythmic movements of fingers, knuckles, hands, or even the forearm, the child pushes and manipulates the paint to produce patterns. Each pattern can be erased as it is made simply by smoothing the paint out on the paper, and the operation repeated or further possibilities explored. Wet finger paintings can be placed on newspaper to dry or hung on a folding clothes-horse, and afterwards stored flat; some wrinkling might occur during drying, but this generally comes out under storage.

It is not essential that finger painting be done on paper; in practice, because the technique is a quick one, it can consume considerable supplies of paper. Any non-absorbent white surface can be used. Sheets of masonite enamelled white, or white plastic sheeting, can be used and washed after use. Sheets of cartridge paper rubbed over with bleached bees-wax, or painted with white enamel, can be used many times.

There are several recipes for making finger paint, and it must be emphasised that all ingredients used should be non-poisonous and non-irritating to children, either through the mouth or through the skin. A quick and satisfactory mixture can be made by mixing powder colours or food dyes with school paste; the colour of the mixture should be strong and vivid to give maximum contrast with the white of the paper. Another simple recipe uses 4 tablespoons of dry starch to 1 pint of water. The starch is mixed with a little water to make a paste. The water is boiled, added to the paste, and the mixture cooked until it is clear and thick. When cool, powder colour or food dye in powder form is added and stirred in.

A third recipe blends 12 level tablespoons of cornflour with 1 cup of cold water. Sufficient boiling water is added to bring the whole to 1 quart. The mixture is then boiled for 1 minute until it becomes clear and thick. Next, 1 level tablespoon of food dye is blended in 3 level tablespoons of cold water, and dissolved in 4 level tablespoons of boiling water. This colouring is added to the hot cornflour mix. Lastly, add 1 tablespoon of antiseptic to the paint, and store in clean, covered jars, pressing the mixture down while warm to eliminate air bubbles.

A period of finger painting usually produces a surplus of colourful patterns. Their disposal sometimes presents a problem. One solution is to use them to create new patterns by cutting or tearing them, forming bright abstract arrangements from the pieces, and pasting them on a backing sheet.

Wet finger paintings also can be used to make prints using a monoprint technique. A sheet of absorbent paper such as newsprint, bulky newsprint, or litho paper (rough side) is placed over the wet finger painting. A piece of strawboard larger than the sheet of paper is placed on top and pressure exerted by rubbing with the hands. When sufficient pressure has been exerted to obtain a clear print, the strawboard is removed, the print is gently lifted away, and hung up to dry or placed flat on newspaper.

Older children can use the finger painting technique to create monochromatic pictures. In addition to fingers and hands, cardboard combs, sticks, and other tools can be employed for special effects and for the expression of detail. As indicated under Book Decoration (see p. 33) finger painting can be used also as a means of creating colourful and decorative coverings for books, folios, and boxes.

FLORAL ART ACTIVITIES

A number of simple activities involving the use of flowers and related materials should be included in an art programme and introduced into the classroom as opportunities occur. Some are suitable for any number of children providing adequate materials and containers can be provided; others are best taken with smaller numbers operating in groups. Some are more suitable for girls, but a number can be done equally well by boys.

MATERIALS

The materials will vary according to the nature of the activity but all can be provided by the children, who bring them as required for a particular activity and then take them home afterwards.

TECHNIQUE

The techniques involved are all simple and, like the materials, vary according to the nature of each activity. The following list indicates the kinds of activities that can be introduced successfully with primary school children. In all cases an individual response should be encouraged.

1. *floral arrangements in suitable containers.* Pleasing arrangement and massing of flowers in suitable containers can make a valuable contribution to the appearance of the classroom, and much can be done to improve current practices.
2. *decorated saucers.* A mound of wet sand is built up in a saucer. Into this wet sand masses of small flowers or portions of flowers are stuck in concentric or geometric arrangements to produce colourful floral patterns.
3. *decorated egg cups.* Here, a mound of wet sand is built up in the egg cup, and miniature flowers or portions of flowers are used to make a pattern in the manner indicated in 2 above.
4. *floral mosaics.* A flat dish or tray is filled to level with wet sand. Flowers, portions of flowers, and small leaves are pushed into the wet sand to form bold, abstract arrangements with mosaic-like effects.
5. *miniature flower arrangements.* Portions of flowers, tiny leaves and grasses are used to make miniature arrangements in lipstick containers, toy jugs, salt cellars, and the like, which are fixed with plasticine to the surface of a mirror.
6. *novelties using fruit and vegetables.* Humorous and quaint three-dimensional interpretations of nursery rhymes and stories are created using fruit and vegetables. Dolls, fairies, and elves, for instance, can be made from peanuts, acorns, walnuts, chestnuts, corn-husks, and pipe-cleaners, and little birds from seed pods, cotton-wool, and soft wire.
7. *dried arrangements.* Dried leaves, seed cases or pods, grasses, small branches, and small pine cones, can be tastefully arranged to form a group on a plywood panel and glued into position using a colourless cement. Both the arrangement and the panel can be varnished with a soft brush to impart a finish.
8. *all-green arrangements.* Evergreens, succulents, green leaves and stalks are used to create an arrangement that can be attractive and interesting despite its limitation of colour.

9. *table decorations.* Comic or novelty items can be made for special occasions such as parties using waste materials and odds and ends to decorate cucumbers, pineapples, coconuts, oranges, and the like.

10. *Christmas decorations.* Appropriate decorations for Christmas can be made from pine cones, seed pods, ti-tree, driftwood pieces, and similar materials, garnished with patching plaster, Santa Snow, indoor silver enamel, silver glitter, coloured ribbons or coloured glass balls, and attached to decorated bottles and other Christmas novelties.

GADGET PRINTING

Gadget printing is a variation and an extension of the cork printing technique, and because a greater variety of printing implements is employed, the possibilities for making interesting patterns are increased. The technique makes use of easily obtained household gadgets or appliances such as keys, washers, nuts, heads of screws, wiggle nails, salt shakers, small metal brackets, table forks, cotton reels; in fact, any small object possessing a surface which can be inked with thick paint or ink. No cutting is involved, and this forms the only significant difference from cork printing. The printed impressions from various gadgets should be distributed in a regular order to form a pattern, and greater interest can be imparted because of the variety of shapes employed.

For details of the inking of the gadgets, materials, and technique, see Cork Printing (p. 58).

HOOKED RUG MAKING

The making of hooked rugs is an old activity which is enjoying a revived popularity because it has been placed on a creative basis. It now presents a challenging problem in contemporary abstract design, and the designing and making of rugs as a creative exercise comes within the capacity of older primary school children. The technique is suitable for boys and girls, and if the simple wooden frames and other materials can be provided in adequate quantities, all children in a class can participate.

MATERIALS

Backing material, such as hessian or coarse canvas; coloured wools and yarns; simple wooden frames, from 1 inch or $1\frac{1}{2}$ inch strips of softwood (of a size which will enable the child to complete the rug in a reasonable time, say 28 inches by 16 inches, or smaller); rug hooks; scissors; drawing pins, or flat headed tacks; a range of common art materials and scrap paper to prepare designs.

83

While it is not essential to prepare a preliminary design, this practice generally leads to a better designed article showing a relationship of shapes and colours and an ordered appearance which are sometimes lacking when the child works directly in the materials. The activity should be regarded as a creative experience from start to finish, each rug showing an individual performance. The child should prepare his own design, working out his own arrangement of abstract shapes and colour scheme; this design can be worked out in paint, chalk, oil pastel, or torn paper. The torn paper pieces in assorted colours, when pasted down, more closely resemble the hooked rug than the other media indicated. When the child is satisfied with his prepared design, it is transferred by hand to the hessian backing using chalk, pastel, or crayon, to draw the lines.

The hessian is now stretched across the wooden frame and tacked firmly in position, and the hooking can begin. The hooking needle is threaded, held in a vertical position, and pushed through the hessian, forming a loop or hook of wool. Each time the needle is used a loop is formed, and in this way the colour areas are built up. As each coloured shape, or a reasonable area, is filled in, the loops are cut with scissors to form the pile of the rug.

If a genuinely creative approach to the rug making is adopted, using combinations of abstract shapes and bold colours, the resultant articles can show a striking variety of colourful, individual designs.

INK DRAWINGS

Ink drawings, using both Indian ink (which is black) and coloured drawing inks, or even school writing ink if nothing better is available, can be done in a variety of ways using a number of simple drawing implements. Most of these can be provided relatively simply and there are few technical difficulties, so that drawings in ink can be done with large numbers of children if adequate materials are available. The techniques are direct and rapid, offering excellent means of producing either quick or detailed sketches showing wide individual variation.

MATERIALS

Indian ink, coloured inks, or writing ink; mapping pens, writing pens, and improvised drawing implements such as sharpened sticks, stiff string, and the like; sable-type brushes; cartridge paper or suitable light coloured paper, size 10 inches by $7\frac{1}{2}$ inches, or smaller; water in suitable containers; newspapers.

TECHNIQUE

Drawings in ink can be made using orthodox implements such as soft brushes in several sizes, mapping pens, and the steel-nibbed school pen, or the possibilities of improvised tools such as sharpened or broken sticks, pieces of stiff string, feathers, and other common materials for making lines and marks can be explored. Children should be encouraged to experiment with implements other than the traditional, for a greater variety of lines and special effects becomes possible and scope for varied and creative personal expression is considerably extended. Each drawing tool used should produce a different quality of line. Thus, the child should discover that, while a mapping nib can make an extremely fine line, a piece of stick can make a line more varied and of entirely different character, and a soft flexible brush offers even further possibilities in line treatment. With the pen, variations in pressure control the type of line so that very thin to bold lines are possible. With the brush also variations in pressure produce differences in line, and additional qualities can be produced by rotating the brush, using it almost dry, and so on.

Drawings should be made directly on the paper, without preliminary sketching. Some pencil "blocking in" is permissible when children lack experience of the ink techniques, but the direct approach generates confidence and a sureness in handling the materials.

Coloured inks can be superimposed on the paper to produce rich and varied colour effects. Indian ink can be diluted with clean water to produce monochromatic brush drawings ranging in tone from delicate grey to dense black. With pen and Indian ink, or brush, washes of transparent water colour can be applied over the pen treatment in the well-known pen and wash technique.

JEWELLERY MAKING

People of all ages are fascinated by jewellery. But most people associate jewellery with diamonds, pearls, platinum or gold, and with expensive tools and intricate techniques. Yet there is much that can be done in the classroom by primary school children using primitive tools and simple techniques. Simple activities, like making bead necklaces from coloured plastic tubing or dyed macaroni pieces, can be introduced with young children, while older children can make more skilled necklaces, ear-rings, bracelets, and brooches. Children enjoy making jewellery, and the activity can become a truly creative experience. They should select their own simple materials, process them, and assemble them to a design they themselves have originated; there should be no copying of designs or following of stereotyped instructions.

There are jewellery making activities that can be introduced from infant grade level upwards. For most of them children can supply their own materials and simple equipment, so that, in most cases, they can work individually in their desks. There will be times when participation can be on a whole class basis, on a group basis, or a child may work individually on a particular piece of jewellery.

The range of materials for making jewellery virtually is unlimited; they can be natural, such as pebbles, or manufactured, such as pieces of melted glass. The one requirement is that the material must contain and reveal an inherent beauty. If the child can recognise beauty in some small item of material, then probably it can be used in jewellery making; and the child's environment abounds in such items.

MATERIALS

Any small piece of material possessing a natural beauty that can be developed further, and including pebbles, seeds, buttons, beads, wire, metals, wood, glass, metal foil, plaster, dyed egg shell, felt, seashells, pieces of tooth brush handle, leather, plastic, nails, tube plastic, cork, macaroni, and so on; safety pins of various sizes; soft, thin, rustless wire or nylon line; side-cutting pliers; scissors; pocket knives, trimming knives; adhesives such as tube cement, fast-drying model cement; processing materials such as sharpening stones, files, sandpaper, glasspaper, rouge and felt; finishing materials such as clear varnish, white shellac, clear nail lacquer, opaque paints, matt and gloss; additional materials, according to the nature of the jewellery; newspaper.

TECHNIQUE

There is no set technique in view of the immense variety of materials that can be used. Each material, or combination of materials, will indicate a logical method of processing, assembling and finishing, according to the nature of the piece of jewellery. Frequently the nature of the material will suggest a certain item of jewellery, and the suitability of the material in terms of the piece of jewellery should always be considered.

Necklaces, for instance, can be made from fine wire or line on which are threaded, in plain or coloured arrangements, any of the following materials or combinations of them; short pieces of coloured plastic tubing of different lengths; macaroni pieces dyed in food dyes: cut-up plastic tooth brush handles; large dry seeds, such as melon seeds, dipped in clear nail polish; plastic thonging tied in regular bunches; wood pieces, cut into identical shapes, and clear varnished or dipped in gloss enamel; small pieces of flat metal in identical shapes dipped in enamel; sea shells arranged in sizes. Where holes are required through materials they should be drilled with a fine drill, and the full number of pieces should be prepared before threading commences. Each necklace will require a small fastener, which the individual child either must purchase or bring from home.

Brooches or clasps require a pin, and a safety pin of appropriate size will hold to the back of most materials with fast-drying model cement. Brooches can be made from the following materials: pebbles, polished first on a sharpening stone, then with felt and rouge, and cemented or wrapped in soft wire; decorative buttons cemented to a section of an ice-cream stick, and clear varnished; pieces of melted coloured glass, cemented on flywire partly rolled and dipped in gloss enamel; or superimposed abstract felt shapes high-lighted with drops of plaster.

The possibilities for jewellery making are endless, and children can be encouraged to invent uses for all kinds of common materials in which they see beauty. With

86

imagination and nimble fingers these common materials can be transformed into items of fascinating jewellery, originated by the child as a creative and satisfying experience.

LEAF PRINTS

Prints from leaves and grasses can be made using an inked roller or, in some instances, by hand inking. The technique is not difficult, and results can be attractive and artistic. But the activity requires printer's ink and can be messy, so that it is suitable only as a group activity for older children.

MATERIALS

Flat leaves and grasses, of distinctive shapes and textures; printer's ink or student quality oil paint, in several colours; rubber rollers; $\frac{1}{4}$ inch plate glass sheet, or tin or masonite, size 12 inches by 10 inches; white or light coloured paper, such as thin cartridge paper, or litho paper, of a size slightly larger than the arrangement of leaves; cleaning materials (mineral turpentine, kerosene, clean rags); newspapers to cover entire working area.

TECHNIQUE

Leaf prints can be produced in several ways, all of which require some form of inking. Printing is best done on a flat-topped table or bench, covered with newspaper. Printer's ink or student quality oil paint is squeezed onto the plate glass and rolled in all directions to ink the roller evenly and thoroughly. A varied collection of leaves and grasses is arranged on a piece of newspaper, inked by lightly rolling the inked roller across their surface so that raised portions and textured prominences take ink. If one or two colours are blended on the plate glass, a varied colour effect is produced. A top sheet of paper is now placed over this inked arrangement and a clean roller used to apply pressure gently so that a print of the inked leaves is produced on the underside of the paper. By gently lifting the top sheet the quality of the printing can be checked, and further pressure applied by rolling, if necessary. If care is exercised, sometimes more than one print can be obtained from the one inked arrangement of leaves. A variation of this process is to ink each piece of grass or leaf separately and to build up an arrangement on a sheet of paper as each piece is inked. (The use of a pair of household rubber gloves protects the hands from excessive ink). When the inked arrangement is completed, a sheet of paper is placed over it, and a clean roller used to produce a print, as before. When several colours and rollers are in use, this variation allows different colours to be used in the inking stage and the inked leaves can be placed with accuracy so that the distribution of colour can be controlled by the child. In this way, unusual but interesting pictures can be made.

Another way to make leaf prints is to place an arrangement of leaves and grasses on a sheet of paper, as before, but in this case the arrangement is not inked. A second sheet is placed immediately on this arrangement, and rolled with a lightly inked roller. An impression of the raised portions of the underlying leaves shows on the top sheet. The inking of the roller and the amount of rolling determine the final appearance of the print, for not only can an impression of the leaf arrangement be obtained on the top sheet but areas of background can be delicately tinted also.

Leaves which can be held in the hand, and flowers such as marguerites and other members of the daisy family, can be inked by hand by pressing them face down on the inked glass. They can then be pressed, inked side down, onto paper to make interesting patterns; the impressions should be distributed to repeat regularly or the effect of the pattern will be lost.

The leaf printing technique can be used to produce pictures as well as patterns. A combination of both rolling and hand pressing can produce prints which suggest a bushland or garden setting, or other landscape types. To complete the picture, suggestions of figures or architectural details are added by using a brush.

After printing, rollers and other inked surfaces should be cleaned initially on newspaper and finally wiped clean with cloths moistened in turpentine or kerosene. Inked leaves should be wrapped in newspaper and deposited in garbage cans.

Completed leaf prints make attractive and decorative panels if mounted in appropriately coloured mount paper. Details of mounting are given under Etching (p. 75).

LEAF RUBBINGS

Leaf rubbings are simpler than leaf prints, make little mess, use common materials, and can be done by any number of children sitting at tables or desks, if sufficient materials are available.

MATERIALS

Flat leaves and grasses, of distinctive shapes and textures; soft crayons, such as marking crayons or soft-coloured pencils; white or light coloured paper, such as thin cartridge paper, litho paper, or even duplicating paper, size 10 inches by $7\frac{1}{2}$ inches, or smaller; newspapers.

TECHNIQUE

As with leaf prints, an arrangement of leaves and grasses is made on a sheet of paper, and a second sheet placed over this. Soft crayons are rubbed backwards and forwards over the top sheet to obtain an impression of the raised portions of the underlying arrangement. Several colours can be used to produce special effects. For example, by blending several colours of crayons over an arrangement of selected leaves and grasses, a colourful and charming impression of autumn can be created, either as a pattern or as a picture.

The technique, of course, need not be confined to leaves; coins, string, paper or cardboard shapes, and so on, can be used under the top sheet to produce rubbed impressions.

LETTERING

The study of lettering as a human activity and as a vital means of communication can embrace fascinating subject-matter and a number of interesting and beneficial activities. This study can be commenced virtually at grade 3 level with simple calligraphic exercises using both traditional and improvised tools, graduating to the making of lettered symbols and words as the child progresses through the grades. With older children in the upper grades, where the study of lettering can be pursued more seriously, a strong case can be made for the teaching of lettering as a group activity to, say, 12 or 15 children. Continual supervision and individual guidance will be necessary to develop the necessary skills, in the setting out of work, and in the proper use and maintenance of materials; to attempt the study of lettering with a large class under normal conditions is to jeopardise the chances of achieving results of acceptable quality and lasting benefit.

MATERIALS

The materials will vary according to the nature and purpose of the activity, and the following materials can be used as the occasion warrants: soft pencils, black and coloured; powder, poster, or tempera paints, with flat bristle brushes in a variety of sizes; pens, speed-ball nibs; Indian ink, or writing ink; paper, white or coloured, such as cartridge paper, cover paper, bulky newsprint, or even thin card, of a size appropriate to the purpose of the lettering exercise; coloured papers for cutting and pasting; scissors; school-paste or mucilage; newspapers.

TECHNIQUE

An important requirement to the successful study of lettering is that the study be made meaningful to the child by relating it to the role of lettering beyond the classroom. The indispensability of lettering and printing (which is lettering mechanically reproduced) as a means of communication, with an enormous range of application from tram tickets to huge posters, should be emphasised by the use of visual material and actual examples, and by reference to magazines, newspapers, and books. While

89

the teaching emphasis necessarily should be on neatness of execution and arrangement, legibility, satisfactory spacing, proportion and well-formed letters, every effort should be made to make the study interesting and realistic.

The materials indicated can be used separately or in combination, according to the stage of development of the individual child. The type of paper will depend largely on the nature of the activity but normally a smooth, plain, non-absorbent paper, such as cartridge paper, gives satisfactory results. For the lettering of signs, posters, and cards for special occasions tinted papers of a heavier quality, or card, are preferable. Nibs for the use of older children must be undamaged and clean; ordinary steel nibs can be used, or special lettering nibs can be purchased, especially if the activity is conducted on a group basis. Writing ink and Indian ink of good quality should be available, and coloured drawing inks can add variety and interest to the work. If other types of ink are not available a beneficial unit of study can still be introduced using ordinary school ink. The approach to the study and the nature of its presentation are more important than the actual materials, and when interest, purpose and reality are infused into the activities splendid results can be achieved using only existing classroom materials.

In introducing the experiences listed teachers must be prepared to accept performances and appraisals appropriate to the age level of the children; it should be remembered that they are employing adult skills and allowance must be made for this fact. This does not imply, however, that ill-formed, careless or untidy work is acceptable; it simply requires the individual child to perform to the best of his ability at his own level. The activities which follow are considered suitable for primary school children.

1. *experience with line.* The study can commence in grades 3 or 4 with experimental exercises and explorations of the nature and types of lines, using broken sticks, improvised quills (cut from drinking straws) and small brushes, as well as pencils and pens. These exercises use lines in endless variety to form doodles, scribbles, in-filling of Scribble Patterns (p. 163), "queer writing," and the like, the aim being to encourage an individual, free use of line and to develop a confidence in the basic skills.

2. *interesting stories.* Encyclopaedias and books of knowledge can supply interesting stories to explain to children the evolution of the written alphabet and the numerals from their primitive origins; the human element in the development of writing to meet man's needs of communication through the ages should be stressed.

3. *class dramatisation.* Class dramatisations of the material indicated in 2 above can be performed using improvised models of primitive writing implements and materials which have been made by the children; suggestions of the dress appropriate to the historical period also might be included.

4. *displays of the uses of printing.* Examples, ranging from tram tickets, labels, menus, programmes, catalogues, pamphlets and the like to books, magazines,

newspapers, and small posters, can be collected and arranged by children on a group basis, the purpose of the activity being to emphasise the importance of lettering and printing in everyday living.

5. *displays of clippings from newspapers and magazines* (see Fig. 32). These also can be arranged by the children as a group experience to illustrate the characteristics of good lettering; such characteristics as legibility, simplicity, good spacing, consistency of size, angle, weight, and so on, can be taught informally and incidentally by reference to the displayed material.

6. *the making of a suitable, single-line alphabet*. The design of a suitable alphabet incorporating the characteristics indicated in 5 above can be undertaken as a class or a group exercise, and the alphabet can be used for the lettering of name plates on school books; the making of labels for folios, projects, displays of work or illustrative material, shelving, cupboards, and other situations where clear labels are desirable; for posters and signs; and for the lettering of cards for special occasions, such as birthdays, invitations to Education Week, and the like.

LIFE DRAWINGS (see Fig. 30)

The drawing by children of one their classmates, especially if the selected child is dressed suitably in a fancy costume, is always accompanied by heightened interest and adds a certain glamour to a classroom activity. It affords an excellent exercise in guided observation and in the use of varied line effects to express personal reactions. Provided simple drawing materials are available in quantity, any number of children can participate, working in their desks. Because some ability to convert visual observations into pictorial terms is needed, the activity is more appropriate for older children who have reached a stage of realism in their work.

MATERIALS

Any simple drawing materials, such as soft pencil, pen and ink, brush and ink, charcoal, crayon, pastel, or oil pastel, in one colour only; white or light coloured paper, such as newsprint, bulky newsprint, litho paper, thin cartridge paper or coloured cover paper, depending on the media being used; improvised drawing boards, such as pieces of plywood, masonite, or even school-paper covers to which the drawing paper can be attached by paper clips or rubber bands; sable-type brushes, small sizes, if brush and ink technique is being used.

TECHNIQUE

First, a reliable child is selected to pose, in ordinary clothes or in a simple costume such as a newsboy, a nurse, or a fairy; a child who is irresponsible and unlikely to

91

pose well can destroy the whole experience. Children should be encouraged to "play at artists" and to approach their drawing in serious and creative mood. The model should pose for pre-arranged periods, with brief rests between, and two unrelated poses are possible within a 30 minute period. Having arranged the model in a position which offers all children a view, the teacher can make chalk marks on the floor to ensure that the same position is adopted each time.

Drawing from a posed model, by a girl, aged 11
Highett Primary School.

FIG. 30. LIFE DRAWING

The children work in the vicinity of their desks, sitting or standing so that they can see the model, and using any of the simple drawing materials indicated. The activity produces more varied and individual interpretations of the model if a variety of media is used; different effects and treatments can be compared when the drawings are exhibited at the close of the period. Children should be encouraged to interpret individually the pose by expressing main lines of contours and folds, and significant detail. The capacity of line to suggest rather than to rigidly define should be stressed in simple terms.

A variation of this type of lesson is the drawing of portraits, using the same simple materials indicated for life drawing. One child in a desk poses by simply sitting still, to enable the other child to complete a drawing of his face or head in either profile, three-quarter, or frontal aspects. When the portrait is completed, the children change roles, so that each takes a turn at posing and drawing. Children enjoy this kind of drawing lesson, and the resultant portraits are full of interest and keen observation.

LINOLEUM BLOCK PRINTS

The cutting of linoleum to make a block from which to take prints is a well-known and popular activity which offers unlimited scope for design possibilities and individual expression. By nature the activity is closely related to Block Printing (p. 30), and although the basic material of the block differs, other materials and the printing technique remain substantially the same. The activity involves the use of cutting tools and ink, and is necessarily messy. For this reason adequate precautions to minimise the mess should be taken, and the activity should be introduced only with small numbers of children who should operate at a work centre prepared by the teacher. Continual guidance and supervision will be required if children are to produce worthwhile results. The technique comes well within the performance range of older primary school children, especially those who desire an activity which is somewhat technical and challenging.

MATERIALS

Suitable linoleum, such as brown "battleship" quality, of a size which will enable the children to complete the whole process in a reasonable working time, say, 6 inches by $4\frac{1}{2}$ inches; lino-cutting tools, purchased or improvised (see below); a variety of papers, white or coloured, such as newsprint, litho paper, ticket paper, cover paper, or cartridge paper, cut to a size slightly larger than the block; printer's ink in tubes or student quality oil paint; piece of $\frac{1}{4}$ inch plate glass, or substitute, size 12 inches by 10 inches; rubber rollers; pliable knife; cleaning materials (mineral turpentine or kerosene, clean rags); newspapers to protect furniture and to cover working area; brushes and Indian ink and scrap paper, to prepare preliminary designs.

TECHNIQUE

Because the distribution of light and dark areas, and the contrasts they afford, determines the appearance and effectiveness of the print, it is sound procedure to commence by preparing a working design. Brush and Indian ink, or black crayon, can be used for this purpose, or cut and torn pieces of black paper on a white sheet might be preferred; the latter permits easy manipulation as different arrangements of shapes are tried. Some children, on the other hand, might like to cut directly in the lino with no preliminary planning, allowing the design to evolve as a result of the cutting process. Children should be encouraged to keep their designs simple and to aim for a flat two-dimensional treatment, relying on the combination and placement of dark and light areas and textural effects for interest and variety. Both linear and mass cutting should be incorporated. Realism and natural appearances should not be attempted, and detail in the design simplified and adapted to the cutting technique; intricate cutting involving skilled techniques is beyond the attainment of primary school children.

Cutting tools (such as V-shaped and U-shaped gouges, in sets) can be purchased and generally are necessary for the major part of the cutting, but much can be done with additional tools such as safe razor blades, trimming knives, sharpened nails, large sewing needles, and the like. Excellent cutting tools can be made from pieces of umbrella rib, sharpened and set in wooden handles or knobs of insulating tape to permit easy handling. Any mark or line incised in the linoleum, by any tool, should register on the print. All cutting tools should be sharp, and kept sharp during the cutting process. The need to concentrate while cutting should be stressed, for pieces removed or cuts made by mistake cannot be repaired. Before cutting the block proper, most children benefit from a short experimental period of cutting in pieces of scrap linoleum.

When the block has been cut to the child's satisfaction, it is ready for inking and printing. Printer's ink is squeezed onto the plate glass and rolled vigorously to ensure thorough inking of the roller. The inked roller is then rolled several times across the linoleum block so that all uncut areas of the surface are inked. A piece of paper larger than the block is placed on the inked surface, covered by a piece of packing paper, and printed using either a wooden spoon or a book press to exert the pressure. Spoon printing is probably the better method for children to use, for the reasons indicated on p. 74. The top papers can be lifted gently to check the quality and clarity of the printing before the print is removed. The first print obtained should then be examined to consider the distribution of light and dark areas and to decide whether further cutting is necessary. If the child is satisfied with the print as produced, several impressions can be printed using papers of different types and colours so that a range of effects is obtained. A selection can then be made, and the final printing undertaken. If heavier papers, such as cartridge paper or coloured cover paper, are being used they should be dampened first to make printing easier. Effective prints have been taken on surfaces as diverse as sandpaper, textured wrapping paper, and hessian; pieces of fringed hessian, on which suitable motifs are printed, can be made into dinner mats, coasters, and book marks.

Linoleum block prints, of course, can be made in full colour, but the use of multiple blocks to produce such prints is beyond the capacity of primary school children. Two, or even three, coloured inks can be blended in bands on the glass and applied to the block to add a limited colour interest, or if several areas and shapes of coloured paper (cut from poster paper or surface squares) are pasted on the paper and the print taken over this, colour can be introduced and interest increased without a change of ink; these background shapes, however, must harmonise with the design cut in the block. Otherwise they can prove distracting and can spoil the effect of the print.

Successful prints are displayed to best advantage when they are mounted in an appropriately coloured mount. Details of mounting are given under Etching (p. 75).

LITTLEMAN LECTURES

Older children can derive satisfaction and benefit from the preparation of brief talks (say, of 3 to 5 minutes duration) on some aspects of art which interest them. This activity should be introduced on a voluntary basis, and frequently can be undertaken by a child as a result of an interest developed by the making of a Cuttings Book (see p. 62). Some guidance no doubt will be required from the teacher, who can assist also in locating and organising illustrative material if this is required.

Apart from developing and extending interests in art, these brief talks can assist personal assurance and poise, the ability to think logically and to express thoughts clearly in public, and there exists an obvious correlation between this art activity and Spoken English.

MAGAZINE MONTAGE PICTURES (see Fig. 33)

The word "montage" comes from the French "monter", to mount, and refers to a cinematographic technique in which separate shots taken during the making of a film are selected, cut, and pieced together as a consecutive whole. A simplified adaptation of this technique, using separate coloured illustrations and advertisements cut from magazines, becomes a creative activity permitting satisfying personal expression for the children participating. The materials are simple and easily procured, and the activity of cutting and pasting is popular with both boys and girls. The technique can be introduced with any number of children if precautions are taken to ensure satisfactory working conditions; newspapers should be used to contain mess and off-cuts, and simple classroom routines established for the use and exchange of magazines, so that children engage individually in a creative experience. At no time should the activity be allowed to degenerate into a period of free reading.

MATERIALS

Old magazines and periodicals, especially those published on a weekly basis; scissors; school paste or mucilage; pasting brushes; backing sheets of cartridge paper, coloured cover paper, or ticket paper, size 15 inches by 10 inches, or smaller, according to the time available; newspapers to contain waste and to restrict mess.

TECHNIQUE

The activity is, in effect, a variation of the technique of making Coloured Paper Pictures (p. 55), the only difference being in the nature of the coloured papers used. Here, the better quality purchased coloured papers are not used; the picture is composed entirely of pieces and areas cut from coloured covers, illustrations, and advertisements which appear in popular magazines. But simply to cut the pieces out and to paste them at random, as some children are inclined to do, does not produce an effective magazine montage. A satisfactory magazine montage picture should present a composed and coherent pictorial statement expressing the child's personal interpretation of the assigned topic. To accomplish this considerable thought

95

must be given to the selection of the pieces and to their fitting together on the backing sheet, so that they relate to each other and contribute to the final effect. Where both selection and arrangement are approached in a thoughtful, creative manner, as indicated, surprisingly realistic and individual expressions can result.

As the other details of technique and pasting remain as shown for Coloured Paper Pictures, the reader is directed to p. 55.

MARBLING

The production of colourful, nebulous patterns on paper by the process called marbling is a simple though messy technique best introduced to a small number of children working as a group at a work centre. Time is saved and the activity more satisfactorily carried out if the working area and the materials are prepared beforehand by the teacher. The technique is quick, so that children can take turns to experience the activity; those children not actively engaged in marbling can be working on other activities conducted simultaneously in the room. In this way, all children in the class can produce marbled patterns on the single occasion that the materials are prepared and available. Adequate measures to minimise mess are essential.

MATERIALS

Student quality oil paints or ordinary oil-base house paints; mineral turpentine; several small containers such as lids of tins; a large flat container such as a baking dish or an enamelled hand basin; water; glue size; white or light coloured paper such as cartridge paper, litho paper, or bulky newsprint, cut a size smaller than the container; newspapers in generous supply to cover the working area.

TECHNIQUE

The container is almost filled with clean water, to within 1 inch of its top, and to this a small quantity of glue size is added. Student quality oil paints or house paint in a selection of three or four harmonising colours, are diluted separately with mineral turpentine in the small lids, and dropped onto the surface of the water where they form a floating colour film. This film is then stirred lightly so that the separate colours run together, forming a variegated combination.

A sheet of paper, cut to a convenient size, is now gently placed on the water. As it is withdrawn, the colour film adheres to the paper to form unusual marbled minglings. The process is repeated with additional sheets until the film of diluted colour is consumed, the marbled pattern each time becoming fainter. More diluted colours can then be dropped on the water, and the activity continued.

FIG. 31.
Finger Paint
Pattern.

Student, Burwood Teachers' College.

FIG. 32.
Collection of Clip-
pings from news-
papers to show
letter forms and
variations.

Student, Burwood Teachers' College.

FIG. 33.
Magazine Montage
Picture.

Girl, Grade 5, Box Hill South Primary School.

FIG. 34. Coloured Paper Mosaic Picture.

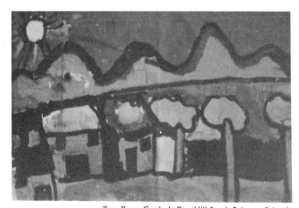

Student, Burwood Teachers' College.

FIG. 35. Newspaper Picture, with black
crayon accents.

Two Boys, Grade 1, Box Hill South Primary School.

FIG. 36. Painted Mural Picture.

The marbled patterns produced can be used as decorations on exercise books, folios, and for other classroom purposes. If large sheets are required, for example, for puppet theatre decorations, a large container such as a watertight sandtray is necessary to hold the water. The large sheet of paper is then drawn through the water rather than simply dropped on its surface.

The technique is messy, but children enjoy it, and newspapers and cleaning materials should be provided for those participating.

MASK MAKING

The making of simple masks as a classroom activity can correlate with the social studies programme and with Costume Making (p. 59) to add interest and appeal to class dramatisations. Masks can be made by individual children using simple materials and painting techniques, and the skills involved make the activity more appropriate for older children at the primary level. Because there are few occasions when every child requires a mask, mask making is perhaps more successfully introduced to 10 or 12 children operating as a group. Three simple types of mask, the Card Mask, Paper Bag or Box Masks, and Papier Mache Masks are recommended.

Card Masks (see Fig. 37)

MATERIALS

Large pieces of light-weight card, such as sides of cereal packets; scissors; paste and mucilage; cellulose tape and gummed paper; poster, powder, or tempera paints, and suitable brushes in several sizes; water; rubber bands, or lengths of thin elastic or wool to hold masks in position; selected waste materials for significant details, if desired; stapling machine; newspapers to cover working area.

TECHNIQUE

The child first should form a clear visualisation of the human character or animal which the mask is to represent. Preliminary sketches on scrap paper should assist the child to clarify his concepts, to plot eye and mouth openings in suitable positions, and to evolve a simple, appropriate design; this then is transferred to the piece of card as a firm outline drawing as large as required. The drawn outline and the plotted openings are now cut out, using scissors. Facial features in bold simple colour areas and bright accents are painted on, and selected waste materials and coloured papers to express significant detail can be added by pasting, if desired. Finally, to complete the simple card mask, a hole is punched at each side, through which a rubber band is passed and fixed in position by looping it around a short piece of match stick; the child simply slips the rubber bands over his ears to hold the mask securely in place. A less satisfactory method is to use an elastic or wool tie which is worn over the child's head; this should be stapled at both sides of the mask to prevent tearing of the card.

FIG. 37. CARD MASK

rubber band

FIG. 38. SHOPPING BAG MASK— pumpkin used in health lesson.

FIG. 39. PAPIER MACHE MASK over crumpled paper or clay base.

SIMPLE MASKS

Paper Bag Masks (see Fig. 38).

MATERIALS

Large paper shopping bags; scissors; paste and mucilage; cellulose tape and gummed paper; poster, powder, or tempera paints, and brushes; water in suitable containers; selected waste materials to add expressive details, if required; stapling machine; newspapers.

TECHNIQUE

Large paper bags can be used to make the masks, or light-weight cartons and boxes such as shoe boxes or cereal cartons; in the latter case the masks produced are called Box Masks.

A prerequisite to successful effort by the child is a clear concept of the type of mask to be made, and children should be encouraged both to visualise the form, colours and detail, and to associate the proposed mask with a specific character, human or animal. So that masks can be used and worn successfully by the children, it is important that eye and mouth openings are located in positions convenient to the wearer. To do this, the bag is pulled over the child's head and the child himself, or another child, marks the position of eye and mouth openings with the fingers dipped in chalk or pastel dust, water, or any other substance that will make temporary marks. The openings as marked are then cut. This should form the first stage of the

99

process; it must be emphasised that if these openings are not fixed in convenient positions, the successful wearing of the completed mask in class dramatisations is jeopardised.

Facial features can now be painted around the eye and mouth openings or they can be made and pasted on, if required. Thus, long ears for a rabbit mask, white cotton-wool whiskers for an old man, a snout for a pig or horns for a devil, are created using appropriate waste materials and pasted or otherwise fixed to the mask, preparatory to painting. Children of primary school age reveal great ingenuity and imagination in their use of selected waste materials to convey detail and to assist the interpretation. Poster or other opaque paints, and both bristle and sable-type brushes, are used in the final stage to paint additional details and to colour the mask to complete the characterisation. When dry the masks are ready for wearing.

Papier Mache Masks (see Fig. 39).

MATERIALS

Newspapers, in large sheets, and also in strips, cut or torn, about 1 inch wide; paper-hanger's paste or flour paste; bowls or dishes; at a later stage, poster or other opaque paints, and brushes; water in suitable containers; gummed paper; newspapers to cover working area; (if clay is used instead of crumpled paper to form the base, modelling clay and improvised boards also will be required).

TECHNIQUE

As indicated for paper bag mask making, a clear notion of the characterisation and nature of the proposed mask is essential to successful performance.

The child's first task is to form a base on which to build the papier mache mask. This is done by crumpling large sheets of newspaper into the approximate shape and size of the mask to be made, or a form can be modelled in clay, but the use of the newspaper is cheaper and easier. Wall-paper adhesive is mixed to a thin cream and put out in bowls or basins which provide easy access. Strips of newspaper about 1 inch wide, cut on a guillotine or simply torn, are dipped in the paste (or the paste can be applied by a $1\frac{1}{2}$ inch paint brush to the strips laid flat on a sink or board) and draped over the prepared base to form a criss-crossed covering layer. Four or five similar layers are required to build up a strong mask, and the layers can be distinguished one from another by alternating layers made from classified advertisements with layers cut from picture pages, pink pages from old telephone books, and the like. During this stage, noses, foreheads, and other protruding features can be built up using smaller pieces of paper. When the child is satisfied with the form and detail of the mask, it is allowed to dry, and the crumpled paper or clay base pulled out.

Any rough edges can be covered with gummed paper or additional paper strips to prevent discomfort to the wearer. Eyeholes and a mouth opening are now cut in the dry mask in convenient positions, and rubber bands attached to hold the mask in place (see p. 98).

The mask is then ready for painting and the addition of expressive detail to complete the characterisation, in the manner indicated for paper bag masks.

MATCH STICK SCULPTURE (see Fig. 40)

The creation of three-dimensional bird, animal, human, or abstract forms using matches and tooth-picks is a simple technique using materials easily procured by the children, enabling them to work in their desks. Thus, it can be introduced as an activity for the whole class. The technique, however, is painstaking and requires finer muscular movements, and while many children enjoy it others can find it tedious and frustrating. It is, therefore, not suitable for young children. It is adaptable to small, simple creations and to large complex structures, and both boys and girls can participate.

MATERIALS

Boxes of matches or bundles of tooth-picks; model aeroplane cement or similar quick-drying adhesive; sharp pocket knives; pieces of plywood or strawboard to form bases for the sculptures; newspapers.

TECHNIQUE

Match stick sculptures are built from the base upwards. Therefore, small holes are made in the strawboard or plywood base into which the leg shapes (or main supports if the form is abstract) are glued. The form is then built up, gluing stick to stick, with a fast-drying adhesive. The aim is to create a free-standing, three-dimensional expression which, whilst standing securely on a base,

FIG. 40. MATCH STICK SCULPTURE

presents a balanced appearance and structural unity. Children in the upper grades can reveal surprising skill and imagination as they work individually to create these intriguing sculptures.

101

MELTED CRAYON ACTIVITIES

During the school year, ends and pieces of drawing crayons accumulate, often to constitute a usable quantity. When such a supply is adequate, a number of activities to use them in different ways can be introduced on a group basis, with small numbers of children. These activities, all using crayons in melted form, are more suitable for older children who wish to extend their interests and their abilities. The activities which follow offer unlimited opportunity for the child who wishes to experiment and to explore the possibilities of new techniques, or of familiar materials used in new ways. The materials, naturally, will vary according to the activity, but all employ some heating implement to melt the crayons.

Melted Crayon Painting

MATERIALS

Crayon pieces, in sorted colours; old bristle brushes; patty-cake tray; heating implement (portable radiator, inverted electric iron, or even a large light globe); paper such as cartridge paper or cover paper, or cloth such as cotton or calico, of medium size, approximately 10 inches by $7\frac{1}{2}$ inch; newspapers.

TECHNIQUE

The paper or cloth is fixed to an improvised drawing board of plywood or strawboard with drawing pins; cloth should be stretched to present an unwrinkled surface. The sorted crayons, in their separate colours, are then placed in the divisions of the patty-cake tray and melted to a liquid state by holding the tray over the heat of a large light globe fitted to a lead, or of a radiator, or of an electric iron, inverted and propped in position. Powder colours can be added to the melted crayons at this stage and mixed in to intensify the colours. If reasonable precautions are taken and the process supervised by the teacher, the melting of the crayons need not be dangerous; most wax crayons melt at a low temperature, and the heat is needed in short periods only. Should the melted crayons have to be carried to a working area, great care should be exercised; if possible, the heating should be done at the working area to eliminate the need for carrying.

When the crayons are melted, they are applied by brush directly to the paper or cloth in bold strokes and colour areas. The painting should be done quickly, using old bristle brushes which should be cleaned in very hot water immediately after use. Should the melted crayons cool and thicken, they can be re-heated. The technique produces paintings different in surface quality and interesting in effect, and rough textures of heaped-up crayon can be contrasted with smooth areas. The completed painting can be given a polish by rubbing lightly with a soft cloth. Great scope exists for experiment and personal variation.

Melted Crayon Patterns

MATERIALS

Wax crayon pieces; food grater; electric iron; white or coloured paper, such as cartridge paper or cover paper (white or black are particularly effective background colours); newspapers, both to use in the process, and to minimise mess.

TECHNIQUE

A piece of paper to form a backing sheet is placed on newspaper. Crayon pieces in various colours are then grated and allowed to drop at random over this backing sheet. A sheet of newspaper is placed over the grated crayon, and by running a warm iron over the top the crayons below are melted, causing them to run and to mingle. Nebulous patterns in unusual and charming colour combinations are produced, and these can be used for colour observation and discussion.

Melted Crayon Masks

This activity uses Papier Mache Masks (see p. 100) as bases for the application of melted crayon. Papier mache masks are either made for the purpose, or old masks can be used and their appeal revived.

MATERIALS

Papier mache masks; wax crayon pieces; old saucepan or tin, or patty-cake tray; heating appliance; old bristle brushes; newspapers.

TECHNIQUE

The selected papier mache mask is placed on a board or backing sheet. The crayons are melted, as indicated above. If separate colours are required the crayons should be melted in the divisions of a patty-cake tray, but sometimes a mottled or marbled effect can be obtained by melting them in mass in an old saucepan or tin. The melted crayon, in liquid state, is then applied to the papier mache mask using old bristle brushes to build up layers of crayon. This, in itself, produces an interesting surface quality, but different colours can be superimposed, dribbled or splashed on, allowed

103

to cool, and polished by rubbing to a high gloss. Brushes and containers should be washed immediately after use in very hot water.

Melted Crayon Modelling

MATERIALS

Wax crayon pieces; paraffin; old saucepan; heating appliance; modelling boards (small pieces of masonite, plywood, or strawboard); newspapers.

TECHNIQUE

This process produces a coloured modelling medium that is useful for modelling on a small scale; it is rarely available in a quantity that permits large models.

Wax crayon pieces are melted as indicated in an old saucepan or tin and while melted mixed with paraffin to form a plastic medium. When cool it should remain plastic, and can be used to model small coloured forms which can be given an attractive surface quality by polishing.

Melted Crayon Mosaics

MATERIALS

Wax crayon pieces, sorted into colours; heating appliance; small tins or similar containers; shallow containers such as lids of shoe boxes, chocolate boxes, and the like; patching plaster or Plaster of Paris, and dish or small container in which to mix it; newspapers to cover working area; adhesive such as colourless cement or wood glue.

TECHNIQUE

Wax crayon pieces, in their separate colours, are melted in small tins, as indicated, and the liquid colours poured into small, flat box lids to cool. On cooling, the solidified colours can be broken into pieces and used to form mosaic designs, by gluing the broken pieces to a backing such as a piece of plywood, masonite, or even the lid of a shoe box. Patching plaster is mixed and used to fill the interstices between the pieces; the plaster can be smoothed with a patching knife or other pliable blade, and wiped clean with a damp cloth or sponge. If the lid of a shoe box, or similar box, is used it can be dampened after the plaster has set, and removed. By inserting hair pins or wire paper fasteners in the plaster while wet, near the top of the panel, hooks can be formed so that the completed crayon mosaics can be hung to form wall decorations.

MOBILE MAKING (see Figs. 41 to 44)

Mobiles, a relatively recent art form, now are widely accepted in adult art, and most teachers are familiar with the appearance of these intriguing constructions which apply principles of balance to shapes and objects in space and motion. Children enjoy making them, and the activity can be beneficial if it is introduced with purpose as a problem-solving experience. Complex shapes involving intricate problems of design in space normally are beyond the capacities of primary school children, who are able, however, to create simple hanging constructions. As a range of easily procured materials and simple tools is used, and as ample working space is necessary so that children can operate freely, the making of mobiles becomes hazardous with large numbers of children working in congested conditions. A group of 6 or 8 older children, with adequate guidance and stimulation from the teacher, can serve to demonstrate the activity to the remainder of the class who can experience the activity at a later date. Some, no doubt, will be inspired to construct mobiles as an extra-curricular interest.

MATERIALS

While the range of materials that can be used virtually is unlimited, they should be linear in nature to obtain the best results; thus, soft clean wire, pieces of dowelling, plywood strips, cardboard strips, skewers, and the like, can be used for arms, while string, wool, thin wire, nylon thread, cottons, etc., can be used to carry the pendants. Pendants can include shapes cut from coloured paper or card or thin metal, bottle tops, buttons, shapes in flywire, paper forms, and so on. Tools and equipment needed are: pliers; scissors; tube glue and colourless cement (a fast-drying cement is desirable); paints and brushes, to paint component parts; newspapers on desks or tables.

TECHNIQUE

An essential requirement to the making of a mobile is a *theme* to give the activity a direction and so that the child has something to interpret. In this way the mobile becomes not only a problem of construction and balance but also a form of creative expression. The themes for primary school children should be simple, such as Fluttering Leaves, Insects, Sky Forms, Fish Swimming, or Flying Birds. The forms and shapes used, however, need not be realistic; in fact, the theme can be better interpreted and expressed in semi-abstract and simplified shapes. By basing the making of mobiles on the use of themes as indicated the child is able to form mental concepts and to work with purpose. The resultant mobiles generally reveal satisfactory organisation of materials, imaginative interpretation of the theme, and individuality in performance, in contrast to the shapeless and unorganised constructions of wire and unrelated materials frequently seen suspended in classrooms.

Mobiles can be constructed from the bottom upwards, or from the top down. Some authorities recommend the former approach, claiming that it permits an easier attainment of physical balance. Experience suggests that primary school children find the latter approach more suitable under normal class conditions; they seem to handle problems of construction more satisfactorily when standing to work with their mobiles suspended at convenient heights, say, along the side of the room.

Commencing from a wire hook, the mobile evolves as a rhythmic arrangement in balance and motion. Laterals or arms of linear materials, like wire or dowelling, are introduced to carry pendants, and each arm and the pendants it carries must be balanced (see Fig. 41). The organisation and combination of many suspended forms in balance constitutes one of the main problems which the child has to solve. Balance can be achieved by altering the position of the fulcrum, or by introducing heavier or lighter pendants as needed, or by adding small spheres of clay, varying in size, to the ends of the arms to serve as weights; when dry these can be painted in bright colours, thus contributing to the final appearance of the mobile. Children will discover that a difference exists between visual balance, which concerns the size of the form, and physical balance, which concerns the weight, and they will have to adapt their construction accordingly to achieve perfect equilibrium. Motion is an integral part of a mobile, and should be considered simultaneously with construction and balance; the word "mobile", in fact, suggests movement. Parts of the mobile can be anchored so that they are static, while others, freely suspended, are enlivened and turned by movements of air in the room so that the construction is in a continual state of animation. The teacher should be on hand to suggest ways to control both motion and balance.

The value of simplicity in both the number of forms and the range of materials should be stressed, and the tendency to overload the growing mobile with pendants in excessive numbers should be discouraged. Main unions in wire should be neatly finished with a twist of the pliers, and ends of knots in threads or wool should be trimmed with scissors. As well as showing sound construction, balance, and controlled movement, the mobile should exhibit a tidy and an attractive appearance if it is to be an effective art form.

As a variation from the suspended mobile, mobiles can be constructed so that they spring from a base piece (see Fig. 43). From a block of wood or similar base, a long wire arm is protruded in a swinging arc, from which a wire hook is suspended so that the construction of the mobile can proceed as indicated. However, these mobiles can create problems of display and storage in a crowded classroom.

MODELLING

There are several modelling media which can be introduced successfully into primary classrooms. These are considered in their alphabetical order, and for details the reader

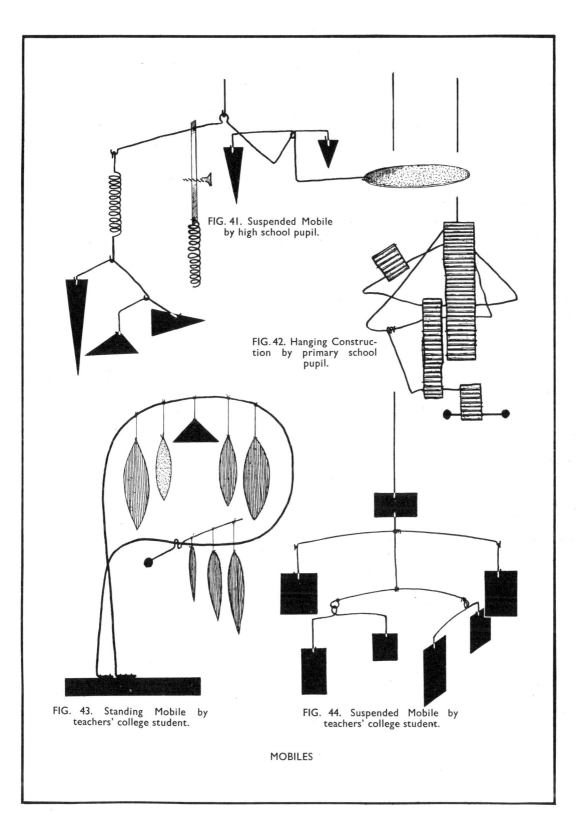

FIG. 41. Suspended Mobile by high school pupil.

FIG. 42. Hanging Construction by primary school pupil.

FIG. 43. Standing Mobile by teachers' college student.

FIG. 44. Suspended Mobile by teachers' college student.

MOBILES

is referred to Clay Modelling (p. 48), Melted Crayon Modelling (p. 104), and wet sand modelling (p. 156).

In addition to these modelling techniques, there are available several brands of self-hardening modelling material. These are more expensive, and are rarely used in primary schools; information concerning their use usually is available in leaflet form from the supplier.

MODEL MAKING

Older boys in the 9 to 12 years age group develop absorbing interests in mechanical objects such as aeroplanes, warships, trains, sports cars, earth-moving equipment, and the like. Some accumulate a considerable body of knowledge in their field of interest and show skill and initiative in the making of models. An art programme can accommodate this interest and provide for these developing skills, and the child can be encouraged to make original models so that the activity is transformed from simply a display of skill into a creative experience.

MATERIALS

Common materials such as cardboard, plywood, balsa wood, and other soft woods, tins, wire, and plastic, can be used with a range of simple tools, including scissors, sharp pocket knives, trimming knives; pliers; fret saws, tenon saws; tack hammers; a hand drill; and a wide range of adhesives and fast-drying cements, such as model aeroplane cement.

Materials should be provided on an individual basis by the children participating, and the necessary tools brought from home as required if adequate supplies are not available at the school.

TECHNIQUE

No method can be prescribed for the techniques will evolve from and be influenced by the nature of the model and the materials being used. Most boys in the age group indicated are resourceful and imaginative both in their approach to the problems encountered and to the use of the materials. They should be allowed to work individually and independently, and the teacher's main function will be to encourage creative endeavour and to stimulate performance. While the construction of the models, as far as possible, should be the unaided work of the children, they will require guidance in the use, purpose, and maintenance of the tools they are using. Mishandling of tools, which can lead to damage or injury, should be corrected and proper working habits demonstrated. All cutting should be done on boards, and simple precautions and procedures introduced to restrict mess.

In the primary school organisation, the making of models by boys frequently can be done in association with needlework activities by the girls, but there seem good reasons why girls should be be permitted to participate in these model making activities if they so desire.

MONOPRINT PICTURES

The making of pictures by monoprinting is a simple and stimulating technique which demands spontaneous work and an individual response. It is more suitable for older children and because it uses rollers and inks, it can be messy. For this reason the number participating should be small, a working area well protected with newspapers should be arranged, and precautions taken to protect both furniture and clothing.

MATERIALS

Printer's ink in tubes, student quality oil paints, or thick poster colour (if nothing better is available); rubber rollers; piece of $\frac{1}{4}$ inch plate glass, or substitute, size 12 inches by 10 inches, one piece per child participating; wooden spoons; reasonably absorbent paper such as bulky newsprint, ticket paper, cover paper, or litho paper (rough side); drawing implements (see below); cleaning materials (kerosene or mineral turpentine, clean rags); newspapers to protect working area.

TECHNIQUE

It is desirable that each child making monoprints should have his own smooth, working surface which he can ink to produce his print; hence, the advantage of the group approach. On a smooth flat surface such as plate glass, tin, laminex, or linoleum, printer's ink of a suitable colour is squeezed out and rolled to secure an even distribution of ink. More than one colour can be used to obtain a blending.

A drawing is then made directly on the inked surface using any pointed tool such as a hard pencil, top of a ball-point pen, edge of a piece of cardboard, sharpened stick, nail file or other simple improvisations. This drawing should be simple in concept and boldly executed. Lines made on the inked surface displace the ink to expose the working surface, so that areas exposed, having no ink, do not print. The inked background areas, however, will register an impression on the printing paper.

A sheet of paper is now gently placed over the inked surface and pressed with the fingertips so that it adheres. A clean roller rolled evenly over the paper should produce a clear print, or the back of a wooden spoon can be used; this permits gradations in tone and variations in surface effect. The completed print is then peeled away. Normally, the process produces only the one print, hence the name "monoprint", but sometimes two or three prints can be taken from the one inking, each one becoming successively fainter. Children should be encouraged to experiment with various types of paper and different textures; by doing this the possibilities of the technique are extended and an interesting variety of prints can be produced.

A variation of this technique is to ink lightly the surface of the plate glass (or substitute) as previously, and to place a piece of paper gently over the inked surface. A pencil drawing is now made on the paper, and the pressure of the pencil picks up the ink on the underside of the paper. Fingers, a rubber eraser, or even a blunt stick, can be used to exert a soft pressure to produce areas of tone, adding interest and variety. The print produced shows a combination of dark lines with background areas partially tinted.

Monoprints also can be taken from paintings in full colour made on the surface of the glass. Student quality oil paints should be used, but if these are not available, thick poster paint can be used with absorbent paper. The painting, on completion, is covered with a sheet of paper, and pressure exerted by rubber roller or spoon to obtain a print.

After use, glass and rollers should be cleaned as much as possible with newspaper, and wiped with rags moistened in kerosene or turpentine.

Selected monoprints can be displayed in appropriately coloured mounts. Details of mounting procedures are given under Displays of Pictures (p. 66) and Etching (p. 75).

MOSAIC PICTURES (see Fig. 34).

The making of mosaic pictures, in which the design is built up of small rectangular pieces, or tesserae, of coloured material cemented to a backing substance such as a wall, is an ancient art form of which some notable examples exist. In the true mosaic the tesserae provide visual and tactile textures which sparkle with colour, giving the mosaic its characteristic surface quality.

Simplified versions, using groups of readily procured and cheap materials, have been evolved for use in school, and some of these can be introduced at infant grade level. The techniques vary little, and are relatively slow and laborious; if attempted on backing sheets that are too large, the activity can become tedious and the children tired of it. If individual children collect and provide their own materials, enabling them to work in their desks, mosaic pictures can be introduced with large numbers of children and at any grade level. However, the activity is likely to cause mess, and should be introduced with large numbers only when adequate precautions to contain the mess have been taken.

Young children in the infant grades can be introduced to mosaic making by creating shell, bead, or button mosaics in sand trays, or in dishes or boxes filled with sand, but older children require more advanced techniques.

Button mosaics, coloured paper mosaics, and pebble mosaics are discussed below; information on melted crayon mosaics appears on p. 104. Other materials, of course, can be used. Children can make mosaics, for example, using beans, dried peas, and grains of various kinds arranged and glued to a backing sheet, but whatever the materials the technique remains substantially the same. Teachers, or children, can introduce different materials or combinations of materials as they desire. The three types listed are considered sufficient to demonstrate the nature of the activity as a creative experience.

Button Mosaics

MATERIALS

Collected buttons of all kinds, large and small, plain and coloured, smooth and textured and covered, and sorted into separate colours; backing sheets of plywood, masonite, strawboard, or lids of boxes, of a size which will enable the child to complete the mosaic in a reasonable time, say, 10 inches by 8 inches, or smaller for younger children; adhesive such as plastic tile cement, liquid woodworking glue, or household colourless cement; pliable knife; common art materials to prepare preliminary designs; patching plaster or water putty; newspapers.

TECHNIQUE

A design is prepared first, in simple shapes and colour areas to emphasise the two-dimensional character of the mosaic. Large simple areas assist the pattern, and provide striking line and textural contrasts. Colour areas should be flat, without gradation, and the colours chosen on the basis of the colours available in the sorted buttons. Realistic treatments are both impossible and undesirable, and should not be attempted. The subject-matter should be simple—one or two objects in a suitable setting, a simple landscape, a figure, or the like.

When a design appropriate to the technique has been evolved, it is transferred using chalk or pastel to the backing material. The buttons in their separate colours are placed in small boxes or lids ready for use. Adhesive is squeezed out and spread by knife or ice-cream stick over one area or shape at a time, and selected buttons pressed into position to fit closely together. This process is repeated until all the design shapes are filled in with suitable buttons. Small rectangular pieces cut from plastic tooth brush handles can introduce some variety in shape if circular buttons only are being used. The small spaces between the buttons are now filled with a thin mixture of patching plaster or water putty, spread over the fixed buttons with a knife, and allowed to set. When almost set, a damp sponge or cloth can be used to wipe away the excess plaster and to obtain a level surface. The plaster provides additional security for the buttons and, because of its whiteness, contributes to a characteristic mosaic-like finish. The completed button mosaics can be edged with a narrow beading attached to the backing.

Coloured Paper Mosaics (see Fig. 34)

MATERIALS

All kinds of coloured papers, collected or purchased, printed or plain, including colour patches cut from paint colour cards (collected in quantity by the children from hardware stores), and cut by guillotine into small square or rectangular pieces no longer than $\frac{1}{2}$ an inch; school paste or mucilage; pasting brushes; scissors; backing sheets of ticket paper, cover paper, cartridge paper, or card, size 10 inches by $7\frac{1}{2}$ inches; newspapers on working surfaces.

TECHNIQUE

The technique is similar to the making of button mosaics. A preliminary design, again emphasising the two-dimensional nature of a mosaic, is drawn in pencil on the backing sheet. The coloured paper pieces in assorted colours can be distributed in chalk-boxes or similar small boxes, one box to a group of 3 or 4 children operating as a group around a work centre. If a sheet of newspaper is spread in the middle, the contents of the box can be tipped out to give the children ready access to the required colours while working, and funnelled back into the box at the close of the lesson. The small pieces can be pasted individually and placed in position, or separate areas of the design can be pasted and the coloured pieces pressed quickly into position. The latter technique is faster. Each shape is pasted and filled in, until the design is completed. Children should be discouraged from working too precisely when placing the pieces; a certain "deliberate carelessness" produces a more animated surface quality, and the tiny irregular back-ground spaces which show through give a sparkle in keeping with the true mosaic. Variations of colour should be incorporated in large areas; a blue sky, for instance, need not be composed of pieces of identical blue, but dark blues, light blues, even greens and purples can be worked in to produce a rich and lively colour area.

Subject-matter, again, should be simple although the technique offers greater possibilities for picture making than most mosaic methods. Pieces of coloured paper may be cut a second time using scissors, and this permits the expression of finer detail not possible in button or pebble mosaics, but complex subjects and realism are still unattainable, and should be avoided.

112

Pebble Mosaics

MATERIALS

Pebbles, interpreted loosely to include small stones collected from seashore, creek bed, or schoolground, chips of brick or tile, chips of ceramic tile, broken coloured glass, pieces of broken crockery and vases, shattered windscreen glass, and so on; backing sheets of plywood, masonite, strawboard, or lids of boxes, of a suitable size as before; adhesives, as indicated for button mosaics; patching plaster; common art materials to prepare preliminary design; newspapers to contain mess.

TECHNIQUE

A technique similar to that described for Button Mosaics (see p. 111) can be used. However, as the making of pebble mosaics lends itself to the making of decorative tiles, or tops of tables and pot stands, an even flat surface sometimes is required. This can be obtained by gluing the pebbles and other small "tesserae" (as indicated above) onto a piece of paper on which the design is drawn in outline. When the gluing of the pieces is completed, the piece of paper is enclosed in a temporary box or fence made from old rulers or similar flat boards held in position by lumps of clay or plasticine; this device permits quick alteration of the size of the box to accommodate different sized mosaics. Plaster is then poured, as previously described, and allowed to set to form a plaster slab in which the "tesserae" are firmly embedded. When the plaster is set hard, the slab can be reversed and the original paper backing dampened so that it can be removed with the aid of an old tooth brush or similar tool, to reveal the desired flat surface.

MURAL PICTURES (see Fig. 36)

Mural pictures generally necessitate the collective efforts of a number of children and are merely larger versions of the types of pictures which can be produced on an individual basis at any grade level using any of the common classroom art media. Thus, murals can be done on large sheets of brown wrapping paper, Kraft paper, litho paper, or other papers in large sheets which can be joined if necessary, in any of the following media, or in combinations of them: chalk, opaque paints, coloured papers, waste materials, cloth applique, embroidery, or mosaic (using sample chips from paint colour cards). Details of these materials and techniques are given under each of the separate headings in the alphabetical list.

One aspect of the making of murals requires emphasis. For a child to derive the full personal and social benefits from his participation, the activity should be conducted as a genuine group experience, each member contributing according to his capacity

113

and special ability and sharing responsibility for the whole mural. For this reason the number of children should be restricted to, say, 3 or 4, and each child then is made responsible, not for an assigned panel, but for certain features of the subject-matter; one child, therefore, assumes responsibility for the sky area and everything in it: colours, clouds, birds, aeroplanes, branches, and so on. Another child becomes responsible for the background, a third child for the foreground and its contents, and so on. If the subject-matter contains numerous buildings, for example, in a street scene, these can become one child's responsibility. By adopting this approach the making of the mural becomes a truly co-operative activity. Each child must work over the entire surface area, co-operating with other children, encountering difficulties, discussing them to arrive at mutual solutions, revealing initiative, giving assistance, showing tolerance, comparing his own performance with that of the other participants, making judgments and evaluations. These, of course, are results in terms of personal growth. The artistic result is a mural showing consistency in treatment and unity in both design and appearance—qualities often lacking in murals produced by children working in assigned panels or compartments, so that, in practice, several children simply are working as individuals on the one large sheet.

MUSIC INTERPRETATIONS

The use of art materials, especially fluid media, to interpret selected musical excerpts, while it forms a useful correlation of the arts, should be used in moderation and as a change of activity. Used in this way, it can be a useful and stimulating imaginative exercise, but it defeats this purpose entirely if employed too frequently. If adequate art materials can be provided, and also suitable recordings and a record player, almost any number of children can participate, and satisfactory results have been obtained at all levels from grade 2 upwards.

MATERIALS

Selected records; record player; art materials, preferably fluid media such as poster or powder paints and large brushes, or pastels on wet paper (see p. 130), but oil pastels, marking crayons or pastels can be used if fluid media cannot be provided; large sheets of paper, such as bulky newsprint or litho paper, size at least 15 inches by 10 inches, but larger if possible; water in suitable containers; newspapers.

TECHNIQUE

The type of music to be used requires some thought. Simple definite rhythms, such as those produced by percussion instruments, appear most suitable for younger children, while compositions expressing a definite mood or atmosphere are appropriate for older children. The mood should be constant throughout the recording or excerpt, and there should be sufficient repetition of both melody and rhythmic pattern to enable these to be recognised by the children. The playing time for the selection should be less than 5 minutes for young children, and no longer than 8 minutes for older children.

The art materials should be distributed beforehand so that the transition from aural reception to graphic interpretation is accomplished with the minimum of disruption. The selection should be played at least twice. The first playing simply is to enable the children to appreciate the music and to absorb it; the teacher can encourage them to close their eyes and to give their undistracted attention to listening. During the second and subsequent playings, children individually take up the art materials and complete their personal interpretations as they listen, using appropriate colours, lines and shapes in rhythmical patterns and arrangements. These arrangements are essentially abstract and are in no sense pictures; the exercise is not a picture making one. It is more than likely that young children in infant grades, associating the music with its subject matter, will produce recognisable pictures, but this tendency should disappear gradually under encouragement from the teachers as the children pass through the grade levels. In the upper grades the interpretations should be decidedly non-objective.

The experience as described can be completed in 15 minutes or so. This permits the playing of two selections in a 30 minute period. If two contrasting excerpts are selected, one lively (such as the traditional Sicilian tarantella) and one quiet and tranquil (such as a pastorale by, say, Handel), corresponding moods should be evoked in the children and their interpretations should vary accordingly. A display of these interpretations, in their pairs, should demonstrate the extent of the variation shown in individual children's reactions.

NEWSPAPER PICTURES (see Fig. 35)

The making of pictures using newspaper cuttings pasted onto a backing sheet uses a technique similar to that used for making coloured paper pictures and magazine montage pictures, the only significant difference being the lack of colour. Newspaper pictures essentially are pictures in black and white. Nevertheless, the technique holds considerable interest for children, who exercise imagination and resourcefulness in their use of newspaper pieces for pictorial purposes, and interesting individual expressions are possible. The activity thus becomes a creative expression. Materials cost little and are readily available, and any number of children can participate providing routines are introduced to restrict mess. The activity is suitable for all grade levels.

Old newspapers, especially news-pictorials, collected on the basis of one whole paper per child participating; school-paste or mucilage; pasting brushes; scissors; backing sheets such as cartridge paper or coloured cover paper, size 15 inches by 10 inches, or smaller; newspapers to contain off-cuts and waste.

TECHNIQUE

Areas of print, columns of classified advertisements, sections of pictorial advertisements, portions of illustrations, and even headlines, are cut or torn, arranged on a backing sheet to form a statement in black and white, and then pasted. For details of the technique, the reader should refer to Coloured Paper Pictures (p. 55) and Magazine Montage Pictures (p. 95).

Children should be encouraged to use imagination and to select their newspaper cuttings in terms of the subject-matter; certain pieces of newspaper, used in a particular manner, might admirably suggest some aspect of the topic. Thus, tall city buildings might be represented convincingly by columns of lottery result lists, or the weatherboard walls of a house suggested by lines of type. When the pasting is completed, the picture can be allowed to dry (a portable electric heater saves much time at this stage), and accents and defining touches added with soft black crayon or oil pastel to complete a statement both creative and individual.

NUMBER PATTERNS

Number patterns are contrived from combinations of numerals arranged to form a coherent pattern, and coloured, and the activity relates naturally to the making of Writing Patterns (see p.198). Common art materials, fluid or dry, can be used, so that the creation of number patterns can be taken as a class exercise in the upper grades where the children can be expected to show a developing appreciation of pattern and to use simple applications of design principles. The activity assumes greater interest for the children if the numerals selected hold some significance for them; thus telephone numbers, car registration numbers (with or without letters), the school number, and similar meaningful numbers can be used. At other times, patterns can be based on a restricted span of numerals, such as the numerals 1 to 6 inclusive or 5 to 0 inclusive.

As the activity essentially is a design activity, children should be permitted and encouraged to distort the number forms in the interest of the pattern; and numerals as they are used can vary in size, depart from their customary proportions, be inverted or reversed or overlapped, as the needs of the pattern dictate. It should be remembered that the numerals are being used creatively and imaginatively as *motifs* in a pattern-making experience, and not as in a writing lesson or an arithmetic lesson where the traditional numeral forms must, of necessity, be employed.

MATERIALS

Common art materials, such as powder, poster or tempera colours and sable-type brushes, crayons, pastels, oil pastels, or felt-tipped pens; cartridge paper, cover paper, ticket paper, or similar paper, white or coloured, size 10 inches by $7\frac{1}{2}$ inches, or cut to a square if desired; water in suitable containers, if necessary; newspapers.

TECHNIQUE

The child should be encouraged to create the number pattern directly on the paper, evolving the relationships and the necessary coherence as the exercise progresses, although some preliminary "blocking in" in a light colour might prove of assistance to individual children.

A random scattering of the numbers in the middle of the page should be discouraged and the whole surface of the paper used. Lines in the arrangement should extend to touch all sides of the paper so that the surface is broken up into bold shapes and areas. To do this, it may be necessary to extend, say, the foot of figure 2 or the top bar in figure 5, or to distort the curved forms in numbers 3 or 6. Interest is introduced by planned distortion, and complexity by overlapping or inversion. The spaces and shapes which result can be coloured, though not necessarily in flat colours, with any of the common art media indicated. Children can exercise considerable imagination in the in-filling employed, and lines, dots, tiny circles, hatching, and combinations of these can be used as well as areas of colour.

While number patterns should reflect a use of imagination in their colour, interest, and variety, the arrangement should be developed around a dominant centre of interest in order to achieve a unity of appearance, and this dominance can be supplied by a shape, or a strong colour, or a method of in-filling.

OUTDOOR OBSERVATIONS AND SKETCHING TRIPS

Outdoor observation walks not only provide opportunities for the study of beauty both in nature and in man-made things such as buildings, but they supplement the work done in picture-making and numerous other art activities. To obtain maximum benefit from such trips the teacher should make a preliminary reconnaissance to select material for observation and to anticipate difficulties and hazards. Children should be told the object of the walk and what is required of them, and the excursion should be undertaken with purpose.

Sketching trips, similarly, should be undertaken with purpose, and to a specific location. The teacher is advised, again, to carry out a preliminary survey, to select vantage points, to recognise difficulties or to plan a convenient route if travelling is involved. Travelling, however, should be kept to a minimum, and the actual sketching commenced without waste of time. Paper can be fixed by drawing pins to sketching boards of plywood or strawboard, or simply fixed by rubber bands to school-paper covers. Dry media which can be carried easily should be used, and the range includes crayons, oil pastels, pastels, coloured pencils, black pencil, ball-point pen, or ordinary fountain pen.

On returning to the classroom, an exhibition of results should be held so that individual children can see the work of their classmates, to show whether or not the object of the exercise was attained, and to give opportunity for remedial teaching or further guidance, if needed.

OIL PASTEL PICTURES

Oil pastels or crayons are a recent addition to the range of art media suitable for use in primary schools, and they come in an attractive colour range. They are non-poisonous, easy for children to hold, blend freely, and are remarkably responsive to children's needs of expression. They provide a much freer approach to colour work than the traditional pastels, and in the hands of older children they can achieve surface effects similar to those of oil paintings. They need no fixing other than a light polishing with a soft cloth.

Oil pastels therefore are an ideal medium for the primary school child, and can be introduced at any grade level, with any number of children. As they are inexpensive, children can supply their own sets.

MATERIALS

Oil pastels, in boxes of assorted colours; cartridge paper, cover paper, ticket paper, litho paper, bulky newsprint, or similar papers, size 10 inches by 7½ inches, or larger according to time available; newspaper to cover desk-tops.

TECHNIQUE

The technique is simple, personal, and direct. The child makes his drawing directly on the paper using the oil pastels in the full colour range, experimenting with them to discover their possibilities and limitations (if any); ways of blending colours and of suggesting detail likewise can be explored.

PAINTING (see Fig. 53)

There seems little doubt that painting is the most popular art activity with young children; few activities or processes induce the same degree of excitement and eagerness to participate or offer the same absorbing pleasure and satisfaction. Yet painting as a school activity, pleasurable as it is, can make an invaluable contribution to many aspects of the personal growth of the child, including the physical, the mental, the emotional, and the social.

Depending on the nature of the materials painting can be taken as a class activity or as a group experience, and it makes its appeal to children of all ages and stages of development. Children can work at desks or tables, at easels, or even on the floor.

MATERIALS

Poster, powder or tempera paints; long handled bristle brushes, round and flat, and smaller sable-type brushes, in a range of sizes; almost any kind of paper except paper with a glossy surface, of a size appropriate to the kind of painting and the stage of development of the children; portable easels, if available. (For detailed information on these materials, the reader is referred to the author's other work, "Modern Art Education in the Primary School," Macmillan and Co. Ltd., Melbourne, 2nd. edition, 1960, pp. 71 to 78 inclusive.)

TECHNIQUE

Paints for use by young children must be easily handled, must be responsive to children's needs of expression, must allow them to work spontaneously and quickly, must permit corrections and overpainting, must have good covering qualities, must be suited to the child's stage of development, and must be relatively inexpensive. The paints which meet these requirements are opaque water paints such as poster colours, tempera colours, or the dry powder colours to which water is added. Transparent watercolours in sets of tubes or cakes meet none of these requirements, and, therefore, are not recommended for use at the primary level.

Young children in the lower grades should paint directly on large sheets of paper, at least 18 inches by 12 inches, using mainly large brushes. The best physical position is standing, either at easels or at paper pinned or attached to walls or chalkrails. Colours need not cover an extensive range, but they must be strong to produce bold colour areas on the paper. They should be put out in suitable containers which permit the child security of use; poster colours are available in stable, 10 ounce jars, and tempera colours come in tins or pans ready for use. Powder colours can be mixed to a creamy consistency and put out in jars in sets of 5 or 6 colours, with a brush to each jar. Occasionally powder colours can be put out in dry form so that children can gain experience in colour mixing; enamelled patty-cake trays or plastic palettes, with 6 or 12 divisions, are useful for this purpose. Small children work spontaneously and with great imagination; they need little or no assistance in their creative expression, and each child paints according to his personality and stage of development. The use of personally devised symbols is perhaps the dominant feature of their paintings.

Older children can work in desks or at tables, but even here the occasional use of easels (providing they are of a suitable height) can have a stimulating and beneficial effect on individual performances. The size of the paper will vary according to the nature of the painting and the topic, and brushes of different sizes and types should be available. Paints should be prepared and distributed in such a way that each child painting has his own set of colours. Again, there is no single technique. Most art processes allow several variations, and frequently there are several ways in which a child can solve a problem of expression; thus there is no "right" technique. Paintings can be done in any way using available materials providing the technique evolved satisfies the individual child's requirements; and, in fact, children should be encouraged to experiment with the paints provided in order to discover more adequate or more effective ways of expressing their concepts. The introduction of a particular technique or skill becomes necessary—and then on an individual basis only—when a child reveals a need for it in order to express himself more satisfactorily. The paintings of older children generally show a developing awareness of physical reality and visual appearances, and vision becomes more important to them than imagination. They become concerned about attributes of visual realism such as perspective, proportion and scale, light and shade, foreshortening and overlapping, and this is reflected in their paintings. The teacher can assist by encouragement and stimulation, and by adequate guidance, suggestion, or demonstration, as requested.

PAPER APPLIQUE PICTURES (see Fig. 54)

The making of paper applique pictures and Coloured Paper Pictures (see p. 55) are similar activities, and both are related closely to Magazine Montage Pictures (p. 95) and Newspaper Pictures (p. 115). Collectively the four comprise variations of a technique based on selection, cutting, arranging and pasting, and they differ only in details of materials. The names of the latter three activities, themselves, make clear the type of paper used in the respective techniques. In the paper applique technique, however, virtually any type of paper and card is legitimate material; thus, coloured papers of all kinds, purchased and collected, wrappings of all kinds, wallpapers, magazine and newspaper pieces, coloured cellophane, coloured crepe paper and tissue, pieces cut from coloured boxes and cartons, pieces of tinted pasteboard and coloured surface boards, corrugated cardboard, and the like, can be cut or torn, arranged on a backing sheet and pasted to form the picture. This broadening of the range of papers, to increase not only the surface interest but also the pictorial possibilities, constitutes the only significant difference between the paper applique technique and the other three activities. As the technique remains virtually the same, the reader should consult the activities and pages indicated for details of procedure.

A variation and development of the technique employs an applique ground in the range of papers suggested, but distributed over the backing sheet in an interesting arrangement of coloured areas and textures, either at random or to form a loose interpretation of the selected topic. On this applique ground the picture is developed, using poster, powder or tempera colours to define forms and details, but the coloured and textured background arrangement is not completely obliterated; pieces of the ground, as desired, are allowed to show through to contribute to the final effect (see Fig. 54). The combination of painted areas and applique ground gives a richness and surface animation than can produce charming pictorial treatments. Defining accents and smaller details can be added in Indian ink with a small sable-type brush.

PAPER FOLDING PATTERNS

Paper is a basic material in an art programme, both as a carrier of other art media and in its own right for it lends itself to numerous uses. One of these is the making of patterns obtained by folding, and then cutting and punching. The patterns can be simple in nature and therefore suitable for young children in infant grades, or complex and intricate. The activity can be introduced at any grade level, the nature of the folding being determined by the stage of development of the children. The materials are readily available, and can be supplied on an individual basis so that any number of children can participate.

MATERIALS

A suitable thin paper, such as duplicating paper, thin litho paper, ticket paper, or thin cartridge paper, white or coloured, the size depending on the nature of the fold (see below); scissors, on the basis of I pair per child; several revolving punch pliers (6 punch); pencils are desirable but not essential; newspapers to contain off-cuts and to restrict mess.

TECHNIQUE

The technique essentially is one of folding and cutting, and while technical difficulties are few, there is considerable scope for personal variation and the use of imagination.

Perhaps the simplest pattern to produce is the border pattern (see p. 34) based on one longitudinal fold. For, say, a 30 minute period, a piece of paper 12 or 15 inches long and 3 or 4 inches wide is folded down the middle longitudinally. Using the line of the fold as a base line, a series of varying triangular and curved scissor cuts, or combinations of these, is projected upwards. Interest can be added to the cutting by the use of punch pliers to make small holes of varying sizes. Pencils can be used at this stage, if desired, to plan cuts or to locate holes to be punched. This unit or motif of cuts and holes is then repeated regularly, using free cutting, along the fold until the end of the paper is reached. Opened out, the paper shows a pattern arranged symmetrically above and below the fold line, and remarkably interesting and intricate border patterns can be cut, depending on the age of the child. Displayed against a dark ground such as a dark wall or black cover paper, the full effect of the folded pattern is seen.

A variation of the technique is to use a 6 or 8 inch square, or rectangle of equivalent size, folded in half, and in half again; or in other words, quarter-folded. The four sides of the shape produced again can be used as base lines for the projection inwards of scissor cuts, used as before in conjunction with punched holes. When opened out, a more complex pattern is obtained, and these can range from intricate self-contained units resembling table centres and doyleys to four-pointed star patterns. This technique can be complicated further by using 8 or 10 inch squares of white or coloured paper, quarter-folded as before. The square form produced is now folded along one of its diagonals to produce a triangular shape of two sides and a longer base. From either end of this base a shallow arc, or two straight cuts meeting at a point, are cut inwards. The shape remaining is cut and punched as described above, using any or all of the sides as base lines. When opened out, intriguing eight-pointed star patterns, somewhat like snow crystal designs, are produced. Cut from brightly coloured papers, and pressed with a warm iron to remove fold marks, these patterns can be hung on cottons to form gay and colourful decorations for Christmas or other special occasions.

It is possible also to make five-pointed and six-pointed star patterns, but the folding to obtain these shapes is more difficult; the simple folds indicated prove satisfactory for children of primary school age.

PAPER SCULPTURE (see Figs. 45 to 50)

Another creative activity for which paper can be used is paper sculpture. While it may lack the permanence and solidity of other forms of simple sculpture, the making of free-standing, three-dimensional forms in paper of various kinds is a flexible and adaptable technique which can offer an additional method of self-expression for the primary school child, challenging both his imagination and his inventiveness. Although simple creations in paper can be made by young children at the lower grade level, the activity is more suitable for older children who show imagination, skill in cutting and manipulation, and judgment in choice of subject. The range of simple tools needed and supplies of paper can be provided without difficulty. If paper supplies are available in quantity to enable children to work individually in their desks, equipment other than scissors can be shared, thus permitting paper sculpture to be introduced as a class experience. Precautions should be taken to restrict mess resulting from cutting; newspapers should cover desks, and off-cuts should be retained for possible use as attached details and decorations.

head in two
pieces

FIG. 45. Simple Paper Sculpture based on
one fold with head and tail units pasted
on.

FIG. 46. Simple Paper Sculpture using
strips held with slide fasteners.

FIG. 47. Paper Artist
based on single cylinder
held with brass fasteners.

FIG. 48. Toy Soldier
based on a combination
of cylinders.

FIG. 49. Chinese Coolie
using a combination of
cones.

brass fastener eyes

FIG. 50. More Elaborate Bird Form based
on cones, and showing the use of fringing.

PAPER SCULPTURE

MATERIALS

Paper that is stiff, strong, and flexible, such as heavy cartridge paper, heavy litho paper, or thin board such as manila, in sheets of a convenient size to enable the child to work comfortably at his desk; coloured papers such as poster paper, foil paper, flint paper, and the like for trimmings; trimming knives and safe, one-edged razor blades; pocket knives or vegetable knives; metal rulers; improvised cutting boards; household colourless cement, mucilage, cellulose tape; wire paper fasteners; stapling machine; large sewing needles and cottons; newspapers to cover desks.

TECHNIQUE

The very flexibility of paper makes it a suitable medium for creative expression, for the child will soon discover that he can process it by curving, rolling, twisting, folding, scoring, cutting, tearing, crumpling, piercing, interlacing, fringing, inserting, stitching, and even continuous cutting to produce spirals and similar forms. Thus, almost anything can be done with it, and opportunities for personal experiment in the expression of detail appropriate to the form virtually are unlimited. Paper sculptures, in construction, can range from simple creations based on one fold (see Fig. 45) to complex detailed forms based on cylinders and cones (see Figs. 48 and 49).

Young children can make simple animal sculptures based on one central fold in a piece of stiff paper such as cartridge paper or black cover paper. Keeping the paper folded, so that the fold forms the line of the back of the animal, it is shaped by cutting with scissors to form, say, the squat body and thick legs of a quaint little bull, or of a Scotch terrier. Details such as head, tail, ears, horns, and the like, are cut separately and affixed by colourless cement, staple, tape, or other means. Colour interest can be introduced by the addition of paper pieces to both sides of the folded paper. When the fold is slightly spread, the sculpture should stand upright on its four legs. Paper as a medium imposes certain limitations, and children should be encouraged to disregard realistic proportions and appearances. They should design their forms to suit the nature of the material; and leg shapes in paper should be wide to gain strength to support the body above.

From the simple fold, children can progress to the creation of upright forms, human, animal or bird, based on cylinders. Thus, a toy guardsman in red and blue cover paper requires a thick cylinder for the body, longer and thinner cylinders for the legs and arms, small cylinders for the head and tall cap, and so on, the parts being joined as before by tape, paper fasteners, staples, or by insertion, and by other means devised by the child. Expressive details such as belt, buttons, rifle, decorations, trouser stripes, etc., are added in coloured papers, pasted on. Girls (or boys) making witches, nurses, Christmas angels, and other female characters, might find the simple cones a convenient base shape from which to start; the cone lends itself to the representation of skirt and dress forms.

Older children can create complex paper sculptures using combinations of cylinders and cones to build basic shapes, and subjecting additional paper to the various processes indicated to express detail and essential characteristics. Thus, a bird form might consist of a cylinder or cone for the body, a cone for the head, while wings, feathers, and tail, are created from paper rolled, twisted, fringed, or cut, and pasted or fixed by other means in position (see Fig. 50). Various surface treatments and textures can be obtained by slitting and curling the resultant strips around a pencil, by notching, by cutting triangles and semi-circles which can be lifted, and even by punching holes with a revolving punch.

Children should be encouraged to explore the full range of processes possible, and to experiment with ways of joining component parts. Frequently ways can be evolved to join parts without external aids at all, as by slotting, inserting, and interlacing. The value of scoring, pleating, fringing, and serrating to secure special effects should be fully examined; scoring to secure clean precise folds is best done with a dull-pointed instrument, such as a vegetable knife, old compass point, pointed nailfile, or the like. All scoring and cutting should be done on cutting boards, and cutting tools should be sharp to secure precise edges. To avoid waste of materials and time, patterns can be cut from cheap papers (such as newspaper) and used as guides when cutting better quality paper, especially when the paper sculpture comprises complex forms and detail. Children should work with all kinds of papers and similar materials which can extend the possibilities of the technique and offer increased scope for personal expression.

Paper sculpture is a creative activity, and the use of prepared patterns or cut-outs, or working drawings, as they appear in reference books and magazines, should be avoided. Children should plan their own designs and evolve their own techniques as they work, with the minimum of assistance. Subject-matter, which can include human forms, animals and birds, simple buildings and vehicles, floral forms, and special decorations, should be simple in concept and familiar to the child. As with other forms of three-dimensional expression, a clear visualisation or "mental picture" of the proposed sculpture is an essential prerequisite to successful performance.

PAPIER MACHE SCULPTURE (see Fig. 51)

Papier mache sculpture is the building up of forms in newspaper pieces or strips using a prepared paste such as wall-paper adhesive. A simple treatment using hand modelling can be introduced with young children while older children can create more completely realised and detailed sculptures around a wire frame. The activity is popular with children of primary school age, and boys and girls can participate with equal satisfaction. The technique is simple but messy, and children need several items of equipment and ample working space. Papier mache sculpture, therefore,

125

is best taken with small numbers of children, operating at a work centre prepared beforehand by the teacher, who should also prepare sufficient paper strips in advance so that the full working time is available for the creative activity. Generous use of newspapers should be made to protect working surfaces and furniture.

Papier mache sculptures, when dry, are strong and durable, and can be painted. In addition to its use for creative expression, however, the technique lends itself to the making of teaching aids, and correlations are possible with other curriculum areas such as social studies, nature study, and literature.

MATERIALS

Newspaper, in small pieces or cut by guillotine into strips approximately 1 inch wide; paper towelling or toilet crepe for finishing layers is desirable, but not essential; adhesive such as flour paste or wall-paper adhesive; bowls or basins in which to mix paste; 2-inch paint brushes are useful, but not essential; soft, clean wire, and pliers; newspaper in sheets, to use in the process and to cover furniture; at a later stage, poster or other opaque paints, and brushes; appropriate waste materials.

TECHNIQUE

The fact that newspaper takes on a plastic quality and can be modelled when soaked in adhesive is basic to the technique. A preconceived concept of the object to be made and a clear visualisation of its shape and detail assist materially in the creation of successful papier mache sculptures.

Crumpled Paper Method

The adhesive is mixed to a thin cream and put out in wide bowls or basins to permit easy access. Young children can commence by taking several sheets of newspaper, crumpling them, dipping the crumpled form into a basin of adhesive, and modelling the wet paper into a suitable basic shape. More adhesive soaked paper is then added, and further modelled by hand until the desired representation is achieved. This model is then put aside to dry, and at a later date, the child can paint it using opaque paints and bristle brushes, and, if desired, paste on coloured paper decorations or simple waste materials, such as buttons for eyes, and so on.

Wire Frame Method

Older children generally show more skill and desire a more detailed and convincing representation. The use of soft wire to create a frame or skeletal arrangement (or armature) enables them to attain this aim. The main lines and contours of the object, say, an animal, are built up virtually as Wire Sculpture (see p. 194), to form a strong structure which will serve as internal support for the layers of papier mache; if desired, it can be attached by brads to a base block to display more effectively the completed sculpture. Strips of newspaper, cut or torn into 1 inch widths, are dipped in the adhesive (or the adhesive can be applied by a 2-inch brush to the strips laid flat on a sink or board) and draped or wrapped like bandages over the wire frame to form the first rough "blocking out" of the model. The wire frame should be covered completely, and greater cohesion and strength is obtained if the strips are criss-crossed as they are applied. Four or five similar layers are required to build a strong sculpture, and they can be distinguished from one another by alternating layers made from picture pages or comic strips with layers cut from classified advertisements. The final two or three layers can be pressed and shaped with the fingers to define contours and to build up protrusions. If desired, a final layer of paper towelling or absorbent toilet crepe applied in the same way makes a satisfactory finish layer; and a coat of thinly mixed water putty applied by brush gives a hard but pleasant texture when dry. The model is now put aside to dry, and a sunny, windy location hastens the drying rate.

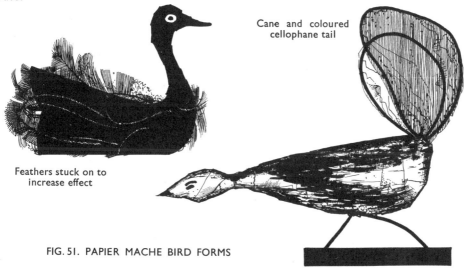

Cane and coloured cellophane tail

Feathers stuck on to increase effect

FIG. 51. PAPIER MACHE BIRD FORMS

When dry and hard the sculpture can be painted in opaque paints to express detail and other distinguishing surface characteristics. Waste materials, selected because of their suitability to represent detail, such as rope for tails or broom hairs for whiskers, can be added by pinning or gluing, or, if the sculpture is a human form, it can be dressed in appropriate and specially made miniature costume of paper and cloth. Several older girls, for instance, can participate as a group to create a number of human forms in papier mache which they dress to show costumes of other lands ("How Other People Dress").

127

The papier mache technique also can be used to make contour maps. Wet, crumpled paper is used to rough in the desired geographical build and paper pieces are then applied and hand-modelled to define the physical features. When dry, the three-dimensional map can be painted in the symbolic colours of the atlas map.

PASTE GRAINING PATTERNS

This simple technique, using opaque paints such as poster or powder paints or even finger paint on large sheets of paper, can produce patterns of limited artistic possibilities, but large in scale. If large sheets of paper are being used, the activity requires considerable working area, and is therefore more suited to a restricted number of children making the patterns at a prepared work centre. As the technique can result in mess being made, adequate precautions are necessary.

MATERIALS

Paper such as cartridge paper, litho paper, bulky newsprint, or similar papers, in large sheets at least 15 inches by 10 inches, but larger if possible; opaque paints such as powder paints, poster paints, or finger paint; large bristle brushes; water in suitable containers; graining or texturing implements, such as cardboard combs, sponges, crumpled paper, or other improvisations which can be drawn through the paint; newspapers to cover working areas.

TECHNIQUE

Paste graining requires a large working surface such as the top of a bench or table; desk-tops generally are too small, restrict movement, and cause accidents. The working surface should be covered with newspaper and a large sheet of paper, as indicated, placed in position to receive the pattern. Sufficient opaque paint to cover the sheet, in one colour, is then tipped onto the paper, and smoothed out with the palms of the hands or by brush to form a smooth, even layer.

The graining or texturing, which produces the pattern, should repeat in a regular arrangement to form a distinct pattern, and a variety of effects can be obtained either by single manipulations or by combinations of several. Thus, a piece of crumpled paper can be drawn through the paint in parallel movements to produce a simple striped grain, or the crumpled paper can be used in conjunction with a cardboard comb or a piece of sponge. A sponge can also be used to make a stippled grain. A second piece of paper placed over the wet paint, and rubbed by hand to expel the air between, shows the effects of suction when peeled away, and this makes a useful background on which other more striking graining can be made to produce patterns of added interest.

128

The activity has limited artistic appeal, although children should be encouraged to explore fully the possibilities of the technique. Individual children can show considerable inventiveness and initiative in improvising ways and means of creating special effects and unusual grainings. The completed patterns can be used to cover folios and exercise books, or as backings to displays of three-dimensional work (see p. 68), as decorations for puppet stages (see p. 149), or elsewhere in the classroom.

PASTEL DRAWINGS

Pastels form one of the most common drawing media found in schools, although surveys suggest they are not as popular with children as teachers and other adults would think. They form a hard and somewhat unresponsive medium for children's needs, and certainly lack the pictorial possibilities and flexibility of paint. Nevertheless, pastels are cheap, easily provided, and have become a standard item in the range of art materials provided for school use. They simplify storage and distribution, need no preparation, and can be used at any grade level by children working in their desks. The chief disadvantage associated with pastels is the overuse of them as a drawing medium. They have a place in the school art programme, but they form only one of the great many materials and processes that can be used, and to depend on pastels exclusively is to restrict seriously the child's creative expression and growth.

MATERIALS

Pastels, in sets of 12 sticks; cover paper, in the full colour range of 11 colours, size 15 inches by 10 inches, or smaller, depending on the time available; fixative; fixative spray; newspapers.

TECHNIQUE

Drawing in pastels, like charcoal drawing (p. 44) and crayon drawing (p. 61) is a simple, direct technique. The child should be encouraged to work directly on the paper, and the habit of making an outline preparation in pencil should be avoided; if any preliminary planning is necessary, it should be done lightly in the colours to be used. Both the end and the side of the pastel stick can be used, each giving a different effect, and children should press firmly to produce bold colour areas. Line and mass treatments are possible, and children can blend colour areas and soften edges by rubbing with the fingers, although this should be kept to a minimum and used for specific effects only. The range of possibilities of the medium, and its limitations, and also means of expressing detail and surface interest, should be explored to meet the child's needs of expression. Children should be given the experience of working on a variety of coloured grounds, and the common use of dull grey or uninteresting brown exclusively is regrettable. Cover paper, which is used for pastel work, comes in an attractive colour range, and the colours can be obtained simply by specifying "full colour range" or "in assorted colours" when ordering supplies. Cover paper, of course, is used in many art activities other than pastel drawing, and the full colour range is essential to a varied programme.

Pastels are prone to smudging, and drawings selected for display or other special purposes should be sprayed with fixative, a common fly spray making an effective spray.

PASTEL DRAWINGS ON WET PAPER

The limitations and disadvantages of pastels can be largely overcome by using them on wet paper, so that they are transformed from a dry to a fluid medium, making them more responsive to children's needs. However, the essential equipment, though simple, is increased and preparation becomes necessary, so that pastels on wet paper is a technique best taken with reduced numbers of children, say 15 to 20, although it can be introduced at any grade level.

MATERIALS

Pastels in sets; cartridge paper, or cover paper in assorted colours, size 15 inches by 10 inches or half-size, depending on time available; water in bucket or large basin; several large brushes or sponges; newspapers under bucket and covering furniture.

TECHNIQUE

The paper should be well wet, either by dipping in the bucket or dish, or by each child individually using a small sponge or sharing the use of a large brush. The use of the sponge is perhaps the easier and more flexible method, and the wet sponge can be kept at hand to dampen the paper as it dries out, especially in warm weather. A number of advantages result from wetting the paper. The use of the water, in addition to transforming the dry pastels into a fluid medium, binds the pigment to the surface of the paper, thus reducing smudging, and generally intensifies the colours used. A variation of the wetting process is to distribute small containers of water to each child, who dips the pastels in the water as they are used, reversing the process so that the wet pastels are used on dry paper.

The technique is simple and direct, and the drawing is made on the wet surface without preliminary sketching. As before, both the end and the side of the pastel are employed, and line and mass treatments are possible. Children should be encouraged to regard the side of the pastel as a brush, and to aim for broad vigorous strokes and bold colour effects, using the end simply for accents and suggesting detail. The finished drawing should show some of the surface characteristics of a fluid medium, and fixing to prevent smudging is not necessary to the same extent.

130

PEG PRINTING

The technique of printing patterns using a variety of household pegs is a simple variation of cork printing, the only difference being in the nature of the printing implement. Materials, and details of the technique, are given under Cork Printing (p. 58) to which the reader should refer.

PEN AND INK DRAWINGS

See Ink Drawings (p. 84).

PEN AND WASH DRAWINGS

Again, see Ink Drawings (p. 84).

PENCIL DRAWINGS

Like paper, the ubiquitous pencil, black or coloured, forms a basic item in the range of materials needed to implement a school art programme. It can be used in its own right or used as an auxiliary to other techniques. If soft and large, the pencil is an excellent drawing medium for young children and a responsive means of self-expression for older children. It needs a minimum of equipment and preparation, and can be used with any number of children working at their desks or tables.

MATERIALS

Pencils, soft black or soft coloured; white or light coloured paper such as cartridge paper or bulky newsprint, of medium size, say 10 inches by $7\frac{1}{2}$ inches; sharpening tools.

TECHNIQUE

The soft black pencil is a simple medium holding no technical problems for children. It offers an expressive line that can range from a soft, delicate grey to a hard, bold black, and almost unlimited possibilities for the expression of detail and textural effects. It is ideal for linear expression, but it can also provide limited mass treatments. It is flexible and responsive, but like other dry media, it cannot offer the pictorial possibilities of paints and brushes in meeting children's needs of expression.

It is a direct medium, and children work on the paper with little or no preliminary planning. Older children, concerned with realism and a more accurate representation,

131

might feel more secure when using a simple "blocking in" as a preparatory step. Children should be encouraged to discover by experiment the range of possibilities, the types of line, and the possible surface effects, especially textural, that can be obtained. Most children are familiar with the pencil as a writing tool, but few have had directed experience of its possibilities for pictorial expression. A great deal can be expressed or suggested by the types and combinations of lines employed, as individual experiment will demonstrate to the children. The teacher can help by devising simple problem-exercises designed to make children use line thoughtfully and expressively; for instance, older children can participate in exercises using black pencils to explain visually the differences between, say, a block of ice and a block of concrete, a tulip and an iceland poppy, or a silk ribbon and a piece of metal strip. Such directed study and experiment in the use of the pencil, initiated by the teacher, can prove advantageous to the child's creative expression.

Coloured pencils, likewise, should be explored fully to discover the types of line they permit, their covering capacity, the colour effects possible, and their capacity for expressing detail and surface enrichment. Children should be encouraged to use coloured pencils firmly; bold colour areas and bright accents should be the aim. A weak pressure producing pale colour effects should be discouraged (unless for a specific reason). As with crayons, small children experience some difficulty in achieving large colour areas; their colour application is uneven and the effort often is accompanied by muscular fatigue and loss of interest. This can be overcome by guiding children to draw their pictures so that large areas are avoided; buildings can be broken into small areas by architectural details, large masses of foliage by patterns of branches, and so on. Working in small areas and applying the coloured pencil firmly, children can achieve the bold bright colour areas so characteristic of children's art.

The richness of coloured pencil drawings made as indicated can be increased and preserved by applying a coat of lacquer to the finished drawing, using a soft brush. The lacquer waterproofs the drawing and gives a durable surface. Appropriate drawings or designs, glued to stout card or plywood and lacquered all over, can be cut to form table mats and similar articles.

Pencils, black or coloured, form a splendid medium for Quick Sketching (see p. 154).

PLASTER BLOCK PRINTS

Blocks from which prints can be taken can consist of several materials. One of these is plaster. Apart from the preparation of the plaster block and the incising of the design, the activity is similar to Linoleum Block Printing (see p. 92). The activity requires considerable equipment and involves several stages over a period of time of more than one day; thus, it is more suitable for older children who wish to experience a process more technical, involved, and challenging. It offers considerable scope for individual performance and experiment, but because of the accompanying risk of mess, it is best taken with small numbers of children operating at work centres prepared for the specific stages. Adequate precautions to control mess and to protect clothing are essential.

MATERIALS

Plaster of Paris, dental plaster, or patching plaster, and a suitable container in which to mix it; lids of boxes such as shoe boxes and large chocolate boxes; improvised cutting tools (see below); steel rules or metal strips; printer's ink in tubes or student quality oil paints; piece of $\frac{1}{4}$-inch plate glass, or substitute, size 12 inches by 10 inches; rubber rollers; pliable knife; a variety of papers, white or coloured, such as newsprint, litho paper, ticket paper, cover paper, or cartridge paper, cut to a size slightly larger than the plaster block; brushes and Indian ink to prepare working designs; cleaning materials (mineral turpentine or kerosene, and clean rags); newspapers in generous supply.

TECHNIQUE

The preparation of the plaster block constitutes the first stage of the process, and the incising of the design the second; the subsequent stages from the inking of the block to the taking of the print are the same as for linoleum block printing.

The plaster is mixed to a cream (see p.135) in the container (basin, old bucket, large saucepan, etc.) and poured into the flat lids of shoe boxes or similar lids to evenly fill them. Each lid should be vibrated gently to settle the plaster, release air pockets, and to secure a level surface. The container should be washed immediately after pouring. The poured plaster is now allowed to set, requiring at least half an hour to harden. When set, it should be scraped level and smooth with a metal ruler or similar tool held in both hands and drawn firmly across the surface. To print effectively, with clear registration of cutting and details, it is essential that a flat surface be prepared.

While the plaster is setting, a black and white design can be prepared to serve as a guide for the later cutting of the block. Considerations effecting the preparation of the design are set out on p. 93. The design, when considered satisfactory in terms of the technique, is now transferred using soft pastel or chalk to the smooth surface of the plaster block.

Stage two involves the cutting of the design in the plaster. Simple and improvised tools such as sharp pocket knives, vegetable knives, safe one-edged razor-blades, sharpened nails, nailfiles, old scissors, large needles, even old compass points, can be used to produce a variety of line effects and surface treatments. Any scratch, cut, hole, or impression made in the plaster should register correspondingly in the print. The plaster is a soft, yielding surface on which to work, and children should be

133

encouraged to experiment with a range of improvised cutting tools to explore fully the pictorial possibilities of this stage of the process. Ample scope is provided for individual expression and personal treatment of the subject-matter.

The block is then inked and the print taken in the manner indicated for Linoleum Block Printing (p. 94), to which the reader should refer. After printing, all inked tools should be cleaned thoroughly.

The inked plaster block, if no longer required for printing, can be allowed to dry. If both cutting and inking have been done carefully, the white incised design on the dark inked surface can make a decorative wall panel characterised by dramatic contrasts, unusual textural detail, and a personal interpretation of the subject-matter. Should ink have been forced by pressure during printing into any of the cuts or incised detail, it can be scraped out carefully with an appropriate cutting tool, as indicated. Edged in narrow timber beading attached to a backing, the dry plaster block can then be hung as a wall decoration.

PLASTER CARVING (see Fig. 52)

The carving of plaster blocks, using simple cutting tools, is a form of self-expression for older children in the primary school. Plaster is a responsive carving medium, and both boys and girls can cut it easily providing they are familiar with the use of simple tools such as pocket knives, old rasps, and the like. It is a subtractive process in that the form is carved from the original block; because of this off-cut plaster accumulates, and the technique can be messy. It is best introduced to small numbers of children, and the activity should take place at a work centre prepared with newspapers to contain the mess.

MATERIALS

Plaster of Paris, dental plaster, or patching plaster, and a bucket in which to mix it; small boxes such as chalkboxes, or chocolate boxes, or similar boxes, providing the material of their manufacture is not too thin; simple carving tools such as pocket knives or vegetable knives; several rasps of different sizes; old chisels, files, and hacksaw blades; large nails and similar tools for incising details; a hand drill with several drills of large diameter is useful but not essential; cutting boards of strawboard and plywood; newspapers in generous supply to cover working area.

TECHNIQUE

The first task is to make the plaster blocks. A number of small boxes (generally on the basis of one per child, although larger blocks of plaster can be sawn in two) are placed in a row, or rows, on a newspaper-covered table or bench; they are then ready for pouring. The plaster can now be mixed. A quantity of water is placed in the bucket, say to half-full, and plaster is added by the handful until the growing heap of submerged plaster finally breaks and just clears the surface of the water. The mixture is then stirred to a cream, and poured quickly into the prepared boxes to a depth of at least 1 to 2 inches. Immediately the plaster has been poured, each box should be gently vibrated by hand to settle the plaster, to release air pockets, and to level the surface. The bucket then should be washed before the residue plaster sets. The small boxes of poured plaster, meanwhile, are allowed to stand until the plaster sets, in approximately 30 minutes, depending on climatic conditions and the consistency of the plaster. The wet sides of the box containers are peeled away to obtain the blocks.

FIG. 52. PLASTER CARVING

The block should now be studied and its dimensions and proportions considered; the child should be encouraged to select a form that can be accommodated agreeably within the mass of plaster as a free-standing, three-dimensional carving. This mental preparation in which the child "senses" the form and detail of the subject-matter is as essential to plaster carving as it is to all creative expression. Some children, however, will prefer to carve abstract shapes. But when recognisable subject-matter, such as human, animal or bird forms, is being carved, it should be adapted and designed to fit the block, touching all sides and using as much of the plaster as possible to

135

minimise cutting and effort. A useful practice at this stage is to lay the block on a sheet of paper, trace around it to secure a shape of the same dimensions, and to prepare a pencil design within this shape; such a device helps to clarify and to simplify the child's concepts. Natural proportions and appearances should be disregarded. One of the limitations of plaster is that it is liable to fracture. Carvings, therefore, should appear squat and blocky; legs must be thick and strong, and all thin projections eliminated or accommodated within the general contours of the body. Thin unions between masses, such as necks, are bad carving; proportions must be modified as the technique dictates.

Carving is done using sharp pocket knives, vegetable knives, old hacksaw blades, and similar tools to cut away the plaster in small pieces at a time. To try to remove large lumps is to risk fracturing the mass. Cutting should be done on a board of plywood or strawboard, and the child should be trained to cut away from his body. The carving should progress on all sides of the form simultaneously, so that after the initial "blocking out," the form gradually emerges, becoming more definite as the cutting continues until contours can be rounded and masses defined by gentle use of rasps or even coarse sandpaper. Surface characteristics and texture can be introduced with any of the simple tools indicated, or with any other tool that seems appropriate to mark the plaster. Children should be encouraged to experiment with means of varying the surface to suggest detail, and the possibilities are extensive. Holes through forms, such as the openings formed by a hands-on-hips pose, or between an elephant's trunk and his neck, or even in abstract compositions, can be pierced initially with a hand drill, and afterwards shaped by a knife or a round file. Cutting tools should be wiped clean after use to prevent rusting.

The sharp whiteness of the plaster imparts a quality to the carving that is both characteristic and attractive, but there occur times when a coloured plaster is desirable. Plaster can be coloured easily by colouring the water *before* the plaster is added; powder colours, food dyes, or cement colouring pigment can be used.

PLASTER RELIEFS

Another activity using plaster is the making of bas-reliefs, a technique that uses both clay and plaster. It is an interesting technique permitting a personal and detailed interpretation of the topic and while it comprises a number of stages, it is not beyond the capacities of older primary school children. Two main skills are involved, those of modelling in clay and of preparing and pouring plaster. A small number of children only should participate, and both boys and girls can successfully handle the process. Mess could prove a serious problem unless adequate precautions are taken, and all work should take place at a working area prepared beforehand with all necessary materials and equipment.

MATERIALS

Plaster of Paris, dental plaster, or patching plaster, and a suitable container in which to mix it; lids of shoe boxes or similar boxes (or shallow wooden boxes can be constructed for the purpose); modelling clay; old kitchen knives; wooden or plastic rolling pins; steel rulers or metal strips; simple modelling tools; modelling boards of plywood, masonite, or linoleum; bucket of water; newspapers to cover working areas.

TECHNIQUE

A quantity of clay is placed on the modelling board and flattened initially with the hands and finally rolled to form a flat slab, in thickness about half the depth of the selected lid. This slab is scraped with a steel ruler (or substitute) to produce a smooth level surface. It is then measured and cut, using a knife along the steel ruler, to fit comfortably into a box lid where it will form the base for a bas-relief. The prepared clay base can be lifted on the modelling board and gently slid into position in the lid. Each child creating a bas-relief should prepare a clay base as indicated.

On this level clay surface a shallow design or picture is modelled, or incised using a range of simple implements such as pocket knives, vegetable knives, ice-cream sticks, nails, sharp sticks, and the like, to cut surface impressions, textures, and other defining details. Some children might like to prepare their design beforehand, while others prefer to cut directly into the clay, allowing the design to evolve as the cutting progresses. The design can range from semi-realistic subject-matter to the non-objective, from a simple statement to a detailed, intricate expression, or from shallow to maximum depth cutting. Unlimited scope exists for personal interpretation and creative expression.

Plaster is now mixed to a thin cream (see p. 135) and poured into the lid to cover completely the clay design to the maximum depth possible. The lid should be vibrated gently by hand to settle the plaster in all parts of the incised design, and to produce a level surface. Before the plaster hardens, hair pins or wire paper fasteners are inserted near the top of the slab to serve as hangers. The plaster is then allowed to set. When hard, the lid is removed and the clay pulled away. The result should be a plaster bas-relief, an accurate reverse impression of the original clay design, but now in more durable and attractive form. The bas-relief can be washed gently under running water to remove particles of clay and to restore the original whiteness of the plaster. The surface should now present strong contrasts of raised portions and cast shadows, and interesting surface textures.

Framed in narrow timber, if desired, or simply hung on the wire hangers, plaster bas-reliefs make fascinating wall decorations, frequently resembling primitive carvings.

137

POSTER MAKING (see Fig. 55)

Poster making is a highly skilled adult art; the production of a successful poster requires considerable knowledge, training, and skill, a fertile imagination, a mastery of many techniques, much effort, and perhaps a measure of luck. All of this would seem to indicate that the making of posters is beyond the capacity of children of primary school age—and displays of posters made by school children would appear to confirm this view. Nevertheless, simplified in method and content, presented as a purposeful exercise in pattern-making and creative design, and illustrated with actual examples, the activity can become a useful problem-solving experience not without some benefit to the young participants. Continual supervision and individual guidance are necessary, so that numbers should be restricted; a group of 10 or 12 children might produce tolerably successful posters, but larger numbers cause performances to suffer, and the results in terms of time, effort, and materials, are questionable. Senior children only should participate, and better results are obtained if the making of posters is centred on a small unit of study, extending over 4 or 5 lessons and incorporating a number of preliminary exercises in lettering and layout before an actual poster is attempted. In conjunction with such a unit of study, a display of selected posters and successful publicity layouts makes an indispensable teaching aid. While a number of common media can be employed, three—opaque paints, coloured papers, and lettering nibs and Indian ink—are more likely to serve the purpose of primary school children.

MATERIALS

Opaque paints such as poster or tempera paints; water in suitable containers; flat bristle brushes and sable-type brushes, in a range of sizes; coloured papers such as poster paper, flint paper, surface squares, or coloured cover paper; scissors; paste or mucilage; pasting brushes; rulers and pencils; Indian ink, pens, and speed-ball nibs; sheets of cartridge paper or cover paper, size 20 inches by 15 inches, but depending on time available; newspaper.

TECHNIQUE

Posters, of course, vary tremendously in size, in format, in style, and in materials employed. Yet in all instances the purpose of the poster, to state a message in clear, simple terms, remains constant. But to describe a single technique or approach is virtually impossible, and just as in picture making the child evolves his own technique to meet his needs of expression, so in the making of a poster he must overcome the problems encountered in his own way to produce a poster bearing the mark of his personality, and unmistakably his own.

Girl, Grade 6, Box Hill South Primary School.

FIG. 53. Painting, using powder paints.

Student, Burwood Teachers' College.

FIG. 54. Coloured Paper Applique Paper, with painted accents.

Two Boys, Grade 5, Scotch College Junior School.

FIG. 55. Poster, using coloured papers.

Student, Burwood Teachers' College.

FIG. 56. Picture by Potato Printing.

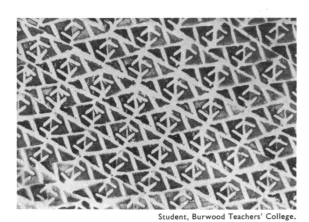

Student, Burwood Teachers' College.

FIG. 57. Pattern by Potato Printing.

Student, Burwood Teachers' College.

FIG. 58. Powder Paint and Paste Picture.

The child may work in any of the media indicated above, or in combinations of them, or in additional materials if he desires. As the techniques of using these materials are familiar to the child, the main problems requiring his attention and solution will be those centred on the requirements of a poster and its subsequent layout.

As a preparatory activity the child can make letter forms and meaningful words, using flat bristle brushes and opaque paints on scrap paper so that he can work without restraint. This can be followed by experience in the use of speed-ball nibs and Indian ink on scrap paper to practise letter forms and spacing, and to discover the need to expand or condense words as the poster demands. Finally the child can take advertising layouts from magazines and periodicals (these layouts initially should be selected for the purpose by the teacher) and reduce them to abstract compositions by blocking out the type areas and illustrations in paints or crayons, so that the layout reveals its basic distribution of areas, divisions, and lines. This exercise serves to demonstrate the importance of pattern and planned layout to the making of a poster. Preliminary activities such as these should be made interesting for the child, illustrated by actual examples and reference material, and terms and problems encountered explained in simple, appropriate language.

The child should then have some background of experience to assist him overcome at his own level the problems of poster making. He can commence by making simple arrangements of intersecting vertical and horizontal lines on the paper, the areas and shapes produced being used to accommodate a minimum amount of wording and illustrations, if any. Children should be shown the value of simplicity to the purpose of the poster, and encouraged to avoid superfluous words and illustrations; an overcrowded poster is not a good poster. They must consider the use of appropriate symbols and shapes, effective space relationships, pleasing colour combinations, the placing of words and detail, the order of priority to be accorded individual words, interest, balance, and similar essential considerations. Above all, they must remember that the purpose of a poster is to transmit a message immediately, clearly, and attractively.

Sometimes an appropriate motif or symbol, cut from a magazine or newspaper, can be used in conjunction with the child's layout and choice of words; such a motif can be more effective than the child's inadequate drawn symbol, and can add interest, colour, and eye-appeal to the poster. The use of cut-outs with hand-lettering and decoration extends the possibilities for primary children to produce successful posters.

Children can produce posters for occasions such as Education Week, Health Week, Library Week, charitable appeals, school fetes and activities, meetings, and the like. Posters produced should be displayed and their merits and defects discussed by the children; those for use should be judged by the children, and posters considered unsuccessful rejected. In this way, the children become critically appreciative, and standards of both evaluation and performance are raised.

POTATO PRINTING (see Figs. 56 and 57)

The term potato printing actually is a misnomer. A more correct term is Vegetable Printing, for besides potatoes, pumpkins, turnips, carrots, parsnips, onions, apples, halves of small cabbages, or any fruit or vegetable with solid flesh, can be cut, inked with poster paint, and used to obtain printed impressions. The activity is popular with children for it is simple, uses fluid materials, produces colourful results, and the products can be as varied and as intricate as the individual child desires. The potato can be used alone, simply varying the cuts or changing the colours, or it can be used in conjunction with other vegetables or printing devices to obtain a rich variety of interesting prints. Materials are easily supplied and the equipment not extensive so that, in most cases, children can work at their desks or tables. However, as opaque paints and printing equipment are employed, the technique can be messy, and children generally need individual guidance and stimulation in the making of the patterns. For these reasons, the activity is perhaps impracticable with large numbers of children, although adequate preparations and arrangements can be made to enable half the class, or, say 20 children, to experience the activity. The activity appeals to both boys and girls, and almost any age group can participate at its own level of performance.

MATERIALS

Suitable vegetables, as indicated; vegetable knives, apple peelers, and similar cutting tools; thick poster paints; spoons; sable-type brushes; improvised printing pads (small pieces of carpet, or cotton wool or blanket in a saucer, or felt or blanket discs cut to fit lids of jars nailed to a flat board); cartridge paper, cover paper, or similar paper, white or coloured, size 15 inches by 10 inches, or smaller according to the time available; newspapers to cover working area and in which to dispose of rubbish.

TECHNIQUE

The inking of the vegetable and its use to print patterns is precisely as described for Cork Printing (see p. 58) to which the reader should refer.

A criticism that vegetable printing is wasteful is not justified. It need not be if children are given the necessary guidance, and cutting techniques are demonstrated by the teacher. One medium to large potato, for instance, properly divided should meet the printing requirements of 6 to 8 children. The piece of potato should be cut to obtain a flat surface, and this itself can be inked and used, or a simple design of two or three cuts can be made on it. This "stamp" is inked and used to produce the first distribution of impressions (see p. 59). It can then be washed, re-inked with a contrasting colour, and reversed to obtain a second set of impressions, if desired, or the original design can be pared away and a new one cut. In this way, the single piece of potato (or other vegetable) can be used many times over, until there virtually is not enough left to hold and to use. With most vegetables there exudes from the cut surface a natural juice which can temporarily dilute the paint to produce a watery print; several initial prints on absorbent paper such as newspaper correct this tendency. To print successfully with the vegetable stamp, the child should press it vertically downwards with a gentle rocking motion, so that the entire uncut surface comes into contact with the paper and the pressure is evenly distributed. The resultant print should be clear and clean, with precise edges. Excessive inking, of course, leads to dirty printing and loss of design. Small vegetables are suitable for the printing of small areas of pattern, while large sheets of semi-absorbent paper can be decorated easily and quickly by using large vegetables boldly cut, such as turnips or half cabbages. The surface effects and design possibilities are increased by using vegetables in conjunction with other simple printing processes such as Cork Printing (p. 58), Gadget Printing (p. 83), Stick Printing (p. 175), or Tin Can Printing (p. 185).

In addition to the production of patterns, the potato printing technique can be used to make pictures. Small rectangular stamps are cut, inked, and used rapidly to print the forms and areas of the picture; colour gradations, superimpositions, and unusual minglings can be obtained, and the surface quality frequently can resemble that of an oil painting. Small wedges of potato can be inked and used to obtain linear effects, outlines, accents, and the like (see Fig. 56).

POTTERY MAKING (see Figs. 59 to 62)

While few primary schools possess pottery wheels or kilns to fire the clay, there are nevertheless several simple pottery techniques which primary school children can use to create pottery forms which can be air-dried and waterproofed. Sometimes satisfactory arrangements can be made with a local firm to have a selection of the children's work fired, or a simple kiln might be constructed in the schoolground, especially in a country area. A simple earth kiln can be constructed with little difficulty by digging a hole 12 to 15 inches square and of the same depth, and lining the sides and bottom with pieces of tin. The pottery to be fired is stacked neatly in the hole, and covered lightly with sand until the hole is filled level with the ground-surface. A fire is then made on the sand, commencing with small sticks and twigs and increasing the size of the fuel (and the heat) up to big logs after about 2 hours. To complete the firing, the fire should burn for about 5 hours. When cold, the ashes are scraped away, the sand is removed, and fired pottery recovered.

Boys and girls of all ages enjoy using clay, but the making of pottery forms is more suitable for older children who possess a more developed design sense and greater manipulative skill. The simple vases, bowls, and dishes which they make assume a

certain utilitarian value so that they can be taken home on completion. To avoid
excessive consumption of clay at any one time and also to minimise storage problems
that can prove serious, pottery as a classroom experience is more satisfactorily
undertaken when the number of children participating is restricted to 10 or 12.
Clay should be used on modelling boards of masonite or linoleum placed on
newspapers; if reasonable precautions are taken, little mess results.

Clay for pottery making should be of good quality and should be thoroughly wedged
before use. Wedging is done to eliminate air pockets, to distribute moisture evenly,
and to obtain a smooth plasticity; this is accomplished by individual children kneading
and pummelling the clay, pulling it into pieces and rejoining it, on a modelling board,
or a wedging board can be constructed. Two boards of five-ply or similar board,
size 24 inches by 18 inches, are joined and bracketed at right-angles; from the middle
of the top edge of the vertical board, a fine wire is attached to the middle of the
front edge of the horizontal board. The clay is wedged by pressing it against the wire
to cut it, and then throwing the pieces hard on to the board so that they re-form
into a mass. The operation is repeated until the clay is smoothly plastic.

Four methods of creating pottery forms without the assistance of a wheel are
suitable for the primary school. All require little equipment and the technical problems
are within the capacity of older children. These methods are the primitive or thumb,
the coil or ring, the slab or strip, and the sling method to produce dishes and similar
forms.

MATERIALS

Plastic clay, thoroughly wedged; modelling boards of linoleum, masonite, or
substitute; simple modelling tools; kitchen knife and steel ruler; wooden or plastic
rolling pin; bucket of water; a wedging board is desirable though not essential;
newspapers to cover working surfaces; at a later stage, white shellac, gloss enamels,
and suitable paint brushes. For the sling method, cloth such as tea towel, or cotton
net or cheesecloth of equivalent size; plastic clothes pegs (10 to 12 per child); rolling
pins or lengths of dowelling (1 per child); and a medium sized carton for each child.

TECHNIQUE

1. *primitive or thumb method* (see Fig. 59). This is the simplest technique. A lump of
   clay of convenient size is taken and shaped by finger pressure until a bowl or
   dish of simple form and even contours is produced. Walls should be of uniform
   thickness. The impressions left by the fingers and the particular surface quality
   which results can be used as a decorative feature on the outside of the vessel,
   but the inside should be smoothed with the fingers, moistened in water if necessary.
   In addition, appropriate linear decoration such as lines and zig-zags, can be incised
   on the outside walls with modelling tools, nails, or sticks, if desired.

143

When completed, the wet pottery should be set aside in a breezy location to dry out thoroughly. When dry, it can be painted or dipped in clear varnish or shellac until it is waterproofed, and more than one dipping or application may be necessary. The outside surface can then be painted in a gloss enamel in a single colour, or a second colour can be dribbled or splashed on and allowed to run to form a substitute glaze somewhat resembling the fired article. Pottery made by this primitive method, if handled with care, can last indefinitely; subjected to harsh treatment and knocks, it will shatter just as fired pottery will.

2. *coil or ring method* (see Fig. 60).   In this method the clay is rolled vigorously on the modelling board using both hands to produce a rope of even thickness and approximately $\frac{1}{2}$-inch in diameter. The total length needed will depend on the size of the proposed vessel, but lengths can be joined or welded. A base is made by winding the rope from the middle outwards until a coil of the required diameter is produced. This forms the base of the vessel, so that each wind should be pressed firmly against the next, and the tops welded together and smoothed. The wall of the pot is now built up by superimposing rings of the clay rope on this flat base. The first ring should be joined solidly to the base, and each successive ring should be uniform in diameter and pressed firmly onto the one below. Ends should be moistened with water or liquid clay and joined firmly; ends should be distributed at random around the walls of the pot to prevent the formation of a weak area. As the wall rises, the inside surface of the rings is smoothed and welded together to achieve strength, but the outside surface is left to show the ring formation so characteristic of the method. The rings forming the wall can be arranged vertically one over the other to produce a vase of cylindrical form, or they can be splayed inwards or outwards, as desired, to produce vessels of varying shapes. When the vessel has been satisfactorily formed, it can be set aside to dry, and finished in the manner indicated for the primitive method.

3. *the slab or strip method* (see Fig. 61).   For the slab method, the clay is placed on the modelling board and flattened, initially by hand pressure, and then by rolling until a flat slab of about $\frac{1}{2}$-inch uniform thickness is produced. Against one edge of this slab, the shape of the base is drawn (this can be circular, square, rectangular, or free-form) and cut out with a knife, with or without the assistance of a steel ruler. The rest of the slab is now cut into strips about $1\frac{1}{2}$ inches wide, and used to build the walls which are erected on the prepared base. Strong welds or joins are required at the junction of the walls and the base, at corners, and where lengths of slab meet. Inside corners and junctions can be welded more satisfactorily using simple modelling tools such as ice-cream sticks or spoon handles. The slab method becomes precarious when tall forms are attempted and it is more suitable for low dishes and box vases. The outside panels can be decorated with incised symbols or pictorial designs, and dried, or simply dried, waterproofed, and finished as before.

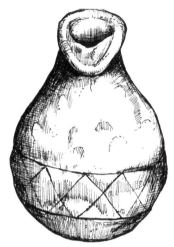

FIG. 59. Primitive or Thumb Method.

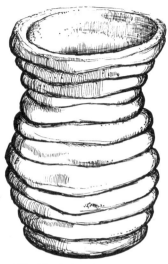

FIG. 60. Coil or Ring Method.

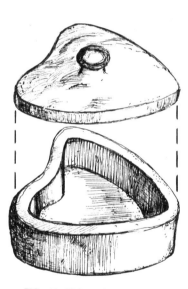

FIG. 61. Slab or Strip Method.

household pegs

tea towel or
cotton net

clay form
shaped by
manipulating
cloth

carton
or box

FIG. 62. Sling Method.

SIMPLE POTTERY MAKING

4. *the sling method* (see Fig. 62). While this method is the most involved and technical of the four, it is still within the performance range of older boys and girls at the primary level. It needs more equipment and increased working space, and introduces a storage problem, so that the numbers participating should be reduced to 5 or 6 children. The method cannot produce vases or tall forms, but it offers children a method of creating interesting dishes and bowls of varying forms.

A tea towel or piece of cotton net is spread over the newspaper-covered desk or table, and on this cloth the clay is flattened and rolled to an even thickness of about $\frac{1}{2}$-inch. If the clay is placed between two parallel strips of $\frac{1}{2}$-inch timber, these can be used as rails along which to run the rolling pin or length of dowelling; this assists the child to obtain an even thickness. Out of this flat slab a large circular or free-form shape is cut, either freehand or by following a prepared paper guide, and the unwanted clay removed. The cloth and the clay form are now lifted carefully and draped over the carton or box so that the clay is suspended inside, the cloth being held by the plastic pegs to the four sides of the box. Now, by carefully manipulating the cloth and adjusting the pegs, the child can alter the shape of the clay to produce a dish or bowl of interesting form. The clay should be left suspended in the box until it dries, and the storage of the boxes over a period of a day or more can present a problem; hence, the necessity for limited numbers of children. When the clay is dry, the cloth is unpegged and peeled from the dish. Very frequently the imprint of the cloth on the outside of the dish leaves an interesting textural effect which can be retained, but the inside should be wiped with a damp sponge to obtain a smooth finish. The dish can be waterproofed and then enamelled as indicated. Pottery produced by the sling method is not so strong as that produced by the other methods and requires careful handling; in fact, breakage can occur when the cloth is being peeled from the back of the dish, or at any subsequent stage, unless the child exercises care. It is desirable to have pottery made by the sling method fired, if possible, and the ground kiln described earlier is satisfactory.

POWDER PAINT AND PASTE PICTURES (see Fig. 58)

This simple process combines the tactile satisfactions of finger-painting with the pictorial possibilities of painting. It is by nature messy, and the working area should be generously covered with newspapers. The dry pigment and the paste required should be placed in the middle of the newspapers so that the children participating have easy access to the basic ingredients. A group of 6 to 8 children is a convenient number, although more than one group can operate if adequate preparation can be made and the materials are available.

FIG. 63. The teacher discusses the making of puppets with a group of children.

Photos by courtesy of
Mr. George Pappas,
English Department,
Burwood Teachers'
College

FIG. 64. The children make, paint, and dress the puppets ready for the performance.

FIG. 65. Sets are designed and constructed by the children.

FIG. 66. The completed puppets are now ready for the performance.

FIG. 67. The stage is completed and the play begins.

FIG. 68. "The Shoemaker and the Elves"
ACT 3
Mrs. Shoemaker: "Tonight we'll hide and watch the elves at work."

PRESENTING A PUPPET PLAY IN THE CLASSROOM

MATERIALS

Dry pigment, in assorted colours, and in suitable containers such as small tins and lids, or patty-cake trays; flour paste, starch paste, or office paste; spoons; wooden ice-cream sticks; pointed implements such as sticks, toothpicks, matches, handles of small paint brushes; a bucket of water for washing purposes; white or coloured paper, such as cartridge paper, cover paper, or similar papers, size 15 inches by 10 inches, but depending on time available; newspapers to cover furniture.

TECHNIQUE

A sheet of cartridge paper is placed on the newspaper. The child then tips or spoons a blob of paste about the size of a walnut onto the paper, and smooths it out with both hands to cover evenly the surface of the paper. Using ice-crean sticks or spoons, small quantities of dry pigment are tipped onto the wet paste, and the child mixes it with his fingers to blend colours and to create shapes and forms. The picture is built up in this way, literally as a hand painting, to produce bold vigorous effects. Detail and surface enrichment can be scratched or incised with any pointed implement such as sticks, handles of paint brushes, and the like, or accents, defining outlines, and finishing touches can be added with a brush.

The technique has limited pictorial possibilities although it permits individuality of interpretation and performance. It lends itself to broad treatments suggesting rather than representing detail, and subjects should be selected accordingly. Topics involving the intricate, the delicate, or the dainty, should be avoided. Seascapes, winter storms, mountain scenes, and similar bold subject-matter, are appropriate.

PUPPET MAKING (see Figs 63 to 68 and Figs 69 to 75)

Probably one of the most satisfying and beneficial group activities that can be introduced into a primary classroom is the making of puppets and the presentation of a puppet play in an improvised stage setting. The imaginary world of puppets gives children an opportunity to use a three-dimensional form of expression and a variety of materials and techniques in a collective effort. It serves to introduce them to play-acting and the theatre. Each member of the group contributes according to his ability, and all must work together. If the project involves a number of puppets and the construction of a stage and backdrops, then almost every member of the class can participate. The actual presentation of the puppet play culminates a period of creative thinking, planning, co-operating, problem-solving, making, constructing, painting, dressing, and rehearsing, from which considerable personal and social benefits can accrue (see Figs. 63 to 68).

There are a number of ways of creating improvised classroom stage settings for simple puppet plays. Perhaps the simplest method is to erect a cord or wire across a section or corner of the room and to pin or peg a bright fabric to the cord, or simply to drape it over; the children operate their puppets from behind the drape. Another simple method is to use a draped table with the puppet operators kneeling at the back; or a table can be turned on its side so that one or two children can squat in between the upturned legs and manipulate their puppets over the edge of the table. A large carton (the larger the better), with a rectangular opening cut in the side facing the audience and the back and bottom then removed, makes a satisfactory stage when placed on a draped table; it can be decorated by painting, or by affixing coloured papers and patterns made in previous lessons. The children kneel behind the table where they are concealed by the drape, and operate their puppets at the hole in the carton.

A range of puppets can be made by primary school children and introduced at the appropriate grade levels according to the capacities of the children. The range includes stick or push puppets, shadow puppets, bag puppets, box puppets, hand puppets of various kinds (such as stocking and cloth puppets), and the articulated stringed puppets or marionettes.

Stick Puppets (see Fig. 69)

MATERIALS

Sticks, such as lengths of dowelling, wooden rulers, wooden spoons, or old paint brush handles; thin strawboard or card that can be cut with scissors; scissors; small tacks and tack hammer; opaque paints and brushes; appropriate waste materials and adhesives, if necessary, to add expressive detail; newspapers.

TECHNIQUE

A human, animal, or bird form, in characteristic pose and action and with some distortion to increase interest, is drawn on the cardboard and cut out with scissors. The cut-out is then painted in appropriate colours to show detail, or selected waste materials can be pasted on to increase interest and appeal; for example, a piece of black fur can be used to represent whiskers on a bearded pirate, and a piece of coloured cloth for his trousers. When the characterisation is complete, the cut-out is tacked to a stick. Another form of stick puppet can be made by dressing an old wooden spoon, using the back of the bowl on which to paint the face.

To operate a stick puppet, it is held in one hand and pushed up from behind an improvised stage, as indicated, to take part in the puppet action; hence, the alternative name, push puppets. Tacked to the stick in a slightly different manner, stick puppets can be operated from the side of a stage, and this, at times, permits more realistic action.

Shadow Puppets

MATERIALS

Sticks, as for stick puppets; thin card; scissors; brass paper fasteners; revolving punch pliers (6 punch); small tacks and tack hammer; silk or nylon screen, and light fittings to illuminate it from behind; newspapers.

TECHNIQUE

As before, a figure is drawn on the cardboard, cut out with scissors, and tacked to a stick. As the puppet is not seen directly by the audience it need not be painted, but details such as eyes, buttons on clothes, or spots on an animal, can be punched so that they show in the light, and edges can be varied by serrating, fringing, tearing, and so on. To introduce movement and action, the puppet can be articulated by joining two or three overlapping sections, each join being made with one brass paper fastener to permit free movement. An additional stick and both hands must be used to manipulate the puppet in action behind the screen (see Fig. 70).

The screen is made by tacking stretched silk or nylon, preferably white, to a simple wooden frame which is set up between the spectators and the puppet operators. Strong lights behind are focused on the screen and the puppets are manipulated close to the screen in the beams of light, so that they throw strong shadows on the screen. The puppets appear to the spectators, therefore, as silhouettes. Stage props such as buildings or trees can be cut from cardboard and similarly placed near the screen so that they also cast strong shadows. The screen should be set on a table, so that the audience has an uninterrupted view and to make the manipulation of the puppets more convenient.

The technique of making shadow puppets can be adapted to obtain colour effects. Instead of using cardboard, the puppet shapes can be cut from stiff sheet celluloid, and coloured as desired using felt-tipped pens, or coloured sheet plastic can be used, although the latter is more difficult to cut and introduces problems for children of primary school age. The coloured forms are attached to sticks, and operated as described above.

Bag Puppets (see Fig. 71)

MATERIALS

Medium sized, narrow paper bags; string; scissors; opaque paints and brushes; suitable waste materials and adhesives; filling, such as cotton waste or crumpled paper; newspapers.

wooden
spoon

wooden
club

cardboard
on stick

FIG. 69. Stick or Push Puppets.

Rear view showing movable head and tail units fixed by paper fastener and operated by stiff wire; body attached to dowel.

FIG. 70. Articulated Puppet.

FIG. 71. Paper Bag Puppet.

FIG. 72. Box Puppet.

table tennis
ball

cardboard
tube

match box

FIG. 73. Finger Puppets.

FIG. 74. Hand or Glove Puppets.

SIMPLE PUPPETS

A string is tied around the middle of the paper bag, leaving an opening to insert the index finger. The portion of the bag above the tie can be partially stuffed with cotton waste or crumpled paper to fill it out, and expressive facial features can then be painted on, using opaque paints in bold colours; and waste materials and coloured papers can be used to add other details, such as a hat or a neck tie. To operate the bag puppet, the child pushes his hand into the bag as far as the string, and inserts his index finger through the opening at the neck to articulate the head. By cutting two "arm-holes" in the lower portion of the bag, and wearing a coloured glove on his hand, the child can protrude the gloved thumb and second finger through the holes as arms, thus increasing the articulation and range of movements.

Box Puppets   (see Fig. 72)

MATERIALS

Small boxes and packets; scissors; pieces of fabric; opaque paints and brushes; appropriate waste materials and adhesives; newspapers.

TECHNIQUE

The lid is glued or taped to the box, and an opening cut in the bottom through which to insert the index finger. The box is then painted, using opaque paints, to show facial features and other details. Selected waste materials can be stuck on; for example, a Red Indian head-dress can be made by sticking the points of the feathers into the box to surround a face painted on the front of the box. The completed head is now attached to a cloth costume in which "arm holes" have been cut. To operate the box puppet, the child thrusts his hand into the cloth, pushing his index finger into the box, and the thumb and second finger through the other holes to simulate arm movements.

Hand Puppets (see Figs. 73 to 75)

MATERIALS

Old stockings, socks, sleeves of jumpers, and pieces of fabric; sewing needles and threads; scissors; appropriate waste materials and adhesives; paints and brushes, if required; prepared papier mache or carved puppet heads, if desired; newspapers, both to make puppet heads and to cover furniture.

152

TECHNIQUE

Hand or glove puppets can be made easily from old socks, stockings, or sleeves of jumpers, appropriately decorated with waste materials and coloured stitching (bright buttons for eyes, coloured felt for fangs or teeth, old jewellery for details, pieces of vividly coloured fabrics or plastic for body markings, and so on) to create fantastic dragon, snake, and lizard forms, as well as heads of other animals and imaginary creatures. One end of the sock or sleeve is cut and stitched to make a suitable mouth opening; the hand is then inserted so that the fingers operate the upper jaw while the thumb manipulates the lower jaw.

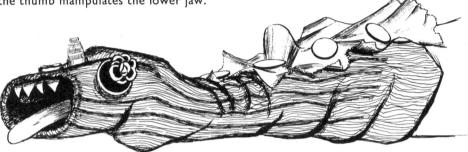

FIG. 75. Sock Puppet.

Heads of human characters and other animal forms also can be made from pieces of cloth or socks, sewn, stuffed, and decorated; from painted tennis or plastic balls; carved from soft wood, such as balsa (see p. 197); or by using the papier mache technique. To make a papier mache puppet head, the child first should construct a simple cylinder, approximately 1 inch in diameter and 6 inches long, made from rolled card held with gummed paper. A length of dowelling standing upright in a bottle serves as a useful support on which the cylinder can be placed to permit modelling. The mass of the head is shaped around the top of the cylinder with crumpled paper bound tightly with string. On this base of crumpled paper, facial features and other projections can be built up and modelled using newspaper pieces or paper towelling soaked in wallpaper adhesive or similar paste. The modelled head is then allowed to dry out, when it can be suitably painted, and hair and other significant detail added. The cylinder, which should be firmly attached to the papier mache head, serves to accommodate the index finger which manipulates the head.

The completed puppet head can be attached to a colourful cloth costume in which sleeves are provided. While the index finger operates the head, the thumb and second finger are inserted in the sleeves to simulate suitable arm actions. While older children can create more elaborate costumes, younger children can make simple costumes from a circle of soft material, such as printed cotton, in which three holes are cut. The middle hole accommodates the index finger which manipulates the head, while the thumb and the second finger are inserted through the remaining holes to serve as arms.

153

Stringed Puppets (or Marionettes)

Stringed puppets, or marionettes as they frequently are called, are articulated and operated by control strings. They provide a greater range of movement and expressive action, but are much more difficult to make and operate. In addition, they require a relatively elaborate and strongly constructed stage, and few primary classrooms have the space to accommodate such a stage. Generally, the range of puppets already described satisfies the needs of primary school children, and their manipulation in puppet plays using simple stages is practicable under normal class conditions.

The reader, therefore, who desires detailed information on the making and operation of marionettes should consult the following reference works:
1. Jagendorf, M. "The First Book of Puppets." Franklin Watts, N.Y., 1952,
2. Beaumont, C. "Puppets and Puppetry." Studio Publications, London, 1958,
3. Seager, D. "Marionettes." Studio Publications, London, 1952.

QUICK SKETCHING

The making of quick sketches is a useful activity to encourage keen observation, rapid working methods, the ability to express essentials only, and the free use of the materials. It can be taken indoors in conjunction with Life Drawing (see p. 91) or out-of-doors in conjunction with Sketching Trips (p. 117). Any number of children can participate, but the skills employed and the objectives of the activity make it suitable for older children only. Any of the common drawing materials can be employed.

MATERIALS

Common drawing materials, including pencils, chalks, charcoal, crayons, pastels, oil pastels, pens, brushes and ink, or felt-tipped pens; paper such as cartridge paper, cover paper, ticket paper, litho paper, bulky newsprint, or other similar paper, size 10 inches by $7\frac{1}{2}$ inches; improvised sketching boards if working out-of-doors.

TECHNIQUE

The method is simple and direct. The drawing is made directly on the paper, without planning or "blocking-in," the aim being to work rapidly and surely, and to practise economy of line and effort. Therefore essential masses, contours, lines, and significant detail only should be suggested; unimportant and extraneous matter should be disregarded. The characteristics of the medium being used should be reflected in the nature of the drawing; thus, differences in technique and in qualities of line should be apparent in, say, a crayon drawing and a pastel drawing.

The practice of imposing 2 minute, 3 minute, or even 5 minute time limits infuses interest and keenness, and assists materially the attainment of the objectives. Subject-matter should comprise familiar objects, which can be displayed for limited periods for visual observation, accompanied by quick sketching, or simply named, and then drawn rapidly from memory.

ROPE SCULPTURE (see Fig. 76)

The creation of simple forms in rope re-inforced with wire is a technique with limited possibilities in terms of expression of detail, but it offers an additional means of expression with few technical difficulties. The materials are easily procured on an individual basis, and little mess is made, so that children can work in their desks. Participation is possible, therefore, by a whole class, if desired.

MATERIALS

Lengths of clean rope, preferably stiff; soft clean wire, such as a thicker florist's wire or baling wire; side-cutting pliers; sharp pocket knives or other simple cutting tools; small cutting boards of plywood, masonite, or strawboard; appropriate waste materials to add expressive detail; newspapers on furniture.

TECHNIQUE

The technique involves the cutting of rope into required lengths, the joining of the pieces, and the use of wire to impart rigidity so that the arrangement stands erect as a free-standing sculpture. Subject-matter should be simple, comprising single objects such as human and animal forms, although the rope pieces can be arranged to suggest the characteristic action or pose of the object. Each pair of legs, in an animal form, is made of a single piece of rope shaped in a parabolic curve passing over or under the rope forming the back line, or, in a human form, through a loop at the end of the piece of rope forming the body. Heads on both animal and human forms, or details such as a camel's hump, can be formed by single or multiple knots tied in the rope. These simple principles of construction serve as a basis for estimating the required lengths of rope, which can then be cut. Unless

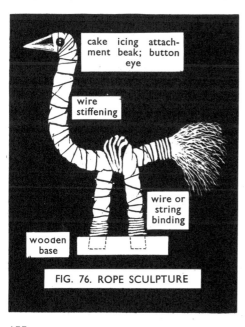

cake icing attachment beak; button eye

wire stiffening

wire or string binding

wooden base

FIG. 76. ROPE SCULPTURE

155

the rope is stiff and self-supporting in short lengths, it should be re-inforced by sufficient wire binding to achieve rigidity, or a wire sometimes can be pushed through short lengths of certain types of rope. The separate, re-inforced lengths are assembled, and joins are made by tight binding in wire, or in coloured wool which adds interest, or even in strips of coloured cloth or old stocking. If visible wire joins prove objectionable, the joins can be made in the wire in the first instance, and then covered with wool or cloth. When the joins are completed, and a standing form results, the various limbs can be arranged as desired in typical pose or to show action. The textural changes and interest possible through teasing ends of rope pieces, or fraying, should be explored by the child; often such processing of the rope can suggest coats of animals, tails, manes, long hair or whiskers on a human form, and so on.

The rope sculpture is finished by adding selected waste materials to suggest significant detail, such as buttons for eyes, scraps of leather for saddles on rope horses, strips of coloured felt for bridles, and so on.

SAND CASTING

Simple relief modelling in wet sand and the taking of a cast or impression of it in plaster is an activity similar to the making of Plaster Reliefs (see p. 136), the wet sand taking the place of the clay. Modelling in wet sand lacks the flexibility and possibilities of clay; nevertheless, simple and boldly effective expressions are possible and interesting textures can often be incorporated. The activity can be undertaken successfully by older children, but in a normal classroom the numbers should be reduced to 5 or 6. Sand casting should take place at a working area prepared before-hand with all necessary materials and equipment, and mess could become a serious problem unless adequate precautions are taken.

Where schools are located close to a sandy beach, the activity can be taken out-of-doors, the children simply creating their wet sand forms at the water's edge. Four small walls (wooden rulers are satisfactory) are built around the sand model to contain the plaster when poured.

MATERIALS

Wet sand; deep containers such as baking dishes and hand basins, or shallow wooden boxes made especially for the purpose; rolling pins; bucket of water; simple modelling tools such as wooden rulers, ice-cream sticks, table knives, or any improvised gadget capable of producing a clear impression in the wet sand; Plaster of Paris, dental plaster, or patching plaster, and a container in which to mix it; hair pins or wire paper fasteners; pocket knives; sandpaper; newspapers to cover the entire working area.

TECHNIQUE

The baking dish or substitute container is half-filled with wet sand, and a rolling pin used to obtain an even flat surface; if the rolling pin is too large for the container, a small bottle can often be used for the same purpose. On this surface the design will be modelled, and a bold treatment of simple forms is more suited to the technique. The child may prepare a working plan on scrap paper or model directly in the sand. Impressions in wet sand can be made with almost anything from fingers to a potato masher, and the simple modelling tools indicated used to define edges, shapes, and details. The modelling can be deep or shallow, and at this stage pieces of pebble, broken glass, wire, etc., can be embedded in the wet sand to produce special textural effects in the plaster cast.

When the sand modelling is completed, plaster mixed to a thin cream is poured gently so that all impressions in the sand are filled; for details of mixing the plaster, see p. 135. If a coloured casting is required, the water should be coloured with powder colours, food dyes, or cement colouring pigment, before the plaster is stirred in. Before the plaster sets, hair pins or paper fasteners are inserted in the wet plaster at the top of the cast to facilitate hanging.

When the plaster is hard, it is carefully lifted and any sand adhering washed away. The granular nature of the sand often imparts an interesting textural quality to the plaster cast, much of which can be retained, but if smooth areas are required as contrasts or in the interests of the design these can be obtained by scraping with a pocket knife or rubbing with sandpaper. Special accents and finishing touches can be added with opaque paints and brushes.

The process normally produces only the single plaster cast; the action of lifting the hardened plaster generally damages the sand model it has reproduced. If more than one cast is required, the model should be made in plasticine, or clay, greasing the surface with vaseline.

SANDPAPER LITHOGRAPH PICTURES

The lithograph technique of the adult artist is a complex process requiring elaborate equipment, but the simplified method used in schools requires little equipment, presents few technical problems, and can be handled successfully by boys and girls at the upper grade level. The taking of a lithograph from a sandpaper base offers children an additional means of self-expression that permits experiment and individual interpretation. As it uses printing inks at one stage of the process, however, it essentially is an experience for restricted numbers, say 8 or 10 children, working at a prepared work centre.

MATERIALS

Fine sandpaper, No. 0 preferably, cut into sheets of convenient size, say 8 inches by 6 inches, or larger; wax crayons, such as marking crayons; printer's ink in tubes;

157

piece of $\frac{1}{4}$-inch plateglass, smooth masonite, or linoleum, size 12 inches by 10 inches; rubber rollers; book press or dessert spoons; paper, white or tinted, such as thin cartridge paper, litho paper, ticket paper, duplicating paper, or similar papers, cut to a size larger than the sandpaper sheets; cleaning materials (mineral turpentine or kerosene, clean cloths); newspapers to cover working area.

TECHNIQUE

A crayon drawing in one colour is made on the surface of the sandpaper, and as the effectiveness of the lithograph will depend on the arrangement of dark and light areas and the contrasts they create, the preparation of a working design so that masses and detail can be distributed satisfactorily often assists the child to achieve a better result. A child may draw directly on the sandpaper, however, if he so desires. Both linear and mass treatments are possible, and the child should explore fully the ways of applying the crayon to express detail and to introduce textural interest.

When the crayon drawing is completed, printer's ink is squeezed onto the plate glass (or substitute) and rolled in several directions to ink the roller thoroughly. The inked roller is then rolled evenly over the surface of the sandpaper so that the crayon drawing is inked. Paper, as indicated, and slightly larger in size than the sandpaper, is placed over the inked drawing and covered with a thin backing paper. Pressure is now applied, either in a book press or by using the back of a dessert spoon, and the original crayon drawing is reproduced as a lithographic print. In spoon printing, a corner of the paper can be lifted gently to check on the quality of the printing in order to control the pressure.

Children should be encouraged to experiment freely to discover the possibilities of the medium. Sometimes more than one coloured ink can be applied to the plate glass and a blending obtained on the roller for transfer to the crayon drawing; this adds a colour interest to the final print. Papers of various qualities and tints should be tried with changes of ink to obtain varying effects, while changes in the gauge of the sandpaper also will influence the final appearance of the print.

The completed print is displayed to advantage when mounted simply in an appropriately coloured mount, and for information on mounting the reader should consult p. 75.

SCRATCHED (OR SCRAPED) PICTURES (see Fig. 82)

The production of pictures by scratching or scraping away a super-imposed dark layer to reveal an underlying white or coloured ground of wax crayons belongs to that group of techniques which are based on the principle that certain materials are repellents, so that a resistance occurs. Other techniques listed which are based on variations of this principle include the making of Batik Pictures (p. 28), Candle and Paint Pictures (p. 40), and Marbling (p. 96).

158

The making of scratched pictures is popular with both boys and girls, and provides unlimited scope for personal interpretation and individual performance; the child has full control of the amount of scratching that is done and so is able to remove the upper layer as the subject-matter requires. While it can be introduced almost at any grade level, the process involves three main stages employing two media, so that preparation and organisation of materials can become a serious problem if large numbers of children are involved. For this reason the activity is perhaps more suitable for reduced numbers, say 10 or 12 children, operating as a row or as a group at a prepared work centre where they can share certain of the materials, and where adequate measures can be introduced to control and contain the accompanying mess. Two distinct variations of the process are available for school use; these are the crayon resist method, which can be introduced at most grade levels, and the plaster base method, which is suitable only for older children.

Crayon Resist Method

MATERIALS

Household candles; wax crayons, such as marking crayons; black powder colour; laundry soap or soap flakes; grating tool or knife; sable-type brushes; small containers such as glass jars; water in suitable containers; white paper, such as cartridge paper, size 10 inches by $7\frac{1}{2}$ inches; scratching implements such as pocket knives, nails, scissors, nail files, small coins, pen nibs, and the like; newspapers to cover furniture. (Indian ink can be used instead of the black powder preparation.)

TECHNIQUE

A number of ingredients can be used for the black coating, and of these Indian ink probably is the most common. However, the activity with a number of children can consume considerable quantities of ink and its use tends to become expensive; in addition, it does not prove as satisfactory as a black powder mix. Black pigment is readily available and cheap, and the mixture is prepared simply and quickly. A soapy water is made by stirring soap flakes or pared or grated laundry soap in a suitable container; to this black powder colour is added and mixed to a cream. The black pigment possesses good covering qualities, and the soap acts as an effective binder. This preparation dries quickly and evenly, gives a pleasant matt surface, spreads smoothly, and is easily scratched away.

Pictures by scraping or scratching can be made using either a white ground, to give a white-lined effect, or a coloured ground, to produce a picture in the full colour range. To make a white ground, a piece of cartridge paper is coated with wax by rubbing the surface with white crayon, household candle or bleached beeswax. Over

159

this the black mix is applied gently to cover the entire surface, using sable-type brushes. This dark layer is allowed to dry. When dry, a variety of improvised scraping tools, as indicated, is used to remove the black layer as desired, to expose the white ground below, the amount exposed depending on the nature of the picture and the effect intended. Linear and mass treatments showing dramatic contrasts of white against black are possible, and striking textural effects and surface interest can be achieved. Detail in unlimited variety can be suggested with an experimental use of the various scratching tools, and few techniques at the primary school level are as responsive and adaptable to the individual child's needs of expression.

To produce scratched pictures in colour, an application of wax crayons is made on the paper, either as a random distribution of colour areas firmly applied, or as a normal crayon drawing (see p. 61) in full colour. In this variation, the effectiveness of the drawing produced depends on the contrasts created between the black layer and the exposed colour areas; hence, the brighter the underlying colours, the richer and more colourful the result. The coloured crayon application is covered with black mix and scratched through as previously described, the amount of scratching, again, depending on the subject-matter and the effect desired. If children are encouraged to work freely and with imagination, the possibilities for individual expression are considerable.

Plaster Base Method

MATERIALS

Plaster of Paris, dental plaster, or patching plaster, and a suitable container in which to mix it; lids of boxes such as shoe boxes, hosiery boxes, or chocolate boxes; steel rulers or metal strips; black printer's ink; rubber rollers; a piece of $\frac{1}{4}$-inch plate glass, linoleum, or masonite, size 12 inches by 10 inches; scratching implements, such as nails, pocket knives, small coins, scissors, large needles, and the like; cleaning materials (mineral turpentine or kerosene, clean cloths); newspapers to cover working area.

TECHNIQUE

The plaster is mixed to a cream (see p. 135) and poured into the lids, which are gently vibrated by hand to bring the plaster to a level surface. When the plaster has set, it is scraped with the steel ruler or substitute to produce a smooth white surface. The plaster block then is put aside to dry. Later, black printer's ink is squeezed onto the plate glass, rolled vigorously to ink the roller, which is then rolled across the plaster surface to produce an even, flat black layer. This should be allowed to dry before proceeding; as the plaster is porous drying should be rapid, but the actual time will depend on climatic conditions. When the ink is dry to touch, it can be scratched away using a variety of implements as previously described, to expose the brilliant white plaster beneath. As before, the child has complete control over the scratching process, and the subject-matter can be interpreted and textural effects and surface detail expressed according to the child's intention.

Scratched pictures on a plaster base, when enclosed in simple wooden frames, make attractive black-and-white wall pictures, in some respects similar in appearance to Linoleum Block Prints (see p. 92) but possessing additional qualities peculiar to the technique.

SCREEN PRINTING

The production of prints of many kinds by the screen printing process is a well-known technique which is adapted to many purposes, from the making of wall pictures and fabric printing to commercial publicity and advertising. The process can vary from simple adaptations to complex procedures. A simplified version is available for school use and can be introduced from grade 3 upwards; older children with some experience of the technique can produce quite creditable prints. Because the process affords opportunities for experiment with different materials, it can offer a challenge to the individual child's developing ability and broaden his means of self-expression.

The technique uses a quantity of simple materials including paint, and ample working space per child is required; screen printing, therefore, is more suitable as an activity involving 6 or 8 children. Newspapers should be used generously to cover furniture.

MATERIALS

Lids of boxes such as large chocolate boxes, hosiery boxes, shoe boxes, and the like; pieces of fabric such as nylon, organdie, fine netting, thin muslin; trimming knives; steel rulers or substitutes; scissors; masking tape; suitable thick paint (see below); pieces of heavy strawboard; improvised cutting boards of plywood or strawboard; stapling machine; wax crayons such as marking crayons; common drawing materials and scrap paper; white paper such as cartridge paper or litho paper (or pieces of cloth), cut to a size slightly larger than the lid screen; newspapers in generous supply.

TECHNIQUE

The first task is to make a screen from the lid of a box. The lid is placed flat on a cutting board, so that a rectangular opening can be cut in it using a trimming knife against a metal ruler; a border at least 1 inch wide must be left around this opening. A piece of any finely-woven stiff material, such as those indicated, is stretched across

161

the opening and either stapled to the surrounding border or fixed in position with masking tape; if tape is used it must be applied evenly and straight because it defines the edge of the print. This completes the making of the screen which is a basic item of equipment, and each child participating should construct his own.

A drawing or design of the same size as the opening in the screen is prepared on scrap paper, and placed under the screen so that it can be seen through the fabric. The drawing is now transferred to the fabric using wax crayons firmly applied; as the purpose of the wax crayon is to prevent the passage of paint at the printing stage, its application must be firm, and in thick lines. If masses or solid areas are incorporated in the drawing, these areas must be completely filled on the fabric with crayon so that no paint can be forced through in the wrong places. When the drawing has been transferred satisfactorily so that it appears as a crayon replica, it is removed and replaced by a piece of cartridge paper which will receive the print. An alternative to the use of crayons at this stage, which older children might try, is to cut a stencil (or stencils) in a suitable waterproof paper (see p. 174) and to cement it to the underside of the fabric screen; the parts of the stencil prevent the passage of the paint, which can penetrate the fabric outside the stencil areas.

Almost any kind of thick paint can be used, including purchased silk screen paint and textile paints, but a mixture of poster paint and starch paste, or powder colour and cornflour paste, or even thick finger paint, proves satisfactory at the primary level. A quantity of paint is placed along the border at one end of the screen, and the paint is then drawn firmly and evenly across the screen using a piece of heavy strawboard, folded card, or even a rubber dish scraper, so that the paint is forced through all parts of the fabric not protected by crayon or stencil. This is the most technical stage of the process, and it is important that the paint should be of the correct consistency. It should be thick and tacky. Thin paint will bleed or seep around the edges or penetrate to wrong places. Care should be taken to avoid over-use of the cardboard squeegee for this also can cause the paint to bleed. Children should be encouraged to adopt careful working habits, and to aim for clean prints. Surplus paint should be scraped up and returned to the border, ready for the next print.

After inking, the screen is lifted and the print is seen on the drawing paper below. Any number of prints can be made simply by repeating the process, or the screen can be cleaned. Most of the crayon can be washed from the fabric by running hot water through the screen, or, if necessary, a cloth moistened in mineral turpentine can be used; this should also be sufficient to remove the stencil.

When older children have gained some experience with the technique, they can experiment with printing on a variety of papers, textured, smooth, glossy, dull, plain, printed, or coloured, to gain special effects. Some might like to explore the possibilities of using several stencils and two or more colours to produce coloured prints. Great scope exists for individual performance, and the teacher should encourage personal investigation by individual children so that they can increase their skills and extend their artistic horizons.

SCRIBBLE PATTERNS (see Fig. 83)

Scribble patterns relate naturally to Number Patterns (see p. 116) and Writing Patterns (p. 198). They use a wide range of common art media, and they can be introduced at any grade level, though the nature of the pattern should become more complex as the child passes through the grade levels. As few materials need be involved, children are able to work individually in their desks so that a whole class can participate, if desired.

When scribble patterns (and the related types of pattern) are properly introduced as problem-solving experiences, they require an intellectual response from the child who must make a series of personal decisions affecting line relationships, space relationships, colour combinations, textural simulations, and the like. The reasoning and the decision-making required in these situations are encountered frequently at the adult level, as in the purchase of furniture, clothing, and household appointments. Thus, participation in these activities can be beneficial to the child if it is made purposeful and the child is made to think.

MATERIALS

Any of the common art media, including black pencil, coloured pencil, crayons, pastels, oil pastels, or felt-tipped pens; white or coloured paper, such as cartridge paper, cover paper, ticket paper, or bulky newsprint, size 10 inches by $7\frac{1}{2}$ inches, depending on time available and the age of the children; newspapers to cover desks; fixative, if pastels are being used.

TECHNIQUE

On a piece of paper of convenient size the child makes a random distribution of lines, in virtually a doodling technique, to agreeably fill the sheet. The resultant scribble, essentially meaningless and non-objective, is the first stage of the activity. The child then proceeds to fill the shapes of the scribble with selected colours and imaginative in-filling to develop a dominant area or centre of interest. The activity now becomes an experience in design, and the child unconsciously uses several common design principles in order to achieve a unified and ordered pattern. All areas of the scribble need not be filled, and the child is required to determine a proportion between filled and unfilled areas. Areas can be filled with bold flat colours to contrast with interesting effects obtained by using combinations of lines, dots, tiny circles, zig-zags, crosses, scumbles, tonal variations, and other filling, to distinguish areas or to suggest textural changes. The problems are made more difficult if the range of colours is restricted to, say, a harmony of three; while to produce a successful and intricate scribble pattern in black pencil, or in any medium using a single colour, the child must explore fully the graphic possibilities of the medium,

163

considering the types of line, and the possible surface effects, especially textural, that can be obtained.

The activity, as the name suggests, normally is used to produce abstract patterns, but as a variation the child occasionally can turn the initial scribble into an imaginative picture. The scribble should be studied from all viewpoints to see if the arrangement of lines and shapes suggests possible subject-matter, such as a human or animal form, known or imaginary, or a familiar object, which can be developed with a further use of art materials to define the imagined form.

SHELL SCULPTURE

The modelling of simple animal and human forms in collected seashells of all types is a simple activity of decidedly limited artistic possibilities, and applicable only to certain areas along the coastline. If children individually can collect adequate supplies of suitable shells they can work in their desks, sharing the other materials required. The skills required make the activity suitable for older children only.

MATERIALS

Collected shells, in a variety of shapes, sizes, and colours; a fast-drying adhesive such as hobby cement; plaster, and a suitable container in which to mix it; simple modelling tools such as spoon handles, ice-cream sticks, or knives with pliable blades; newspapers to cover working area.

TECHNIQUE

The technique is simple, although relatively complex sculptures can be created if shells in adequate variety are available. Subject-matter should be simple, comprising a single human or animal form, and the child should have a clear concept of the proposed form before commencing the sculpture. Shells are selected for their suitability to represent parts of the proposed sculpture, and shapes, colours, and textures must be considered. If possible, all the shells required should be selected and their combination planned, before cementing or fixing takes place. When these initial steps are completed, the child creates the sculpture by sticking shell to shell (or shell into shell) with hobby cement to build up the shapes of the object. When the cement is dry, the child can fill in the crevices between shells with patching plaster, using an ice-cream stick, spoon handle, pocket knife, or similar aid to obtain a smooth application. Excess plaster can be wiped away gently, using a damp sponge or cloth. For display purposes and also to give the shell sculpture stability, it can be set in a lump of plaster which can be painted, if desired, in opaque paints to harmonise with the subject-matter of the sculpture.

SOAP SCULPTURE (see Fig. 77)

Of the various carving materials suitable for use in the primary school, soap is perhaps the softest and most responsive; indeed, its softness is one of its chief limitations, for, being so soft, the carving is easy and some children show a tendency to engage in excessive carving and insufficient creative expression. The range of cutting tools is simple and easily provided, the soap can be brought by the individual child, so that soap sculpture can be introduced to a whole class, if desired, at the upper levels of the school. The process, like all carving activities, is subtractive and off-cut soap accumulates; adequate use of newspapers should contain any mess made. Pieces of off-cut soap can be used for laundry purposes, especially in washing machines, and even the completed soap sculpture can be used in the bathroom; wrapped in coloured cellophane and attractively tied, it can form a useful present for the child to take home.

FIG. 77. SOAP SCULPTURE

MATERIALS

Soft, fresh soap, such as large pieces of laundry soap, cakes of coloured toilet soap, and soft kitchen sand soap; simple cutting tools such as pocket knives, vegetable knives, pen nibs reversed in their holders, nail files, large nails, and similar tools; improvised cutting boards of plywood or strawboard; scrap paper and pencil is useful but not essential; newspapers to cover working surfaces.

TECHNIQUE

The technique of carving from the block of soap virtually is identical with the technique for Plaster Carving (see p. 134), the same principles of design and cutting and the same limitations applying with equal validity. The reader, therefore, should consult the page indicated for details of the technique.

SPACE DESIGNS (see Figs. 78 to 81)

Sculptures in lump clay, plaster, soap, or wood, are all concerned with solid masses of material; the techniques employed, therefore, are techniques of sculpture in the *mass*. The creation of space designs introduces the new dimension of space, so that the techniques used literally constitute sculpture in *space*, and relate the activity to the making of Mobiles (see p. 105). The problem of the space design is to achieve a coherent, unified, interesting construction of lines (in the form of pieces of dowelling, wire, string, wools, and the like) and planes (formed of pieces of paper, card, plastic, cellophane, flywire, light metal, etc.), arranged to manipulate and to animate the space it occupies. When the space design occupies an unrestricted space it is called a *free-standing* design (see Fig. 78); when it is constructed within a limited space such as a small carton or shoe box, it becomes an *enclosed* space design (see Fig. 79). In both approaches the selection and combination of the various materials should be allied to a satisfactory composition or relationship of the parts, and the construction should show structural strength, coherence and unity, variety and interest, and a dominant focal point; hence, the term space *design*.

Both types come within the performance range of older children in the primary school. However, a wide range of materials and tools is required, children need ample space in which to work and to move about, certain items of equipment must be shared, and considerable mess can accompany the activity; for these reasons numbers participating should be restricted, and 6 to 10 children comprise a manageable group.

The introduction of the making of space designs as a purposeful classroom activity can hold considerable benefit for the participants. The production of a successful space design involves a logical approach to the use of materials, the exercise of intellect and imagination, the capacity to think through a series of problems to a feasible solution, and the development of powers of concentration, perseverance, resourcefulness, ingenuity, and the like. In addition, they satisfy a real need of children of the age group indicated to manipulate and to handle materials in building, assembling, and constructing. Details of the two types follow.

Free Standing Space Designs

MATERIALS

Pieces of flat board or small wood blocks to serve as base pieces; linear materials (such as pieces of dowelling, skewers, old paint brush handles, wire, string, wool, plastic thonging, and the like); plane materials (such as sheet plastic, paper, card, cellophane, light metal, flywire, stiff fabrics, etc.); a range of simple tools, including pocket knives, trimming knives, tenon saws, tack hammers, side-cutting pliers, tin

166

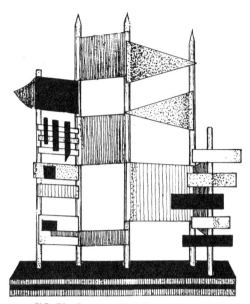

FIG. 78. Free-standing Space Design in wooden skewers and coloured papers.

FIG. 79. Enclosed Space Design in a Shoe Box.

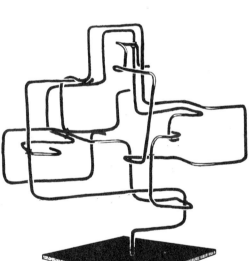

FIG. 80. Free-standing Space Design in wire.

FIG. 81. Free-standing Space Design in wire with coloured paper in-filling.

SPACE DESIGNS

shears, a hand drill, rasps, revolving punch pliers (6 punch); cutting boards of plywood or heavy strawboard; adhesives such as glue, colourless cement, fast-drying model cement, wood-working glue; cellulose tape and gummed paper; stapling machine; brads, tacks, steel pins, lills, drawing pins; opaque paints and brushes to paint component parts; newspapers to cover working area.

TECHNIQUE

Free standing space designs are constructed on a small wooden base and project upwards to occupy and animate an unrestricted space. There is no set technique; the child evolves his method of working in terms of the problems encountered as the design grows. The tools indicated should be available for use as the nature of the construction dictates, and joins in component parts can be effected by gluing, binding, nailing, or inserting. Usually the base block is drilled to accommodate the main supports of the design, which are glued in position in the holes, and from such a start the space design evolves as the child desires. It can grow as a static arrangement of intersecting horizontal and vertical lines and planes (for example, an arrangement of wooden skewers and pieces of coloured card of varying sizes) or as a dynamic construction of diagonal directions and movements checked by transverse lines and planes (for example, skewers and old paint brush handles set into the base at calculated angles, related by stringing and coloured wools, and supporting paper forms cut from cover paper).

As a rule, space designs are more effective when they are simple in concept, employing thoughtfully selected materials in a restricted range; children should be discouraged from overloading the construction with unnecessary and unrelated materials. When the construction is completed to produce a unified design with an established centre of interest, selected parts can be painted in poster paints to add interest and to improve the appearance; thus, the base block might be painted black, and certain linear supports or laterals such as skewers or pieces of wire painted a contrasting white.

Space designs essentially are non-objective. They have no subject-matter or pictorial content. They are simply free-standing, three-dimensional constructions in space, resulting from an educational experience with materials.

Enclosed Space Designs

MATERIALS

The making of space designs enclosed within the confines of boxes, ranging from chalk boxes to shoe boxes to shirt boxes with window fronts, generally involves a reduced use of tools and an increased use of gluing, taping, and pinning in the construction. Base blocks are not required, and with the addition of the boxes, as indicated, the nature of the materials remains substantially as shown for free-standing space designs.

TECHNIQUE

The procedure is somewhat different. The child's first task is to prepare the inside of the box as a setting for the space design. This can be done by pasting in strips, shapes, or areas of coloured paper to serve as a background and to make a contribution to the design, or opaque paints can be used to paint the interior in flat colour areas, in geometric divisions, or the paint can be dribbled, splashed, stippled, or applied in any way appropriate to the proposed design. While the box is drying, the child can be selecting his linear and plane materials, painting or otherwise preparing them for assembly. The problem now is to construct a coherent and interesting design in related materials within the enclosed space of the box. Coloured wools, threads, string, and thin wire, become important ingredients and can be threaded through holes punched in the sides of the box, either to be terminated by taping or stapling, or for return in a different direction or angle. Wooden skewers or lengths of dowelling, can be fixed in position on drawing pins pushed through from the outside.

As with free-standing space designs, however, there is no method that can be described; the child builds the enclosed design within the space, determining his method of working as he proceeds, according to his purpose and intentions. The approach is essentially abstract and no subject-matter is interpreted. In this major respect the enclosed space design differs basically from the diorama (see p. 63), with which it should not be confused.

SPATTER PICTURES

The making of pictures by spattering paint over arranged cut-outs or through masks requires some skill and experience of the technique before satisfactory spatter pictures are produced, but the process is not beyond the capacity of children in, say, grades 5 or 6, and there is considerable scope for individual experiment. Small numbers are advisable, because the technique can create mess and children need ample working space. A range of materials is employed but all are readily available. A vertical surface such as a wall or a display board becomes necessary if the spatter effect is to be produced by spraying.

MATERIALS

White or coloured paper, such as cartridge paper, bulky newsprint, ticket paper, or cover paper, size 10 inches by $7\frac{1}{2}$ inches, or larger, depending on time available and the purpose of the picture; brown Kraft, brown wrapping, or cover paper, from which to cut masks; scissors and safe, one-edged razor blades; steel lills; thinned poster paint or similar opaque paint; old tooth brushes; pencils; several household-type fly sprays; several flywire screens (see below); water in suitable containers; newspapers to use when spraying, and also to cover the working area.

TECHNIQUE

There are several ways to make spatter pictures, ranging from the simple tooth brush and pencil technique which younger children can employ to the use of intricate masks and spraying, which meets the needs of older children.

Simple masks are cut from small pieces of suitable paper such as brown Kraft. Outlines can be drawn in pencil, or the child can cut directly into the paper. Cutting should be done from the middle of the piece so that two shapes are produced, the cut-out, and the shape left, which is the mask. Both pieces may be used, if desired. Shapes cut should be bold, conventionalised, with simple outlines, and a minimum of detail. Small holes required in a mask should be made by punching rather than by cutting. When the mask is completed, it is placed in position on a piece of paper or card, either white or appropriately coloured. The spatter treatment is produced by dipping a tooth brush in opaque paint such as thick poster or powder paint, holding it vertically over the mask, and rubbing a pencil up and down the bristles to disperse the colour on the paper below. The mask can be lifted, moved to a new position (if desired), and the process repeated. In this way, regular patterns of an all-over type (see p. 24) can be made, or self-contained pictorial statements are possible. As children gain in skill and experience, both the cut-out and the mask can be used with changes of colour to obtain more complex results; the spattering is done around the edge of the cut-out, and through the opening in the mask. Any tendency by either mask or cut-out to curl or buckle can be overcome by the use of small lills to pin them down, or they can be dampened first so that they remain limp. The two pieces can be superimposed, overlapped, alternated, inverted, and so on, as the child decides.

A development from the tooth brush and pencil process is the use of the tooth brush with a small plywood frame, say 6 inches by 4 inches, over which rustless flywire is stretched. Masks and cut-outs are prepared as before and arranged on paper to form either a pattern or a pictorial design. The tooth brush is dipped in thick opaque paint, and rubbed vigorously across the flywire screen held horizontally an inch or two above the paper. The rubbing on the wire disperses the paint as a fine distribution on the paper below. If the paint is too thin, the paint is inclined to run and merge, thus destroying the spatter effect. Again, the cut-out can be moved as desired and the spattering repeated with changes of colour, so that involved and colourful results can be obtained.

Older children enjoy using an improvised spray gun to achieve a spattered effect. An area of a wall, a display board, a portable chalkboard, or a sheet of plywood, should be protected by newspapers pinned or taped to cover an area much larger than the piece of paper, which is pinned in a central position. Masks and cut-outs are arranged on the paper as the child desires, taped, or pinned with lills; drawing pins, being larger, can show in the completed spatter, and are best avoided. Thinned poster colour is now sprayed through a fly spray held horizontally, and a fine dispersion of paint is produced on the exposed paper. If the spray is held too close to the paper, or in the one position for too long, the paint is likely to run down the paper; children, therefore, should be encouraged to work with care.

The spatter technique can be used for the making of pictures and patterns, for the decoration of Christmas and other cards, and for the decoration of large sheets of paper which can be used in class dramatisations, for costume making (see p. 59), and in puppet stages (see p. 149). In addition, large paper friezes or mural pictures can be made by arranging cut-outs along a base line, say, to represent buildings and people in combination with natural leaves, branches, bracken fern, and so on, to make a farm scene; the arrangement is then sprayed with two or more colours appropriate to the theme, to produce a bold silhouette picture against a coloured background. Such a project often can be undertaken as a group experience.

SPONGE PAINTING

Sponge painting is a variation of ordinary Painting (see p. 118), the basic difference being that the major portion of the picture is painted with a sponge, and brushes are used only for finishing touches and accents. In this latter respect, the activity is similar to the making of Powder Paint and Paste Pictures (p. 146), and similarly it produces bold, sweeping effects suggesting the mood or character of the topic rather than a detailed representation. The activity can cause mess and children need ample space in which to work at desks or tables. Therefore, 6 or 8 older children, working at a prepared area, comprise a reasonable number.

MATERIALS

Natural sponges, or synthetic sponges in cylindrical or cubic form; poster paints or powder paints in shallow containers such as patty-cake trays, or tempera colours in discs; water in suitable containers; sable-type brushes; paper, white or coloured, such as cartridge paper, bulky newsprint, ticket paper, or cover paper, size 15 inches by 10 inches, or larger; newspapers to cover working area.

TECHNIQUE

The limitations indicated for Powder Paint and Paste Pictures (p. 146) apply equally to sponge painting, and topics should be chosen accordingly. The technique permits broad treatments and bold textural effects, but detailed interpretation of subject-matter is impossible. Topics, therefore, should derive from seascapes, stormy land-scapes, mountain scenes, snowscapes, nocturnes, or from single objects (or small groups) painted as large as the paper permits, such as a vase of flowers, an old tree, and similar things.

Opaque paint should be distributed in wide shallow containers such as saucers, small lids, or patty-cake trays, to permit easy access; these should be placed on newspapers in the middle of the working area. The technique is direct, and the children simply dip their sponges in the paint and use them as improvised brushes. Children should be encouraged to experiment to discover the possibilities of the sponge. The side can be used for broad scumbles, the edge for sharper effects, while corners and curved surfaces can be used to obtain different surface results; sweeping strokes, bold colour areas, delicate stipples and blendings, are possible. When the painting has been finished as far as possible with the sponge, sable-type brushes are used to paint in expressive detail, colour accents, and the deft touches needed to complete the statement. The technique permits wide individual variation.

"STAINED GLASS" PICTURES

The technique of painting or colouring glass is an ancient art, and all teachers and a great many children today are familiar with the beauty of stained glass windows in either the great cathedrals or small local churches, having seen such windows in reproductions or as a result of actual visits. The traditional technique is laborious and involved, requiring great skill and special facilities; it utilises the passage of light through various kinds of glass to intensify and to blend the colours in a rich pattern of pictorial symbolism.

This same principle is basic to a simplified technique which can be introduced in the upper grades of the primary school, in which transparent and translucent papers are arranged as a window and displayed against the light. It involves several stages which children find interesting, and the activity is popular. Although different materials are required at each stage, they generally can be provided with little difficulty. Children will require continual guidance and supervision, so that the numbers participating should be small, say 6 to 10. A working area should be prepared, with the materials required for a particular stage, and the full process is likely to occupy two or three periods.

MATERIALS

Suitable card, such as pasteboard, pulpboard, manila board, or even heavy paper, cut to a size which permits the child to complete the whole process in a reasonable time, say 10 inches by $7\frac{1}{2}$ inches, or equivalent; cutting boards of plywood or strawboard;

cutting tools such as trimming knives, safe one-edged razor blades, sharp pocket knives; Indian ink and wide speedball nibs in holders (or thick black crayon, or black paint and a small bristle brush); mucilage or liquid glue; pasting brushes; sable-type brushes; transparent and translucent papers, white and coloured, such as cellophane, tissue paper, confectionery wrappings, tracing papers, wrapping parchments, and the like; common drawing media and scrap paper; newspapers.

TECHNIQUE

The child should first measure a rectangle on a piece of card or stiff paper of convenient size, leaving a 1 inch surrounding border. A second rectangle of the same dimensions is drawn on scrap paper, and in this the child prepares a thick-lined design in which the lines simulate the leading in a window. At this stage these lines can be made with thick black crayon, pastel, oil pastel, or soft pencil, and they should be so arranged that they form a coherent net-work, leaving no space isolated, and making frequent contact with the edges of the surrounding border. Subject-matter should be interpreted in simple shapes to facilitate cutting, and the representation of fine detail is not possible. Long, thin shapes, which may buckle in the actual window, should be divided and strengthened by transverse lines, and large areas generally should be broken up by lines introduced, if necessary, for the purpose.

When a satisfactory design is prepared, showing no weaknesses and a unified pattern of lines, it is transferred to the card and reproduced in thick, black lines approximately 3/16 of an inch wide, using Indian ink and speedball nibs, or black poster paint and a small bristle brush. The spaces between the lines are now removed, using trimming knives or safe one-edged razor blades, to obtain a framework of "leads" contained within the surrounding border. Fragments of white card showing along the cut edges and the border should be blackened with paint or Indian ink before proceeding.

The card is now turned over, and the spaces filled-in with coloured transparent and translucent papers, as indicated, to establish the forms of the subject-matter. The prepared design should be consulted frequently as a guide during this stage. The paper pieces are cut slightly larger than the window spaces, and fixed with mucilage or liquid glue to the surrounding strips, or "leads." The design is built up in this way, using a variety of papers, and transparent coloured papers, like cellophane, can be overlapped in whole or in part to obtain rich colour effects.

Incidents and characters from nursery rhymes and children's literature, simply conceived in bright colour areas, make suitable subject-matter, and the full effect of the completed stained glass window is seen when it is displayed in front of a source of light, such as a window or a light-fitting.

A less involved method which produces a less spectacular result eliminates the cutting and pasting of transparent pieces, and achieves a measure of translucency by the use of an oil applied to the back of the design. A thick-lined drawing is made in Indian ink on a piece of cartridge paper, as described. Transparent water-colours

173

are used to colour the spaces between the lines to establish the forms of the subject-matter; or if the child prefers, the process can be reversed so that the water-colour painting is made first and the black lines superimposed as outlines and connecting strips. When dry, the paper is turned over and a coating of oil, such as purified linseed oil or paraffin oil, or similar clear oil, is applied by brush to make the paper translucent. The resultant window lacks the colour richness and vibrancy of the former method; nevertheless, its more subdued colours are not without a certain charm.

STENCILLED PICTURES (see Fig. 3)

The making of pictures (or patterns) using a stencilling technique is an activity requiring developed skill in cutting and manipulation, and the ability to plan a design to suit the nature of the technique. It is suitable, therefore, for older children only. The activity is best done at an adequately prepared work centre, with restricted numbers of children. Stencilled impressions can be made on paper using poster or similar opaque paints and special brushes, or on a closely-woven cloth such as cotton, using stencil colours or oil paints. The technique is somewhat limited in its pictorial possibilities and can become tedious; nevertheless, individual children find it satisfying, and can produce successful, personal expressions.

MATERIALS

Purchased stencilling paper, or a strong, waterproof paper substitute (see below); stencil brushes or stiff bristle brushes; poster, powder or tempera paints (or stencil colours or oil paints if cloth is being used); cutting tools such as trimming knives, safe one-edged razor blades, or special stencil knives; cutting boards of plywood or heavy strawboard; paper such as cartridge paper or cover paper, white or coloured, size 10 inches by $7\frac{1}{2}$ inches; drawing materials and scrap paper; steel lills are useful but not essential; newspapers to cover working surfaces.

TECHNIQUE

If special stencil paper is not available, improvised stencil paper can be prepared by waterproofing a heavy paper such as brown Kraft or cartridge paper with an application of shellac or varnish, or by applying a coat of floor polish or furniture wax.

A preliminary design should be prepared with some care, to suit the technique. It should be simple in concept, with a minimum of detail and with bold shapes joined to each other by short, narrow strips of paper to hold the design together when the shapes subsequently are cut out to form the stencil. The child should check carefully to see that sufficient holding strips are incorporated in the design, and if satisfactory it can be transferred to the stencil paper, using a pencil. It is then ready for cutting.

174

The stencil paper should be placed on a cutting board, and the parts of the stencil not required cut out using any of the cutting tools indicated. The child should be urged to cut with care; mistakes sometimes cannot be repaired, and accurate cutting adds to the effectiveness of the stencil. The paper to receive the stencilled picture (or pattern) should be pinned to a drawing board (or substitute) which has been covered with newspaper. The stencil is then placed over the paper, and pinned with lills so that all parts of the stencil are in close contact with the paper. If cloth is being used, it should be stretched tightly over layers of newspapers and pinned in position with drawing pins; the stencil is then placed in position, as described.

Poster or other thick opaque paints should be distributed in shallow containers such as small lids or patty-cake trays. Thin paint is likely to bleed under the stencil, thus damaging the picture; hence, the consistency of the paint is important. Specially-made stencil brushes are available, and while substitute brushes sometimes can be made by cutting down worn bristle brushes, a number of purchased stencilling brushes should be available. The brush is dipped in the colour, and the paint applied carefully with vertical, dabbing strokes through the stencil onto the exposed paper below. Whole areas can be stencilled to make large colour areas, or the stencilling can be done from the edges inwards to produce broad outlined effects. Care should be taken that the stencil does not move, or become torn or damaged. Single colours can be used, or colours can be superimposed to secure blendings. Children should be encouraged to experiment freely to discover the various effects that can be obtained, and it is sometimes a sound practice to carry out these experimental exercises with scraps of stencil paper on newsprint as a preliminary activity; in this way the child is given an understanding of the technique and its possibilities which should benefit his subsequent performance.

When cloth is being used, the stencil colour or oil paint is squeezed in a small quantity onto a small piece of plate glass, dinner plate, linoleum, or similar surface; the brush is then dipped in the colour, and used as previously described. Brushes should be washed after use in mineral turpentine, and other surfaces cleaned thoroughly.

STICK PRINTING

The printing of patterns ranging from simple to complex, using a variety of sticks as printing implements, is an activity similar to cork printing, the only significant difference being found in the change of tool. Sticks in a variety of end sections such as square, rectangular, circular, semicircular, or triangular, or ends of mouldings of different types, can be used as found or cut and inked, and used to print patterns in the manner indicated under Cork Printing (see p. 58) to which the reader should refer.

175

STITCHED PICTURES

See Embroidery Pictures (p. 71).

STONE SCULPTURE (see Fig. 84)

Carving in a variety of soft stones using simple cutting tools is an activity that might be introduced on a small scale in the upper grades, where one or two older boys experienced in cutting techniques might find it a means of self-expression both challenging and satisfying. It rightly can be regarded as an extension of Clay Carving (see p. 46) for the activities are substantially the same, the materials in some cases being harder to carve and therefore less responsive. However, by sensing or "seeing" a form suggested in a piece of stone, or by choosing an appropriate object of simple form, the amount of carving can be reduced to a minimum, so that the activity can come within the ability range of older boys. The types of natural stone that can be carved will vary according to the locality, but the range can include soft mudstone, soft limestone, soft granular sandstone, especially in water-worn forms found on beaches; while manufactured materials such as light-weight insulation brick, artificial stone, black foam glass, or even rock salt, can be used where they are available.

The carving of a satisfactory form requires a considerable working time, and it is probable that stone sculpture commenced as a classroom activity will be continued by the child as an extra-curricular interest. The tools include files, rasps, saws, knives, chisels, large nails, according to the nature of the material, and all cutting should be done either on a board, or the stone perhaps can be held in a vice at a woodworking bench.

As the equipment and approach to the carving remain substantially as indicated for Clay Carving (p. 46), the reader is directed there for further information.

STRING DESIGNS (see Figs. 88 and 89)

The use of strings extensively in the making of free-standing constructions around a simple frame calls for manipulative skill, patience, a developed sense of design, and an interest in assembling and building in common materials. The activity is closely related to the making of Free Standing Space Designs (see p. 166), but it involves a severe restriction in the range of materials used, the chief material, as the name indicates, being string. The activity is suitable for older children, many of whom find the technique interesting and stimulating. It is best introduced to small numbers

FIG. 82. "Scratched" Picture, using wax crayons.

FIG. 83. Scribble Pattern, in black pencil.

FIG. 84. Stone Sculpture in mudstone, Mount Gambier stone, and beach sandstone.

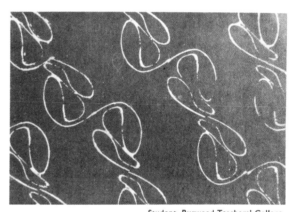

FIG. 85. Pattern by String Printing.

FIG. 86. Waste Materials Picture.

FIG. 87. Writing Pattern, using upper case letter forms.

of children, say 8 to 12, who will need ample working space so that they can work around the design, considering its development from all sides. The first stage of the activity, the making of the frame or support, requires the use of poster paints, so adequate precautions should be taken to minimise mess.

MATERIALS

Smooth white string, preferably in two or three thicknesses to give variety to the design; scissors; large-eyed sewing needles; trimming knives and sharp pocket knives; cutting boards of plywood or strawboard; metal rulers; adhesives such as liquid glue, hobby cement, household tube adhesive; cellulose tape and gummed paper; stapling machine; side-cutting pliers; revolving punch pliers (6 punch); wood files or small rasps; small tacks and tack hammer; steel pins, lills, drawing pins, paper fasteners; poster or powder paints in dark colours, and suitable brushes; small blocks of wood or pieces of board to serve as base pieces; materials to construct supports (see below); newspapers.

TECHNIQUE

Before the string can be used, a frame or support must be constructed, using a technique similar to the making of Free Standing Space Designs (see p. 166). The frame usually springs from a base piece and is constructed upwards, using three main types of material, as follows. With all types, the appearance of the string design is improved if the frame is painted in dark poster colour to contrast with the white string before the actual stringing commences.

Stiff board, such as pasteboard or heavy manila, is cut into strips up to 2 inches wide, but widths should vary to add interest. The strips are arranged in a series of interlocking convolutions, joined or fixed in position by stapling, taping, or sewing, and tacked to the base block. Selected edges can be nicked with scissors, or small holes can be punched parallel to the edges, to accommodate the strings which pass through the holes or over the nicks to converge at a point elsewhere in the design, where they pass through a hole and fan out to another edge. Where strings terminate, they can be knotted, and knots should be trimmed with scissors to present a tidy appearance. The design generally will incorporate a major system of stringing supplemented by two or more minor arrangements; the major system as a rule springs from the base and rise vertically to, or towards, the highest point of the frame, while the smaller systems are placed to achieve a balanced, unified, interesting design, showing both strips and strings held in opposed, dynamic tensions.

Similarly, a frame can be constructed in wire or cane (see Fig. 88) twisted and curved to form an interlocking arrangement, lines of which can be nicked with pliers or a file to prevent strings from slipping. It can be nailed to a base, and painted.

178

When dry, stringing of major and minor systems can proceed as described, holding the wire rigidly in position and imparting interest to the design.

The third type of frame is constructed from wooden skewers (see Fig. 89), pieces of dowelling, wooden strips, or even straight wire pieces. A larger base, such as a piece of flat board, is required, and this is drilled to accommodate the supports of the design which can be glued or nailed in position. The construction then evolves as an architectural arrangement of vertical, horizontal, and oblique lines formed of the materials indicated. Joins can be constructed by tacking, gluing, binding, or by

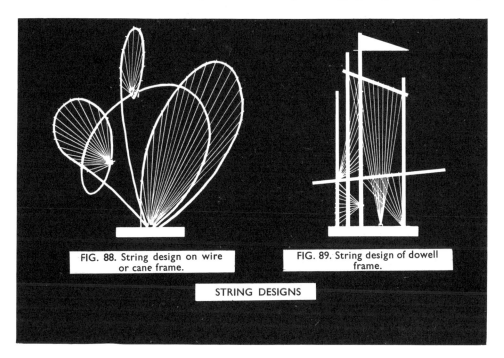

FIG. 88. String design on wire or cane frame.

FIG. 89. String design of dowell frame.

STRING DESIGNS

combinations of these, to achieve a strong, coherent structure. Laterals or arms can be nicked with a file to hold the strings in position. When the frame is completed, it should be painted, using one or more colours, and allowed to dry. Stringing can then commence, several systems being employed, and they can spring from different levels of the frame. Again, the completed design should present an ordered appearance based on sound design.

String designs, basically being a form of space design, similarly are non-objective and should show no pictorial content. They are essentially problem-solving experiences in abstract design in which the child, in his own way and at his own level, overcomes difficulties, forms appraisals, makes decisions, and acts independently, as he works with everyday materials.

179

STRING PRINTS (see Fig. 85)

The use of strings moistened in paint, either by dipping or by brushing, and arranged on paper to produce a print, should be regarded simply as a starting point for an experience in design. The activity is a means to an end. The artistic possibilities of the technique are limited, it can be messy, and a number of materials and tools are required; it is suitable, therefore, for small numbers of children only at the upper level.

A criticism levelled against the activity—in many cases, justifiably—is that the results largely are accidental, and the child is given little opportunity to make a personal contribution to the evolution of the pattern. This need not be so. If the activity is made purposeful and the technique used in conjunction with another printing medium, the child can control the process to such an extent that considerable creative effort and individual variation are possible.

MATERIALS

Lengths of string; poster or powder paints, assorted colours, in wide-mouthed jars; large bristle brushes or small house-painter's brushes; rubber rollers; cartridge paper, cover paper, ticket paper, or similar paper, size 15 inches by 10 inches, or smaller; newspapers to protect clothing and furniture.

TECHNIQUE

The string should be used in manageable lengths, say, 15 to 18 inches; long lengths become difficult to control and cause mess. The paint, in jars, should be well stirred. The child then moistens the strings simply by dropping them into the paint, and holding them over the jar so that the excess paint can run down the string back into the jar; running the string between thumb and index finger helps this process. Strings can also be inked by laying them side by side on a board, or on a piece of paper, and rubbing a paint brush up and down their length. The strings should be moistened, not soaked, in paint.

They can now be arranged on a sheet of paper to form a pattern of repeating rhythms, or as a series of static linear motifs. Changes of colour can be introduced. The child should make this arrangement thoughtfully and creatively; a random dropping does not necessarily produce a pattern nor is it a conscious design activity. When the arrangement of wet strings is satisfactory, a second sheet of paper is placed over the top, and a clean roller used to obtain the print. The top sheet is peeled away to produce one print, and if the strings are removed carefully from the bottom sheet, a second print frequently can be obtained. These prints can remain as they are, or impressions from a second printing process, such as Cork Printing (p. 58), Gadget

Printing (p. 83), or Potato Printing (p. 141), can be alternated or superimposed to form richly varied, colourful, and intricate patterns.

Paint moistened strings, or a longer length of painted string, also can be dropped gradually onto a piece of paper to form a self-contained, static arrangement agreeably occupying the sheet; at this stage, it might resemble a coloured Scribble Pattern (see p. 163). A second sheet of paper is placed over this, and a print, consisting of an arrangement of shapes and lines of varying thicknesses, taken as before. This print is then dried (preferably with the assistance of a portable electric heater). The child now selects certain of the shapes which he paints in colours to contrast with the colours of the strings. In this way bold, colourful non-objective designs, comprising painted areas and printed lines, can be produced.

Short lengths of string can be arranged and pasted or glued in position on a piece of thick strawboard, plywood, or similar material. The string arrangement then can be inked or painted by brush, and used to print all-over patterns and designs in one or more colours. The use of two such "stamps" with changes of colour can produce intricate and colourful superimpositions (see Fig. 85). Children should be encouraged to work with care so that successive impressions are correctly aligned, and to avoid over-inking the string, which is one of the main causes of messy printing.

Painted strings, in addition, are used in Tin Can Printing (see p. 185).

SUN PRINTS

This extremely simple technique using cut-outs and masks as in Spatter Pictures (see p. 169) and sunlight to produce prints on coloured paper, can offer little challenge to the child unless he is encouraged to approach the arrangement of shapes and objects as a design exercise. The technique can be introduced at any grade level, requires few materials, and makes little mess. The actual printing, however, can take as long as a week or more depending on the strength of the sunlight, during which the children's work must be exposed on window sills or similar places; thus, large numbers participating become difficult unless satisfactory arrangements can be made for the exposure of their work.

MATERIALS

Coloured paper which fades in sunlight, such as cover paper, poster paper, and certain sensitised papers used by draughtsmen and architects, of a size adequate to the child's purpose; stiff brown paper from which to cut masks (leaves, flowers, twigs, or materials such as string, keys, coins, etc., can be used in addition); scissors; steel lills; backing boards of plywood or strawboard; revolving punch pliers (6 punch) are useful, but not essential; newspapers.

TECHNIQUE

The technique offers few difficulties. A sheet of fugitive-coloured paper of a convenient size is pinned to a backing board of strawboard so that it can be moved. On this coloured paper the child composes a simple pictorial representation in paper cut-outs or masks, or a pattern of abstract shapes, or even an arrangement of leaves and grasses. The pieces should be manipulated freely to obtain an agreeable composition on the coloured ground, and then pinned in position, using lills. The arrangement then is carried carefully to a location where it can be exposed over a period of days to strong sunlight. The action of the sunlight bleaches the fugitive colour of the background paper to produce the superimposed arrangement in silhouette form. The child should be encouraged to control this bleaching process by checking each day the degree of fade; this can be done by unpinning one shape in the composition, or lifting a corner. When sufficient contrast is achieved, the masks and cut-outs can be removed to obtain the print.

TEXTURE DESIGNS

See Collages (p. 51).

THREE-DIMENSIONAL PROBLEMS IN SPECIFIED MATERIALS

The solving of three-dimensional problems using specified materials in a limited range is aimed not only at assisting the child to understand the properties and characteristics of common materials, but also at encouraging him to think logically and creatively as he analyses the introduced problem in an endeavour to evolve a feasible solution. The different problems devised by the teacher should employ local and familiar materials, natural or manufactured, either singly or in combinations rarely exceeding three materials; indeed, children should be given opportunities to explore freely the characteristics of a single material, say, paper. The introduction of such problem-solving experiences is suitable for older children only, and generally in restricted numbers. When the problems are posed as challenges to the individual child's inventiveness and ingenuity so that he understands why he is doing what he is doing, most children respond with enthusiasm and find the solving of the problems something of a fascinating and absorbing puzzle.

MATERIALS

The materials and simple tools will vary according to the nature of the problem, as indicated below. Generally, simple cutting tools such as scissors and trimming knives, and cutting boards, are the only necessary equipment.

TECHNIQUE

There are no prescribed techniques. Each child will solve the set problem in his own way as a result of his own analysis and subsequent action. The nature of the problems should be such that children are required to think, and the use of tools (cutting tools excepted) and adhesives virtually eliminated. Whatever solution the child employs must be accomplished within the possibilities of the materials; and in this way he comes to understand their varying properties and limitations.

The teacher should explain clearly the nature of the problem, indicating what the child is to make, and, perhaps, some of the limitations of the materials. Some children will work independently, requiring no assistance; others, on the other hand, will encounter difficulties which will block further progress, and the teacher should be on hand to offer guidance by suggestion, advice, or even demonstration. Sometimes selected solutions are required for display purposes or as teaching material; in this case, the exercise should be done on a strawboard base to permit transportation.

The variety of problems that can be devised by the teacher virtually is unlimited, and the following are included as examples only.

Problem No. 1. Using a single sheet of cartridge paper, 15 inches by 10 inches, construct a three-dimensional structure, using folding and cutting only. No additional paper or other materials can be used.

Problem No. 2. Using a piece of stiff card, such as pasteboard or pulpboard, approximately 20 inches by 4 inches, make the tallest possible construction, using only folding and cutting. No other materials, tools, or aids, can be used.

Problem No. 3. Using drinking straws, which can be cut to various lengths, erect a three-dimensional structure wider than it is tall.

Problem No. 4. Using paper drinking cups and drinking straws, construct a recognisable animal form; the drinking cups can be cut and used in any way desired, but no glue, pins, tape, or other fasteners can be used.

Problem No. 5. Using small twigs, dry leaves, and dry grass, construct a simple bird form. No other materials can be used.

TIE-AND-DYE PRINTS

Cloth can be coloured in many ways. Paints or other solid colouring materials, for instance, can be applied by brushes, as in Fabric Painting (p. 76) or by a printing process, as in Screen Printing (p. 161). Cloth also can be dyed, which involves its immersion in a dye bath; and tie-dyeing is perhaps the simplest method. After a period of experiment and trial-and-error, older primary school children are able to manage the technique, and both boys and girls find the activity interesting. A risk of mess accompanies the dyeing, and the whole working area should be generously protected by newspapers. Children participating should wear protective clothing such as old shirts or smocks, and rubber gloves prevent little hands becoming too messy. The nature of the activity precludes large numbers, and 6 or 8 children form a convenient group. Materials usually can be provided with little difficulty, especially if a cold-water dye is used.

MATERIALS

Suitable fabric, white or light in colour, such as muslin, silk, cotton, calico, linen, etc., cut to a convenient size (plain white handkerchiefs are excellent); wide, deep enamelled containers, such as hand basins, for dye baths; old rulers or similar sticks to stir dye; lengths of thread, string, wool, strips of other fabric, or even strong rubber bands, to tie material; simple dyes (preferably cold-water dyes), in assorted colours; running water, or clean water in a bucket; scissors; needles and threads; newspapers to minimise mess.

TECHNIQUE

The technique involves tightly binding cloth and immersing it in dye so that the tied portion resists the dye while the untied areas are coloured. The success and effect of the print depend on the number of ties and the manner of tying. The portions tied must be tied *tightly* using string, wool, or strips of other fabric, in several tight layers, so that dye is prevented from penetrating through or under the tie. The dye is prepared in an enamelled basin or similar container, stirred thoroughly with a stick or ruler, and the tied fabric immersed according to the directions accompanying the dye. When the dyeing is satisfactorily completed, the fabric is removed and untied (using scissors to cut the wet knots), to reveal a print of nebulous shapes, and varied tones and edges.

More than one portion of the cloth can be tied and dyed to produce roughly concentric areas, or the cloth can be re-tied and re-dyed to produce differences in tone, or another colour can be used. A white fabric provides stronger contrasts and offers wider tonal possibilities. If more than one colour is used, dyeing should proceed from light colours to dark; to attempt to dye light colours after dark frequently produces disappointing results. Children should be encouraged to experiment freely on scraps of cloth so that they can investigate fully the possibilities of the technique.

If the child desires, the dyed cloth later can be subjected to additional processes to add to the interest and complexity of the dyed pattern. Thus, the pattern can be outlined or embellished by decorative stitching (see p. 72), or the cloth can be stretched tightly over newspaper and overprinted by linoleum block printing (p. 92) or by stencilling (p. 174), using waterproof fabric colours or oil paints. By combining processes, as indicated, children are able to produce strikingly colourful and richly varied prints.

TIN CAN PRINTING

The printing of freely contrived patterns using tin cans (such as tinned fruit or vegetable cans, or even wooden or plastic rolling pins) is another printing technique suitable for older children at the primary level. Considerable working space and equipment are required so that the activity is more suitable for smaller numbers, and as the technique can cause mess, adequate measures should be taken to protect both working area and participants.

MATERIALS

Tin cans, as indicated; paper, white or coloured, such as cartridge paper, cover paper, ticket paper, or similar paper, size 15 inches by 10 inches, or larger; opaque paints such as poster or tempera paints; sable-type brushes; water in suitable containers; materials from which to assemble patterns, such as felt, string, inner rubber tubing, and the like; scissors; quick-drying adhesive, such as model cement, household colourless cement, rubber cement, and brushes to apply it; newspapers to cover working area.

TECHNIQUE

The child's first task is to remove both ends from the tin, and to make certain no rough edges remain on the inside which might cause injury to the operator. Irregularly-shaped, long pieces can be cut from inner tubing, felt, and similar materials, to be later wrapped around the tin can; lengths of string can be used to provide contrasts and added interest. When pieces of satisfactory length and shape have been prepared, fast-drying adhesive is applied by broad brush to the outside of the can, and the pieces and strings are pressed into position in an arrangement that will produce a bold pattern when printed. Suitable paper for printing should be selected and placed on newspaper in readiness.

The arrangement on the tin can now be inked. Opaque paints such as poster or tempera colours should be used. (Printer's ink or oil paints also can be used, but they require additional equipment; see p. 94). If one colour only is being used, an area of this colour can be painted on a piece of strawboard or cartridge paper, and the tin can inked by placing the hands inside the can at either end and rolling it through the paint until all printing surfaces are inked. When more than one colour is planned, the separate colours are best painted on the various parts of the arrangement, using large and small brushes as appropriate. Care is needed with the painting, particularly when shapes and strings are closely arranged.

The pattern is made on the paper by rolling the can across the surface, slowly and firmly, to produce a clear print, until the end of a run is reached. When re-inking

185

becomes necessary, the child should mark the bottom edge of the can with a pencil, so that after re-inking the pattern can be resumed from the point marked. While a rolling pin can be used similarly for printing and is, perhaps, more comfortable, it has certain disadvantages; it is not so easy to mark when re-inking becomes necessary, and the hands on the handles can obscure the printing in progress. The tin can, being smaller, gives a clear view of the evolving pattern.

The technique offers unlimited scope for individual children to experiment with ways of achieving intricacy. Thus, a pattern can be made by rolling the can in one direction and over-printing in the same colour using a change of direction, or over-printing using the same pattern with a change of colour. The possibilities are further increased by combining tin can printing with processes like Block Printing (p. 30), Cork Printing (p. 58), Potato Printing (p. 141), Stick Printing (p. 175), or by Stippling (p. 58). Children enjoy great freedom in devising suitable patterns, and in operating the cans individually and creatively.

TOOTH PICK SCULPTURE

See Match Stick Sculpture (p. 101).

TOUCH TABLE

The setting up of a "touch table" in the classroom enables children to handle, study, and discuss the surface qualities and textures of the various objects and materials displayed. Such a table might display attractively a heterogeneous collection of things such as pine cones, water-worn pebbles, pieces of driftwood, feathers, a piece of silk, wood shavings, corrugated cardboard, pieces of sandpaper, shattered windscreen glass, and so on, which the children bring. The collection should be readily accessible, and should change continually as children bring new materials, and others are removed.

By encouraging children to utilise their sensory powers, the touch table assists their developing awareness of, and sensitivity to, common things around them. This cultivation and extension of sensory responses is, of course, a vital part of the educative process, for the senses collectively provide the avenue through which the child receives most of the impressions and stimuli that form his concepts and determine his actions.

In terms of aims and purpose, therefore, the use of a touch table in the classroom relates to the making of Collages (p. 51), for both activities are directed towards the development of tactile responses.

186

VASELINE PRINTS

Like the making of Duoprints (p. 70) and String Prints (p. 180), the making of vaseline prints produces two separate prints from the initial drawing. It is an interesting technique involving several simple stages, and older children in the upper grades find it enjoyable. However, it is inclined to be messy; for this reason numbers should be restricted, a working area prepared beforehand, and adequate measures taken to protect clothing and to minimise mess.

MATERIALS

Vaseline; pigment in powder form; piece of $\frac{1}{4}$-inch plate glass or masonite, size 12 inches by 10 inches (preferably, one piece per child participating); rubber rollers; spoons; wooden rulers or similar sticks; pliable knife; pencils; white paper such as cartridge paper, litho paper, bulky newsprint of medium size, say, 10 inches by $7\frac{1}{2}$ inches; scrap paper; newspapers.

TECHNIQUE

A drawing is needed, and most children find it helpful to plan their drawings first on scrap paper, or they may draw directly on the cartridge paper, if they desire.

An ink consisting of a mixture of powder colour and vaseline must be prepared. This can be done simply in two ways. Dry pigment in the selected colour is added by spoon to the vaseline in the jar, and stirred by ruler or stick until thoroughly mixed, or the dry pigment and vaseline can be mixed on the plate glass or masonite, using a knife such as a palette knife in the first instance, and finishing with a roller. The mixture should be rolled out evenly to form a large colour area.

A piece of cartridge paper is placed on the spread colour, and the child makes his drawing on the paper using a pencil firmly, but holding both hands well clear of the paper so that the only pressures on the paper result from the lines of the pencil. When the drawing is finished, the sheet of paper is lifted to obtain a coloured print on the underside which shows a positive impression of the drawing.

Without touching the spread colour on the plate glass, a second sheet of paper is now placed over it and rubbed with the palm of the hand, to produce a negative print, giving two quite different impressions of the original drawing.

Colour interest can be introduced by rolling two or even three prepared colours on the glass to produce a blending, so that multi-coloured impressions are obtained. Children should be encouraged to try different colours on papers of different types to extend the range of possibilities. When all printing is finished, the surplus ink can be scraped up and returned to the jars for future use, and rollers, glass, and other equipment wiped clean with paper towelling and clean cloths.

VEGETABLE PRINTS

See Potato Printing (p. 141).

WASTE MATERIALS PICTURES (see Fig. 86)

Waste materials pictures in many respects are similar to Cloth Applique Pictures (p. 50) and Paper Applique Pictures (p. 120). The main difference lies in the nature of the materials used in waste materials pictures, for, providing the material is of a two-dimensional character, the range virtually is unlimited. Any relatively flat substance or material that can be stuck to a backing sheet using the normal range of adhesives can be used. This extension of the range of materials naturally increases the range of tools and adhesives required, but the technique remains basically one of selecting, arranging, and pasting.

Generally the activity can be introduced at any grade level if the teacher is prepared to accept natural performances. Children can bring individual collections of selected waste materials (in paper bags) and their own adhesives, so that they can work at their desks, sharing other necessary items such as liquid glue or stapling machines. The picture-making possibilities for the individual child are increased if he has access to additional waste materials, and these can be provided through class collection and stored in labelled cartons, as described on p. 53. Newspapers should cover desk-tops so that off-cuts, spoils, and rejected materials simply can be wrapped up and disposed in garbage cans — after non-expendables such as scissors and trimming knives have been collected.

The technique lends itself to the making of large, collective pictures which form splendid co-operative experiences for children working in groups of 3 or 4 (see p. 114).

MATERIALS

Any appropriate waste material of a two-dimensional nature (including papers of all kinds, white, coloured, printed, plain, smooth or textured, collected, or purchased; all kinds of fabrics, cloths, textiles, and woven goods; all kinds of threads, string, or cordage; all kinds of manufactured goods and finished articles of a hard, flat nature; natural materials such as leaves, straw, feathers, shavings, sawdust); backing sheets of cartridge paper, cover paper, pasteboard, manila board and the like, size 15 inches by 10 inches, or smaller; adhesives such as liquid glue, milliner's solution, mucilage, household tube cement, office paste; pasting brushes; scissors; trimming knives; pocket knives and safe one-edged razor blades; long-armed stapling machine; lills; newspapers to contain mess.

TECHNIQUE

The activity, as indicated, is one of selecting, cutting, arranging, and pasting, the aim being to compose the waste materials as a personal and creative interpretation of the topic. The making of Collages (p. 51), on the other hand, is not concerned with the making of pictures, yet the technique is identical; the reader should turn, therefore, to the page indicated for details of procedure.

An aspect of the making of waste materials pictures requires emphasis. The thoughtless pasting of materials by the child defeats an important educational aim of the activity. Children should be encouraged to think about the nature and surface properties of the materials they are using, and to select them in terms of the subject-matter being interpreted. Colour, texture, and general appearance should be considered. Thus, in the making of a picture concerning winter, the dull winter sky might be represented by a piece of coarse grey material, fleeting white clouds by cotton wool, bare trees by dry twigs, puddles of water by washed milk bottle tops, a fence by corrugated cardboard, and so on. In this way, the activity becomes a creative one, the child is encouraged to consider tactile and visual qualities, and the resultant picture is a more convincing personal statement.

WASTE MATERIALS SCULPTURE

Box Sculpture (p. 37) rightly can be considered a form of waste materials sculpture in which the range of materials is limited. Waste materials sculpture, in the sense used here, imposes no limitations on the range of the materials that the child can use; they can be two-dimensional or three-dimensional, manufactured or natural, common or unusual, so long as they are appropriate to the child's sculptural purposes. As with waste materials pictures, children in any grade can participate at their own level of performance. They can supply individually their supplies of materials and work in their desks, sharing other requisites as needed. Additional supplies of waste materials can be obtained from the class storage cartons (see p. 53). Because of the variety of materials there exists a risk of considerable mess unless simple routines and measures are adopted for the collection and disposal of rubbish and unwanted materials. The widest possible scope exists for personal performance and individual variation, and most children find waste materials sculpture a fascinating and absorbing activity, which they can pursue as an extracurricular interest.

MATERIALS

Virtually any material or small object, except those likely to decay and become offensive; the following items may be required according to the materials being used: liquid glue, fast-drying cement, household tube cement, mucilage, office paste;

cellulose tape, gummed paper; scissors; trimming knives, sharp pocket knives, safe one-edged razor blades; cutting boards of plywood, strawboard, or masonite; tacks and tack hammer; side-cutting pliers; tenon saws, coping saws; hand drill; revolving punch pliers (6 punch); steel pins, lills, drawing pins; wire paper fasteners, brass fasteners; stapling machines; sandpaper; rasps and files; opaque paints such as poster, powder or tempera paints and suitable brushes; water; newspapers.

TECHNIQUE

Because the infinite variety of materials that can be collected can be used in numerous ways, it is impossible to provide precise details of working methods. The child creates his sculpture according to the materials he is using, evolving a technique that seems natural for the occasion and which permits him to achieve his intention. He should be encouraged to appreciate the possibilities of the materials being used and to accept their limitations. He should work with the minimum of guidance and assistance, although he should have access to any of the tools and equipment indicated, as needed.

The information given under Box Sculpture (p. 37) is relevant, in view of the similarity of the activities; the reader is directed to the page shown, therefore, for additional guidance.

WAXED PAPER PICTURES

The making of pictures using a waxed paper is similar to the making of Candle and Paint Pictures (p. 40). Both techniques employ the resistance principle by using a wax impression under transparent water paints. Children from infant grade level upwards can make pictures using the waxed paper technique, and it forms a simple and interesting variation in the picture-making programme. Materials are readily available, and a whole class can participate.

MATERIALS

Waxed paper, such as waxed lunch wraps, internal waxed bags from cereal packets, or waxed wrapping parchment, cut to a convenient size; thin white paper, such as duplicating paper, typing paper, thin cartridge paper, and the like, cut to the same size as the waxed paper; hard, pointed pencils; transparent water paints in dark colours; soft sable-type brushes; water in suitable containers; paper clips; newspapers.

TECHNIQUE

A hard smooth surface on which to work obtains best results; children can work on plastic topped tables, or pieces of smooth masonite or even plate glass can be brought from home. A piece of waxed paper is placed between two sheets of thin white paper of the same size, waxed side down, and the three sheets are held together by paper clips. The child now makes a drawing on the top sheet, using firm to heavy pressure on a hard pointed pencil, or similar pointed tool. The drawing can be as detailed as the child desires, but a firm pressure on the pencil must be maintained throughout the drawing. On completing the drawing, the top sheet and the waxed sheet are removed, leaving an invisible wax impression of the drawing on the bottom sheet.

Over this a wash of dark transparent water colour is applied gently with a sable-type brush. Care should be taken that the wax lines are not damaged or removed, as they can be if the brush is used too vigorously. The wax impression repels the superimposed water colour which produces, however, a dark background, so that the wax impression of the original drawing now appears as a white-lined drawing on a dark coloured ground. Scope for individual experiment is limited, but the prints obtained can show considerable variation in performance.

WEAVING (see Figs. 90 to 96)

Weaving is an activity capable of adaptation to procedures ranging from the very simple to the highly complex, and there are looms suitable for every grade level from infant grades to high school. Thus children of all ages can participate.

Weaving as a classroom experience has suffered a decline in popularity in recent years. Large classes, the problems accompanying the storage of looms and incomplete weaving, the cost of wools, the time required to complete a woven article, and the use of prepared, imposed patterns which destroy the creative aspect of the activity, are among the factors which have contributed to this decline. If weaving is to enjoy a return to popularity it must be placed on a creative basis, using simple looms and readily available materials, and originality of design and variety in textures must be emphasised; children should be required to create their own designs and to weave them on looms appropriate to their age level.

A loom is a piece of equipment which supports two set of threads. The *warp* threads generally are stretched from top to bottom, and on these the weaving is done. The cross threads, which pass from left to right, are called *weft* threads. Simple frame, board, and card looms can be constructed easily and are suitable for primary school use; on these children can weave mats, pot holders, scarves, belts, purses, dolls' clothes, and other small items, using a variety of manufactured weaving materials such as yarns and cords, and natural materials such as grasses, reeds, and raffia. Older children at higher levels, as their skills and interest develop, can be introduced to other simple looms, to rigid heddle looms, and ultimately to simple two and four shaft looms.

Weaving can be presented as an activity interesting to both boys and girls, and can be conducted on a group or class basis, according to the availability of materials.

MATERIALS

Simple looms (see below) on the basis of one per child participating; weaving materials which may include thick wools and yarns, lines, strings, cords (jute, rayon, nylon, plastic), ropes, ribbons, strips of cloth, strips of old stocking, grasses, reeds, raffia, and related materials; scissors; large needles, such as darning needles or improvised cardboard needles; rulers; materials to construct looms.

TECHNIQUE

Young children because of immature motor development and a short interest span will not be able to weave very much, and simple frame and board looms can be introduced simply as play things. From playing with the loom and simple weaving materials, and by performing simple experiments, the child discovers the rudiments of weaving and his interest is kindled. As a rule, young children should commence with thick weaving materials, such as cords, ribbons, strips of cloth, ropes, etc., graduating to thinner threads, lines, yarns, and the like, as their co-ordination and skills develop.

The weaving of simple paper mats (see Fig. 90) forms an appropriate activity to introduce the small child to the "over one, under one" technique characteristic of primary school weaving. A 9 inch square of stiff paper or thin card is folded in two, and on one folded side a line is drawn 1 inch from the top edge. Cuts are made at 1 inch intervals from the fold upwards to meet this drawn line. The card is then opened out to show a series of parallel cuts. Strips of paper, 1 inch wide and in contrasting colours, are woven into this using an over-under action, the ends being fixed underneath by pasting. A border on both sides, made from 2 inch strips of coloured paper folded over the four edges and pasted, conceals the ends, and completes the simple woven mat. The preparation of the card should be the responsibility of the teacher, and during their weaving the young children will need continual guidance; the teacher should assist freely both by demonstration and by the use of actual examples.

Perhaps the most suitable looms for the primary school are frame and board looms, and card looms. A frame loom (see Fig. 94) consists of four pieces of timber joined at the corners, or small picture frames or similar frames, say, 12 inches by 9 inches, can be used. Along the top and bottom, about $\frac{1}{2}$-inch in from the edge, a row of large tacks or small nails, $\frac{1}{4}$-inch apart, is nailed to take the warp, or long, threads. Initially, the strings forming the warp threads can be placed 1 inch apart, but later they can be narrowed to $\frac{1}{2}$-inch or even $\frac{1}{4}$-inch as the child grows in skill and ability. Weft threads, consisting of short lengths of heavy rug wool, cord, or rope, can be introduced simply by finger weaving using an over-under action. On such a loom the child can weave small mats, pot-holders, and the like, incorporating colours of his own selection and arrangement. Frame looms, from which the tacks or nails protrude, can cause storage problems and damage to incomplete work; simple board looms (see Fig. 95) can be constructed in such a way that this objection can be eliminated.

192

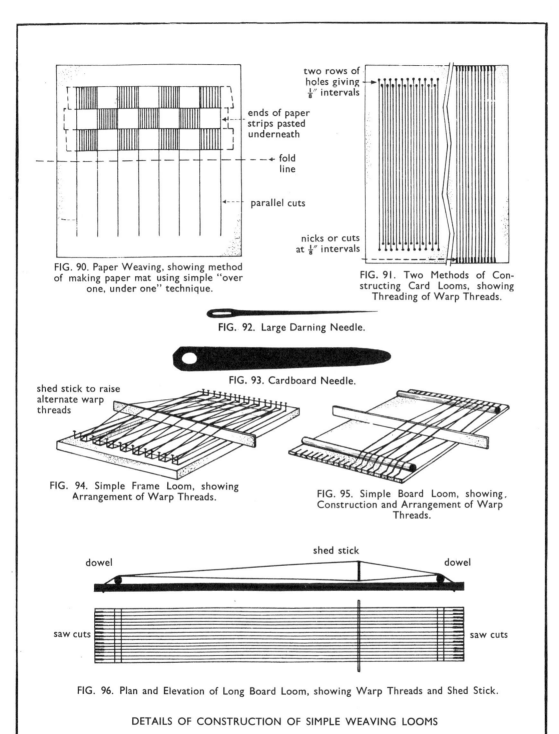

FIG. 90. Paper Weaving, showing method of making paper mat using simple "over one, under one" technique.

two rows of holes giving $\frac{1}{8}$" intervals

ends of paper strips pasted underneath

← fold line

parallel cuts

nicks or cuts at $\frac{1}{8}$" intervals

FIG. 91. Two Methods of Constructing Card Looms, showing Threading of Warp Threads.

FIG. 92. Large Darning Needle.

FIG. 93. Cardboard Needle.

shed stick to raise alternate warp threads

FIG. 94. Simple Frame Loom, showing Arrangement of Warp Threads.

FIG. 95. Simple Board Loom, showing Construction and Arrangement of Warp Threads.

dowel   shed stick   dowel

saw cuts   saw cuts

FIG. 96. Plan and Elevation of Long Board Loom, showing Warp Threads and Shed Stick.

DETAILS OF CONSTRUCTION OF SIMPLE WEAVING LOOMS

On a piece of flat board or plywood of a convenient size, pieces of $\frac{1}{2}$-inch dowelling are nailed at the top and the bottom, parallel to the edge and 1 inch in from it. Along the edge behind each piece of dowelling a series of short cuts, $\frac{1}{4}$-inch apart, is made with a small saw. The warp threads, in pairs, are threaded through each pair of cuts and over the dowelling pieces, so that the threads are raised above the surface of the board. A small strip of wood or cardboard, called a "shed stick," is used to separate the warp threads to permit the weaving of the weft threads in an over-under action, and to push the weft threads together to obtain a close weave. Such board looms stack easily and neatly. A long board loom (see Fig. 96), made from a piece of flooring board or other flat board, constructed as indicated and used in a similar manner with appropriate weaving materials, can be used to produce scarves, belts, and longer articles.

A card loom (see Fig. 91) is constructed from a piece of stiff card such as strawboard or heavy pasteboard, of a convenient size, say, 8 inches by 6 inches. About $\frac{1}{2}$-inch in from each end, a row of small holes, $\frac{1}{4}$-inch apart, is punched. A second row of holes, also $\frac{1}{4}$-inch apart, is punched below and in between the first row, so that a series of holes at $\frac{1}{8}$-inch intervals is provided. The warp threads are threaded through these holes so that a double thread runs between each pair of holes from top to bottom, giving a warp thread every $\frac{1}{8}$-inch. An alternative to the punched holes is to use small cuts or nicks at $\frac{1}{8}$-inch intervals along the top and bottom edges of the card, the warp threads in pairs being passed through each pair of cuts. A large darning needle is threaded and the weft threads woven in with an over one, under one technique. Smaller weaving materials can be used, including finer wools, strings, nylon, lines, raffia, grasses, and the like, to make mats, pot-holders, purses, and small articles showing more intricate weaves and patterns evolved by the child, creatively and on an individual basis.

Other, larger looms can be introduced as they are available, possibly on an individual basis according to children's interests and ability. Children should be encouraged to develop their own weaves and to design creatively, and points such as the suitability of the weaving materials for the article, their selection and colour, the distribution of the colours, variety in textures, and general surface appearance should be considered, perhaps by the individual child and the teacher in discussion.

WIRE SCULPTURE (see Fig. 97)

The use of wire features prominently in a programme of creative activities. It can be used in making components for Dioramas (p. 63), in Papier Mache Sculpture (p. 125), in the making of Mobiles (p. 105), and in Space Designs (p. 166). It is also an expressive medium in its own right, and can be used for what is virtually drawing in wire as well as for three-dimensional sculptures. Wire that is soft, so that children can manipulate it easily with fingers and hands, generally can be supplied in adequate quantities by class collection supplemented, perhaps, by purchased supplies. Wire sculpture uses few tools, makes little or no mess, enables children to work in their desks with a minimum of movement about the room, and is practicable with large numbers; thus, a whole class can participate. It is more suitable for older children who possess the manipulative skills and co-ordination essential to the technique; and because it is less familiar, perhaps, as an art material, many children find it a responsive medium permitting a fresh and direct means of expression.

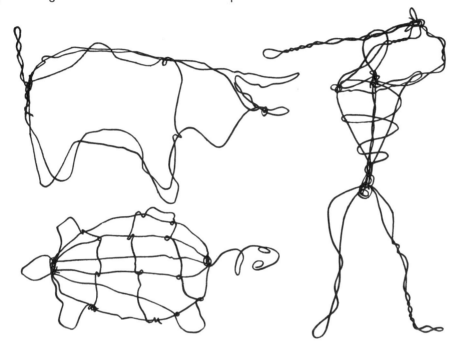

FIG. 97. WIRE SCULPTURE

MATERIALS

Soft, pliable wire, including soft-drawn galvanised wire in gauges from 12 to 24, florist's wire in 18-inch lengths, baling or packing case wire, plastic-coated electrical wire, fuse wire, copper wire, pipe cleaners, old wire coathangers, and similar wire; side-cutting pliers; small rectangular or circular base blocks, if needed; other materials which can be applied to the wire, as indicated in the variations of the wire sculpture technique which follow.

TECHNIQUE

The technique is simple, and the children work directly in the wire to create free-standing, three-dimensional human, animal, bird, or insect forms, using various kinds of wire. Technical difficulties are few, and invariably result from the use of

195

wire that is too thick or hard for the child to manipulate satisfactorily. The main lines of the sculpture are shaped in a thicker wire and bent to express action, or the characteristic pose of the object, while fine wire is used to fill-in and to express detail. Joins are effected by twisting two pieces, or two pieces can be overlapped and bound tightly with a fine wire. Selected waste materials can be incorporated, if desired, to add details and impart interest, but their use should be kept to a minimum; eyes can be represented by coloured buttons, feathers for a tail on a bird form, coloured foil for scales on a fish, and so on. The completed sculpture can be tacked or glued to a base block or inserted in a lump of plaster, painted in a bold colour for display purposes.

Wire sculpture need not be the simple technique described, and there are several variations which increase the complexity of the sculpture and introduce additional tactile and visual qualities, including colour. Having gained some experience in using wire on its own, children should be encouraged to explore these additional possibilities to extend their means of self-expression. Thus, a simple straight-lined wire construction representing, say, the body of a giraffe, can be given three-dimensional form by binding strips of adhesive-soaked paper around the limbs, neck, body, etc., to form cylinders of the required thickness and length. When dry, the angles of the limbs can be adjusted to suggest movement, and the sculpture painted in appropriate colours. A similar, simple wire construction can be bound in coarse knitting or rug wools of various colours to achieve the third-dimension; a human form representing, say, a footballer can be bound in wools to show the club colours, and boys can make themselves delightful club emblems or mascots in this way.

To produce starkly white, heavily textured forms, wire sculptures can be coated in patching plaster or other plaster, thickly mixed and applied by hand; or melted crayons (see p. 102) or enamellised paint can be dribbled on so that it runs down the wire, introducing colour minglings and unusual textures. Older children might be interested in using liquid solder or similar material dribbled over the wire to produce an irregular, metallic effect. Dipped, sprayed, or painted in black poster or powder colour these sculptures take on something of a wrought-iron look. Given a permissive atmosphere in the classroom, individual children can devise further variations and extend the possibilities of wire as a medium for creative expression.

WOOD BLOCK PRINTS

The taking of prints from a wood block is a further variation of an activity described in Block Printing (p. 30), Linoleum Block Prints (p. 92) and Plaster Block Prints (p. 132). It requires developed skill and experience in the use of cutting tools, and can be introduced on a limited scale in the upper grades, where individual boys might find the technique both a challenge to their energies and abilities and a new means of expression. Suitable timber and adequate (if improvised) cutting tools generally can be provided or obtained by those participating.

MATERIALS

Wood blocks, of well-seasoned, even-grained, soft-wood that cuts well, such as balsa or pine; cutting tools such as sharp pocket knives, trimming knives, small chisels, U-shaped and V-shaped gouges (if available); hand drill with a full range of bits; printing materials and other equipment as indicated for Linoleum Block Prints (p. 92); sand-paper, if necessary; newspapers.

TECHNIQUE

The surface of the wood block must be perfectly flat and smooth, and the child should resort to hand-sanding if necessary to achieve a satisfactory surface. Cuts are made in this surface, or areas removed, by any of the tools indicated, or by drilling. While the nature of the block and the cutting tools are slightly different, the technique remains substantially as described for Linoleum Block Prints (p. 92), to which the reader should refer.

WOOD SCULPTURE

Pieces of wood normally are readily available in most areas, and can be introduced as a medium for use in the classroom with little difficulty. The assembling and joining of small pieces of milled and dressed timber, such as off-cuts from carpenters' benches and joinery works, is an activity that can be introduced almost at any grade level of the primary school. But the carving of three-dimensional forms from blocks of dressed timber is an activity suitable only for older children, particularly boys, who enjoy whittling and similar cutting skills. Where a soft wood, such as balsa, is available in block form, the activity lends itself to the carving of heads for hand puppets (see p. 153), thus giving the activity purpose and meaning.

Carving from milled blocks of soft wood, or sculpture in the round as it is called, is similar in most respects to the carving of Driftwood Sculpture (p. 68), the only significant difference being that the latter uses lumps or pieces of wood as they are found in their natural state, without milling, dressing, or processing. Despite this difference, the tools, technique of carving, and finishing, remain virtually the same, and the reader therefore is directed to the page indicated.

The assembling of small pieces of wood of varying shape and size to create a sculptural form is a different activity, being an additive rather than a subtractive technique, less difficult, and suitable for introduction with all age groups if natural performances are recognised. Children can work at prepared work centres, and the numbers participating will depend on the supply of wood scraps available, but as adhesives and other materials are employed, the activity probably achieves best results when small numbers are involved.

MATERIALS

Wood scraps of varying shape and size; tools such as coping saws, fret saws, hand drill, small nails and hammers, trimming knives, sharp pocket knives, rasps, files, sandpaper, according to the ages of the children; improvised cutting boards of plywood or masonite; adhesives such as liquid glue, wood-working glue, tube cement, model cement, and ice-cream sticks to apply them; finishing materials such as furniture polish, clear varnish, shellac, opaque paints, or candles for singeing; selected waste materials; newspapers.

TECHNIQUE

The technique is one of selection and assembling of the wood pieces to make a three-dimensional recognisable form, such as a human or animal, familiar or imagined. The various pieces can be shaped by sawing, carving, rasping or drilling, if desired, before being assembled; thus, to form the head of an animal form, a piece of suitably shaped wood might require a little additional sawing to define the shape, drilling to suggest eyes, and rasping to round edges and soften contours. The component pieces can then be joined by gluing or by nailing. The wood pieces can be supplemented by other scrap wood pieces such as ice-cream sticks, matches, wooden spools and reels, wooden beads, skewers, dowelling and so on to add variety and to extend the possibilities of the technique. Selected waste materials can be affixed to suggest significant details but their use should be reduced to a minimum.

The completed wood sculptures can be surface finished, if desired, in several ways. A lighted candle can be used to singe the wood to obtain brown colour patches, or, if a range of colours is desired, opaque paints, matt or gloss, and bristle brushes can be used, though not to the extent that the nature of the wood is obliterated. Some children might prefer to wax the wood forms with furniture polish, or to paint them with clear varnish or white shellac, to bring out the natural colours and grain of the timbers used. In this way, children are helped to appreciate the inherent beauty of common timbers.

WRITING PATTERNS (see Fig. 87)

Number Patterns (p. 116), Scribble Patterns (p. 163) and writing patterns are related activities, and all three are problem-solving experiences in design and pattern-making.

Writing patterns can be made in several forms such as borders (see p. 34), all-over arrangements (p. 24), or even as self-contained abstract designs (p. 23). Any of the common art media, dry or fluid, can be used so that children can work in their desks and a whole class can participate if desired. Paper on which the patterns are to be made should be placed on newspaper so that the children can work freely and to the edge of the paper.

As with number patterns, words and letter forms used should be meaningful to the child so that he has a personal interest in the pattern he is producing. Letters, for example in border patterns, can consist of the child's initials, car registration prefix letters, and so on, while words that can be used in abstract and free arrangements might include Christian names, surnames, names of suburbs and towns, motor car names, names of football teams, or even names of popular sporting identities.

Substituting the letter form for the numeral, the making of writing patterns becomes an activity similar to the making of Number Patterns (p. 116); consequently the reader should refer to the page indicated for details of technique.